CW01648258

ALEXANDER POPE AND HIS CRITICS

CULTURAL FORMATIONS:
THE EIGHTEENTH CENTURY
Series Editor: Nick Groom

Other titles in this series:

SPENSER'S FAERIE QUEENE:
WARTON'S OBSERVATIONS AND HURD'S LETTERS
Edited with a new introduction by David Fairer

WARTON'S HISTORY OF ENGLISH POETRY
Edited with a new introduction by David Fairer

A COLLECTION OF POEMS BY SEVERAL HANDS
Robert Dodsley
With a new introduction by Michael Suarez

RELIQUES OF ANCIENT ENGLISH POETRY
With a new introduction by Nick Groom

ALEXANDER POPE AND HIS CRITICS

ALEXANDER POPE AND HIS CRITICS

VOLUME II

An Essay on the Genius and Writings of Pope:
Volume II

Joseph Warton

Edited and with an Introduction by
Adam Rounce

Routledge
Taylor & Francis Group
LONDON AND NEW YORK

This edition reprints the fourth edition, first published 1782 by
J. Dodsley, London.

This edition published 2004 by Routledge
11 New Fetter Lane, London EC4P 4EE

Simultaneously published in the USA and Canada
by Routledge
29 West 35th Street, New York, NY 10001

Routledge is an imprint of the Taylor & Francis Group

Selection and Editorial Matter © 2004 Adam Rounce;
individual owners retain copyright in their own material.

Typeset in Times by Keystroke, Jacaranda Lodge, Wolverhampton
Printed and bound in Great Britain by TJI Digital, Padstow, Cornwall

All rights reserved. No part of this book may be reprinted or reproduced or utilised in any form or by any electronic, mechanical, or other means, now known or hereafter invented, including photocopying and recording, or in any information storage or retrieval system, without permission in writing from the publishers.

British Library Cataloguing in Publication Data
A catalogue record for this book is available from the British Library

Library of Congress Cataloging in Publication Data
A catalog record for this book has been requested

ISBN 0–415–30909–3 (Set)
ISBN 0–415–30911–5 (Volume II)

Publisher's Note
The publisher has gone to great lengths to ensure the quality of this reprint but points out that imperfections in the original book may be apparent.

AN
ESSAY
ON THE
GENIUS
AND
WRITINGS
OF
POPE.

IN TWO VOLUMES.

VOL. II.

LONDON:
PRINTED FOR J. DODSLEY, IN PALL-MALL.
M.DCC.LXXXII.

AN

ESSAY

ON THE

GENIUS and WRITINGS

OF

POPE.

SECT. VIII.

Of JANUARY *and* MAY, *The* WIFE *of* BATH, *and* TRANSLATIONS *of* STATIUS *and* OVID, *and the* IMITATIONS *of ſome* ENGLISH POETS.

THE firſt dawnings of polite literature in Italy, appeared in tale-writing and fables. Boccace gave a currency and vogue to this ſpecies of compoſition. He collected many of the common tales of his country, and delivered them in the

the pureſt ſtile, enlivened with intereſting circumſtances. Sacchetti publiſhed tales before him, in which are many anecdotes of Dante and his cotemporaries. Boccace was faintly imitated by ſeveral Italians, Poggio, Bandello, Cinthio, Firenzuola, Maleſpini, and others. * Machiavel himſelf did honour to this ſpecies of writing, by his Belphegor.

To produce, and carry on with probability and decorum, a ſeries of events, is the moſt difficult work of invention; and if we were minutely to examine the popular ſtories of every nation, we ſhould be amazed to find how few circumſtances have

* Machiavel, who poſſeſſed the livelieſt wit with the profoundeſt reflection, wrote alſo two comedies, Mandgragora and Clytia, the former of which was played before Leo X. with much magnificence; the latter is an imitation of the Caſſina of Plautus; " Indigna vero homine Chriſtiano (ſays Balzac) qui ſanctiores Muſas colit, et, in ludicris quoque, meminiſſe debet ſeveritatis." Epiſt. Select. pag. 202. I have been informed that Machiavel towards the latter part of his life grew religious, and that ſome pieces of aſcetic devotion, compoſed by him, are preſerved in the libraries of Italy. Lord Bacon ſays remarkably of Machiavel, that he teaches what men uſually *do*, not what they *ought* to do.

been

been ever invented. Facts and events have been indeed varied and modified, but totally new facts have not been created. The writers of the old romances, from whom Ariosto and Spencer have borrowed so largely, are supposed to have had copious imaginations: but may they not be indebted, for their invulnerable heroes, their monsters, their enchantments, their gardens of pleasure, their winged steeds, and the like, to the Echidna, to the Circe, to the Medea, to the Achilles, to the Syrens, to the Harpies, to the Phryxus, and the Bellerophon of the ancients? The cave of Polypheme might furnish out the ideas of their giants, and Andromeda might give occasion for stories of distressed damsels on the point of being devoured by dragons, and delivered at such a critical season by their favourite knights. Some faint traditions of the ancients might have been kept glimmering and alive during the whole barbarous ages, as they are called; and it is not impossible, but these have been the parents of the Genii in the eastern, and the

Fairies in the weſtern world. To ſay that Amadis and Sir Triſtan have a claſſical foundation, may at firſt ſight appear paradoxical; but if the ſubject were examined to the bottom, I am inclined to think, that the wildeſt chimeras in thoſe books of chivalry with which Don Quixote's library was furniſhed, would be found to have a cloſe connexion with ancient mythology.

We of this nation have been remarkably barren in our inventions of facts; we have been chiefly borrowers in this ſpecies of compoſition; as the plots of our moſt applauded plays, both in tragedy and comedy, may witneſs, which have generally been taken from the novels of the Italians and Spaniards.

The ſtory of January and May now before us, is of the comic kind, and the character of a fond old dotard betrayed into diſgrace by an unſuitable match, is ſupported in a lively manner. Pope has endeavoured, ſuitably to familiarize the ſtate-

lineſs

lineſs of our heroic meaſure, in this ludicrous narrative; but after all his pains, this meaſure is not adapted to ſuch ſubjects, ſo well as the lines of four feet, or the French numbers of Fontaine *. Fontaine is, in truth, the capital and unrivalled writer of comic tales. He generally took his ſubjects from Boccace, Poggius †, and Arioſto; but adorned them with ſo many natural ſtrokes, with ſuch quaintneſs in his reflections, and ſuch a dryneſs and archneſs of humour, as cannot fail to excite laughter.

Our Prior has happily caught his manner, in many of his lighter tales; parti-

* It is to be lamented that Fontaine has ſo frequently tranſgreſſed the bounds of modeſty. Boileau did not look upon Fontaine as an original writer, and uſed to ſay he had borrowed both his ſtile and matter from Marot and Rabelais.

† "Poggius Florentinus in hoc numero eloquentium virorum ſingulare nomen obtinet. Scripſit de nobilitate, de avaritia, de principum infelicitate, de moribus Indorum, FACETIARUM quoque librum unum. Ab adverſariis exagitatus orationes pleraſque invectivas edidit. In epiſtolis etiam laudatur. Cyropædiam, quam Xenophon ille ſcripſit, latinam reddidit, atque Alphonſo regi dedicavit, pro qua a rege magnam mercedem accepit." Facius de viris illuſtribus, Florentiæ, 1745.

cularly in Hans Carvel, the invention of which, if its genealogy be worth tracing, is firſt due to Poggius. It is found in the hundred and thirty-third of his *Facetiæ*, where it is entitled Viſio Franciſci Philelphi; from hence Rabelais inſerted it, under another title, in his third book and twenty-eighth chapter; it was afterwards related in a book called the HUNDRED NOVELS*; Arioſto finiſhes the fifth of his incomparable ſatires with it; Maleſpini alſo made uſe of it; Fontaine, who imagined Rabelais to be the inventor of it, was the ſixth author who delivered it, as our Prior was the laſt; and perhaps not the leaſt ſpirited.

RABELAIS was not the inventor of many of the burleſque tales he introduced into his principal ſtory; the fineſt touches of which, it is to be feared, have undergone the uſual and unavoidable fate of ſatirical writings, that is, not to be taſted or underſtood, when the characters, the facts and the follies they ſtigmatize, are periſhed and

* See Menagiana, Vol. I. p. 368.

unknown.

unknown. Gulliver in the next century, will be as obſcure as Garagantua; and Hudibras and the ſatire Menippeè cannot be read, without voluminous commentaries.

The Wife of Bath, is the other piece of Chaucer which Pope ſelected to imitate: One cannot but wonder at his choice, which perhaps nothing but his youth could excuſe. Dryden, who is known not to be nicely ſcrupulous, informs us that he would not verſify it on account of its indecency. Pope however has omitted or ſoftened the groſſer and more offenſive paſſages. Chaucer afforded him many ſubjects of a more ſerious and ſublime ſpecies; and it were to be wiſhed, Pope had exerciſed his pencil on the pathetic ſtory of the patience of Griſilda, or Troilus and Creſſida, or the complaint of the black knight; or, above all, on Cambuſcan and Canace. From the accidental circumſtance of Dryden and Pope's having copied the gay and ludicrous parts of Chaucer, the common notion ſeems to have ariſen, that

Chaucer's vein of poetry was chiefly turned to the light and the ridiculous *. But they who look into Chaucer, will ſoon be convinced of this prevailing prejudice, and will find his comic vein, like that of Shakeſpear, to be only like one of mercury, imperceptibly mingled with a mine of gold.

CHAUCER is highly extolled by Dryden, in the ſpirited and pleaſing preface to his Fables; for his prefaces, after all, are very pleaſing, notwithſtanding the oppoſite opinions they contain, becauſe his proſe is the moſt numerous and ſweet, the moſt *mellow* and *generous*, of any our language has yet produced. His digreſſions and ramblings, which he himſelf ſays he learned of honeſt Montaigne, are intereſting and amuſing. In this preface is a paſſage worth particular notice, not only for the juſtneſs of the criticiſm, but becauſe it contains a cenſure

* Cowley is ſaid to have deſpiſed Chaucer. I am not ſurprized at this ſtrange judgment Cowley was indiſputably a Genius, but his taſte was perverted and narrowed by a love of witticiſms.

of

of *Cowley*. "Chaucer is a perpetual fountain of good ſenſe; learned in all ſciences; and therefore ſpeaks properly on all ſubjects: As he knew what to ſay, ſo he alſo knows where to leave off; a continence, which is practiſed by few writers, and ſcarcely by any of the ancients, excepting Virgil and Horace. *One of our late* great poets is ſunk in his reputation, becauſe he could never forgive any *Conceit* that came in his way; but ſwept, like a drag-net, great and ſmall. There was plenty enough, but the diſhes were ill-ſorted; whole pyramids of ſweet-meats for boys and women; but little of ſolid meat, for men. All this proceeded not from any want of knowledge, but of judgment; neither did he want that, in diſcerning the beauties and faults of other poets; but only indulged himſelf in the luxury of writing; and perhaps knew it was a fault, but hoped the reader would not find it. For this reaſon, though he muſt always be thought a great poet, he is no longer eſteemed a good writer; and for ten impreſſions which his works have had

in

in ſo many ſucceſſive years, yet at preſent a hundred books are ſcarcely purchaſed once a twelvemonth." It is a circumſtance of literary hiſtory worth mentioning, that Chaucer was more than 60 years old when he wrote Palamon and Arcite, as we know Dryden was 70, when he verſified it. The lines of POPE, in the piece before us, are ſpirited and eaſy, and have, properly enough, a free colloquial air. One paſſage, I cannot forbear quoting, as it acquaints us with the writers who were popular in the time of Chaucer. The jocoſe old woman ſays, that her huſband frequently read to her out of a volume that contained,

Valerius whole: and of Saint Jerome part;
Chryſippus, and Tertullian, Ovid's art,
Solomon's proverbs, Eloiſa's loves;
With many more than ſure the church approves *.

POPE has omitted a ſtroke of humour; for in the original, ſhe naturally miſtakes the rank and age of St. Jerome: the lines muſt be tranſcribed.

* Ver. 359.

Yclepid

Yclepid Valerie and Theophraſt,
At which boke he lough alwey full faſt;
And eke there was a clerk ſometime in Rome,
A cardinal, that hightin St. Jerome,
That made a boke agenſt Jovinian,
In which boke there was eke Tertullian,
Chryſippus, Trotula, and Helowis,
That was an Abbeſs not ferr fro Paris.
And eke the Parables of Solomon,
Ovid' is art, and bokis many a one *.

In the library which Charles V. founded in France about the year thirteen hundred and ſeventy-ſix, among many books of devotion, aſtrology, chemiſtry and romance, there was not one copy of Tully to be found, and no Latin poet but Ovid, Lucan and Boethius; ſome French tranſlations of Livy, Valerius Maximus, and St. Auſtin's City of God. He placed theſe in one of the towers of the old Louvre, which was called the tower of the library. This was the foundation of the preſent magnificent royal library at Paris.

The tale to which this is the Prologue, has been verſified by Dryden; and is ſup-

* Ver. 671.

poſed

posed to have been of Chaucer's own contrivance: as is also the elegant VISION of *the flower and the leaf*, which has received new graces from the spirited and harmonious Dryden. It is to his fables, though wrote in his old age *, that Dryden will owe his immortality, and among them, particularly, to Palamon and Arcite, Sigismunda and Guiscardo, Theodore and Honoria; and above all, to his exquisite music ode. The warmth and melody of these pieces, has never been excelled in our language, I mean in rhyme. As general and unexemplified criticism is always useless and absurd, I must beg leave to select a few passages from these three poems; and the reader must not think any observations on the character of Dryden, the constant pattern

* The falling off of his hair, said a man of wit, had no other consequence, than to make his laurels to be seen the more. A person who translated some pieces after Dryden used to say,

——— Experto credite, quantus
In clypeum assurgat, quo turbine torqueat hastam.

Crebillon was ninety when he brought his Catiline on the stage.

tern of POPE, unconnected with the main ſubject of this work. The picture of Arcite in the abſence of Emilia, is highly expreſſive of the deepeſt diſtreſs, and a compleat image of anguiſh.

He rav'd with all the madneſs of deſpair,
He roar'd, he beat his breaſt, he tore his hair.
Dry ſorrow in his ſtupid eyes appears,
For wanting nouriſhment, he wanted tears:
His eye-balls in their hollow ſockets ſink,
Bereft of ſleep he loaths his meat and drink;
He withers at his heart, and looks as wan,
As the pale ſpectre of a murder'd man *.

THE image of the Suicide is equally pictureſque and pathetic.

The ſlayer of himſelf yet ſaw I there
The gore congeal'd was clotted in his hair:
With eyes half-clos'd and gaping mouth he lay,
And grim, as when he breath'd his ſullen ſoul away.

This reminds me of that forcible deſcription in a writer whoſe fancy was eminently ſtrong. " Catilina vero, longe a ſuis, inter hoſtium cadavera repertus eſt, paululum

* Palamon and Arcite, Book I.

etiam

etiam ſpirans; ferociamque animi, quam habuerat vivus, in vultu retinens." Nor muſt I omit that affecting image in Spenſer, who ever excels in the pathetic,

And him beſides there lay upon the graſs
A dreary corſe, whoſe life away did paſs,
All wallow'd in his own, yet lukewarm, blood,
That from his wound yet welled freſh, alas;
In which a ruſty knife faſt fixed ſtood,
And made an open paſſage for the guſhing flood *.

When Palamon perceived his rival had eſcaped,

—— He ſtares, he ſtamps the ground;
The hollow tow'r with clamour rings around:
With briny tears he bath'd his fetter'd feet,
And dropp'd all o'er with agony of ſweat.

Nor are the feelings of Palamon leſs ſtrongly impreſſed on the reader, where he ſays,

The rage of Jealouſy then fir'd his ſoul,
And his face kindled like a burning coal:

* Fairy Queen, Book I. Canto 9. Stanza 36.

Now

Now cold despair succeeding in her stead,
To livid paleness turn'd the glowing red *.

If we pass on from descriptions of persons to those of things, we shall find this poem equally excellent. The temple of Mars, is situated with propriety, in a country desolate and joyless; all around it,

The landscape was a forest wide and bare;
Where neither beast nor human kind repair;
The fowl, that scent afar, the borders fly,
And shun the bitter blast, and wheel about the sky.
A cake of scurf lies baking on the ground,
And prickly stubs instead of trees are found.

The temple itself is nobly and magnificently studied; and, at the same time, adapted to the furious nature of the God to whom it belonged; and carries with it a barbarous and tremendous idea.

* These passages are chiefly of the pathetic sort; for which Dryden in his tragedies is far from being remarkable. But it is not unusual for the same person to succeed in describing externally a distressful character, who may miserably fail in putting proper words in the mouth of such a character. In a word, so much more difficult is DRAMATIC than DESCRIPTIVE poetry!

The

The frame of burniſh'd ſteel that caſt a glare
From far, and ſeem'd to thaw the freezing air.
A ſtrait long entry to the temple led,
Blind with high walls and horror over-head:
Thence iſſued ſuch a blaſt and hollow roar,
As threaten'd from the hinge to heave the door;
In through the door a northern light there ſhone,
'Twas all it had, for windows there were none.
The gate of adamant, eternal frame,
Which hew'd by Mars himſelf from Indian quarries
came.

This ſcene of terror is judiciouſly contraſted by the pleaſing and joyous imagery of the temples of Venus and Diana. The figure of the laſt goddeſs, is a deſign fit for GUIDO to execute.

The graceful Goddeſs was array'd in green;
About her feet were little beagles ſeen,
That watch'd with UPWARD eyes the motions of
their queen.

But above all, the whole deſcription of the entering the liſts *, and of the enſuing combat,

* The reader is deſired all along to remember, that the firſt delineation of all theſe images is in Chaucer, or Boccace, and it might be worth examining how much Dryden has added purely from his own ſtock.

combat, which is told at length, in the middle of the third book, is marvelloufly fpirited; and fo lively, as to make us fpectators of that interefting and magnificent tournament. Even the abfurdity of feigning ancient heroes, fuch as Thefeus and Lycurgus, prefent at the lifts and a modern combat, is overwhelmed and obliterated amidft the blaze, the pomp, and the profufion of fuch animated poetry. Frigid and phlegmatic muft be the critic, who could have leifure dully and foberly to attend to the anachronifm on fo ftriking an occafion. The mind is whirled away by a torrent of rapid imagery, and propriety is forgot.

THE tale of Sigifmonda and Guifcardo is heightened with many new and affecting touches by Dryden. I fhall felect only the following picture of Sigifmonda, as it has the fame attitude in which fhe appears in a famous piece of CORREGGIO.

Mute, folemn forrow, free from female noife,
Such as the Majefty of grief deftroys:

For bending o'er the cup, the tears ſhe ſhed
Seem'd by the poſture to diſcharge her head,
O'erfill'd before; and oft (her mouth apply'd
To the cold heart) ſhe kiſs'd at once and cry'd.

There is an incomparable wildneſs in the viſion of Theodore and Honoria *, that repreſents the furious ſpectre of "the horſeman ghoſt that came thundering for his prey," and of the gaunt maſtiffs that tore the ſides of the ſhrieking damſel he purſued; which is a ſubject worthy the pencil of Spagnoletti, as it partakes of that ſavageneſs which is ſo ſtriking to the imagination. I ſhall confine myſelf to point out only two paſſages, which relate the two appearances of this formidable figure:

* This is one of Boccace's moſt ſerious ſtories. "It is a curious thing to ſee at the head of an edition of Boccace's tales, printed at Florence in 1573, a privilege of Gregory XIII. who ſays, that in this he follows the ſteps of Pius V. his predeceſſor, of bleſſed memory, and which threatens with ſevere puniſhments all thoſe, who ſhall dare to give any diſturbance to thoſe bookſellers to whom this privilege is granted. There is alſo a decree of the inquiſition in favour of this edition, in which the holy father cauſed ſome alterations to be made." LONGUERUANA, Tom. II. p. 62. a Berlin, 1754.

and

and I place them laſt, as I think them the moſt lofty of any part of Dryden's works.

Whilſt liſt'ning to the murm'ring leaves he ſtood,
More than a mile immers'd within the wood,
At once the wind was laid—the whiſp'ring ſound
Was dumb—a riſing earthquake rock'd the ground:
With deeper brown the grove was overſpread,
And his ears tingled, and his colour fled.

The ſenſations of a man upon the approach of ſome ſtrange and ſupernatural danger, can ſcarcely be repreſented more feelingly. All nature is thus ſaid to ſympathize at the ſecond appearance of

— — The felon on his ſable ſteed
Arm'd with his naked ſword that urg'd his dogs to ſpeed.

Thus it runs——

The fiend's alarm began; the hollow ſound
Sung in the leaves, the foreſt ſhook around,
Air blacken'd, roll'd the thunder, groan'd the ground.

But to conclude this digreſſion on Dryden. It muſt be owned, that his ode on the power of muſic, which is the chief ornament of this volume, is the moſt unrivalled of his compoſitions. By that ſtrange fatality which ſeems to diſqualify authors from judging of their own works, he does not appear to have valued this piece, becauſe he totally omits it in the enumeration and criticiſm he has given, of the reſt, in his preface to the volume. I ſhall add nothing to what I have already ſaid on this ſubject *; but only relate the occaſion and manner of his writing it. Mr. St. John, afterwards Lord Bolingbroke, happening to pay a morning viſit to Dryden, whom he always reſpected †, found him in an unuſual agitation of ſpirits, even to a trembling. On enquiring the cauſe, "I have been up all night, replied the old bard; my muſical friends made me promiſe to write them an ode for their feaſt of St. Cæcilia: I have been ſo ſtruck with the

* Vol. I. pag. 51.

† See his verſes to Dryden, prefixed to the tranſlation of Virgil. Lord Bolingbroke aſſured Pope, that Dryden often declared to him, that he got more from the Spaniſh critics alone, than from the Italian, French, and all other critics put together; which appears ſtrange. This from Mr. Spence.

ſubject

ſubject which occurred to me, that I could not leave it till I had completed it; here it is, finiſhed at one ſitting." And immediately he ſhewed him this ode, which places the Britiſh lyric poetry above that of any other nation. This anecdote, as true as it is curious, was imparted by Lord Bolingbroke to POPE, by POPE to Mr. Gilbert Weſt, by him to the ingenious friend who communicated it to me *. The rapidity, and yet the perſpicuity of the thoughts, the glow and the expreſſiveneſs of the images, thoſe certain marks of the firſt ſketch of a maſter, conſpire to corroborate the truth of the fact.

THE TRANSLATION of the *firſt book of Statius*, is the next piece that belongs to this Section. It was in his childhood only, that he could make choice of ſo injudicious a writer. It were to be wiſhed that no youth of genius were ſuffered ever to look

* Richard Berenger, Eſq.

into Statius *, Lucan, Claudian, or Seneca the tragedian; authors, who by their forced conceits, by their violent metaphors, by their ſwelling epithets, by their want of a juſt decorum, have a ſtrong tendency to dazzle, and to miſlead inexperienced minds, and taſtes unformed, from the true reliſh of poſſibility, propriety, ſimplicity and nature. Statius had undoubtedly invention, ability and ſpirit; but his images are gigantic and outrageous, and his ſentiments tortured and hyperbolical. It can hardly, I think, be doubted, but that Juvenal intended a ſevere ſatire on him, in theſe well known lines which have been commonly interpreted as a panegyric.

> Curritur ad vocem *jucundam* et carmen *amicæ*
> Thebaidos, *lætam* fecit cum Statius *urbem*,

* Writers of this ſtamp are always on the ſtretch. They diſdain the natural. They are perpetually graſping at the vaſt, the wonderful, and the terrible. "Καν ἑκαςον αυτων προς αυγας ανασκοπης, εκ τȣ φοβερȣ κατ᾽ ολιγον ὑπονοςει προς το ευκαταφρονητον.—Κακοι δε ογκοι, και επι σωματων και λογων, οἱ χαυνοι και αναληθεις, και μηποτε περιιςαντες ἡμας εις τȣναντιον ȣδεν γαρ φασι, ξηροτερον ὑδρωπικȣ." Longinus, περι ὑψȣς τμ. γ. Sect. iii. They ſhould read the ſenſible diſcourſe of S. Wedrenfels, of Baſle, *De Meteoris Orationis*.

Promiſitque

Promiſitque diem; tanta *dulcedine captos*
Afficit ille animos, *tantaque libidine vulgi*
Auditur: ſed, cum *fregit ſubſellia* verſu,
Eſurit.———

In theſe verſes are many expreſſions, here marked with italics, which ſeem to hint obliquely, that Statius was the favourite poet of the vulgar, who were eaſily captivated with a wild and inartificial tale, and with an empty magnificence of numbers; the noiſy roughneſs of which, may be particularly alluded to in the expreſſion, *fregit ſubſellia verſu*. One cannot forbear reflecting on the ſhort duration of a true taſte in poetry, among the Romans. From the time of Lucretius, to that of Statius, was no more than about one hundred and forty-ſeven years; and if I might venture to pronounce ſo rigorous a ſentence, I would ſay, that the Romans can boaſt of but eight poets who are unexceptionably excellent; namely, TERENCE, LUCRETIUS, CATULLUS, VIRGIL, HORACE, TIBULLUS, PROPERTIUS, PHÆDRUS. Theſe only can be called legitimate models of juſt thinking and writing. Succeeding authors, as it happens in all countries, resolving to be original and new, and to avoid the imputation of copying, became distorted and unnatural: by endeavouring to open an unbeaten path, they deserted simplicity and truth; weary of common and obvious beauties, they must needs hunt for remote and artificial decorations. Thus was it that the age of Demetrius Phalerëus succeeded that of Demosthenes, and the false relish of Tiberius's court, the chaste one of Augustus. Among the various causes however that have been assigned, why poetry and the arts have more eminently flourished in some particular ages and nations, than in others, few have been satisfactory and adequate. What solid reason can we give why the Romans, who so happily imitated the Greeks in many respects, and breathed a truly tragic spirit, could yet never excel in tragedy, though so fond of theatrical spectacles? Or why the Greeks, so fruitful in every species of poetry, yet never produced but one great epic poet? While on the

the other hand, modern Italy, can ſhew two or three illuſtrious epic writers, yet has no Sophocles, Euripides, or Menander. And France, without having formed a ſingle Epopëa, has carried dramatic poetry to ſo high a pitch of perfection in Corneille, Racine, and Moliere.

For a confirmation of the foregoing remark on Statius, and for a proof of the ſtrength and ſpirit of Pope's youthful tranſlation, I ſhall ſelect the following paſſage.

He ſends a monſter horrible and fell,
Begot by furies in the depth of hell.
The peſt a virgin's face and boſom wears;
High on a crown a riſing ſnake appears,
Guards her black front, and hiſſes in her hairs:
About the realm ſhe walks her dreadful round
When night with ſable wings o'erſpreads the ground;
Devours young babes before their parent's eyes,
And feeds and thrives on public miſeries *.

Oedipus, in Statius, behaves with the fury

* B. I. ver. 701.

of

of a bluſtering bully; in Sophocles*, with that patient ſubmiſſion, and pathetic remorſe, which are ſuited to his lamentable condition.

Art thou a father, unregarding Jove!
And ſleeps thy thunder in the realms above?
Thou, fury, then, ſome laſting curſe entail,
Which o'er their children's children ſhall prevail;
Place on their heads that crown diſtain'd with gore,
Which theſe dire hands from my ſlain father tore.

Ovid is alſo another writer of a bad taſte, on whom Pope employed ſome of his youthful hours; in tranſlating the ſtories of Dryope and Pomona. Were it not for the uſeful mythological knowledge they contain, the works of Ovid ought not to be ſo diligently read. The puerilities and affectations with which they abound, are too well known to be here inſiſted on. I chuſe

* See his addreſs to the furies in the Œdipus Coloneus of Sophocles, beginning at the words, Ω ποτνιαι δεινωπες, at verſe 85, down to verſe 117. And afterwards, when he becomes more particularly acquainted with the unnatural cruelty of his ſons, yet his reſentment is more temperate. See verſe 433 down to verſe 472, of the ſame moſt enchanting tragedy.

chuſe rather to account for Ovid's falling into ſo blameable a ſpecies of writing, in the words of a ſenſible critic *; who after he

* Franciſci Vavaſſoris de Epigrammate Liber. Pariſiis 1672. Pag. 47, edit. 8vo.

About this time it became faſhionable among the wits at Button's, the mob of gentlemen that wrote with eaſe, to tranſlate Ovid. Their united performances were publiſhed in form by Garth, with a preface written in a flowing and lively ſtyle, but full of ſtrange opinions. He declares, that none of the claſſic poets had the talent of expreſſing himſelf with more force and perſpicuity than Ovid; that the Fiat of the Hebrew law-giver is not more ſublime than the Juſſit et extendi campos, of the latin poet; that he excels in the propriety of his ſimiles and epithets, the perſpicuity of his allegories, and the inſtructive excellence of his morals. Above all, he commends him for his unforced tranſitions, and for the eaſe with which he ſlides into ſome new circumſtance, without any violation of the unity of the ſtory; the texture, ſays he, is ſo artful that it may be compared to the work of his own Arachne, where the ſhade dies ſo gradually, and the light revives ſo imperceptibly, that it is hard to tell where the one ceaſes and the other begins. But it is remarkable that Quintilian thought very differently on this ſubject of the tranſitions, and the admirers of Ovid would do well to conſider his opinion. "Illa vero frigida et puerilis eſt in ſcholis affectatio, ut ipſe tranſitus efficiat aliquam utique ſententiam, et hujus velut præſtigiæ plauſum petat: ut Ovidius laſcivire in Metamorphoſi ſolet, quem tamen excuſare neceſſitas poteſt, res diverſiſſimas in ſpeciem unius corporis colligentem." Garth was a moſt amiable, and benevolent man. It was ſaid of him, that "no Phyſician knew his Art more, nor his Trade leſs." Pope told Mr. Richardſon, "that there was hardly an alteration, of

he has censured, what he calls, the *pigmenta*, the *lascivias*, and *aucupia sermonum* of PATERCULUS, of VALERIUS MAXIMUS, of PLINY the naturalist, and PLINY the consul, of FLORUS, and TACITUS, proceeds as follows: " Apud Ovidium, cum in Heroidum epistolis, tum vero præcipue in libris Metamorphoseon, deprehendunt qui ista curant, multa solerter et acute dicta. Sed advertit nemo, quod sciam, unde exorta hæc ei prætor cætoros libido, et quæ causa festivitatis novæ, et prioribus inusitatæ poetis, esse potuerit. Natus Ovidius eodem, quo Cicero mortuus, anno, in hæc incidit tempora, ut ita dicam, declamatoria, hoc est, ea, quibus inductus primum est, et valere cæpit, et in honore esse, strictior is habitus et comptior scripturæ; ubi color sententiarum, plurimi ac densi sensus, et qui cum quodam lumine terminarentur, non tarda nec inerti structura.

of the innumerable, that were made throughout every edition of the Dispensary, that was not for the better." The vivacity of his conversation made Garth an universal favourite both with Whigs and Tories, when party-rage ran high.

tura.

tura. Sic enim nove loqui cæptum eſt de novo genere loquendi. Itaque ejus adoleſcentia iis maxime ſtudiis ac diſciplinis declamitandi traducta, exercitaque tunc, cum Portio Latroni et Arellio Fuſco rhetoribus daret operam, cumque ſeſe non ad forum, a quo laboris fuga abhorrebat, ſed ad poeticam, in quam erat natura propenſior, contuliſſet: detulit una ſecum figuram hanc et formam ſermonis, cui aſſueverat aliquandiu, et inſtitutum jam oratione ſoluta morem retinuit in verſibus."

We are now advanced, through many digreſſions, that I would hope are not wholly impertinent, to Pope's Imitations *of Seven Engliſh Poets*, ſome of which were done at fourteen or fifteen years old. His early bent to poetry has been already taken notice of in the firſt volume *, to which the following anecdote muſt be added, which I lately received from one of his intimate friends. "I wrote things, ſaid Pope, I am aſhamed to

* Pag. 78.

ſay

ſay how ſoon; part of my epic poem ALCANDER, when about twelve. The ſcene of it lay at Rhodes, and ſome of the neighbouring iſlands; and the poem opened under the water, with a deſcription of the court of Neptune. That couplet on the circulation of the blood, which I afterwards inſerted in the Dunciad,

"As man's meanders, to the vital ſpring
"Roll all their tides, then back their circles bring,

was originally in this poem, word for word."

THE firſt of theſe Imitations is of Chaucer; as it paints neither characters nor manners like his original, as it is the only piece of our author's works that is looſe and indecent, and as therefore I wiſh it had been omitted in the preſent edition, I ſhall ſpeak no more of it.

THE Imitation of Spenſer is the ſecond; it is a deſcription of an alley of fiſhwomen. He that was unacquainted with Spenſer, and was to form his ideas of the turn and manner of his genius from this piece, would

would undoubtedly ſuppoſe that he abounded in filthy images, and excelled in deſcribing the lower ſcenes of life. But the characteriſtics of this ſweet and amiable allegorical poet, are, not only ſtrong and circumſtantial imagery, but tender and pathetic feeling, a moſt melodious flow of verſification, and a certain pleaſing melancholy in his ſentiments, the conſtant companion of an elegant taſte, that caſts a delicacy and grace over all his compoſitions. To imitate Spenſer on a ſubject that does not partake of the pathos, is not giving a true repreſentation of him, for he ſeems to be more awake and alive to all the ſoftneſſes of nature, than almoſt any writer I can recollect. There is an aſſemblage of diſguſting and diſagreeable ſounds, in the following ſtanza of POPE, which one is almoſt tempted to think, if it were poſſible, had been contrived as a contraſt, or rather burleſque, of a moſt exquiſite ſtanza in the FAERY QUEEN.

The ſnappiſh cur, (the paſſengers annoy)
Cloſe at my heel with yelping treble flies;

The whimp'ring girl, and hoarſer-ſcreaming boy,
Join to the yelping treble, ſhrilling cries;
The ſcolding quean to louder notes doth riſe,
And her full pipes thoſe ſhrilling cries confound;
To her full pipes the grunting hog replies;
The grunting hogs alarm the neighbours round,
And curs, girls, boys, in the deep baſe are drown'd.

The very turn of theſe numbers, bears the cloſeſt reſemblance with the following, which are of themſelves a complete concert of the moſt delicious muſic.

The joyous birds ſhrouded in chearful ſhade,
Their notes unto the voice attempred ſweet;
Th' angelical, ſoft trembling voices made
To th' inſtruments divine reſpondence meet;
The ſilver-ſounding inſtruments did meet
With the baſe murmure of the water's fall;
The water's fall with difference diſcreet,
Now ſoft, now loud unto the wind did call;
The gentle warbling wind low anſwered to all *.

Theſe images, one would have thought, were peculiarly calculated to have ſtruck the fancy of our young imitator with ſo much admiration, as not to have ſuffered him to make a kind of traveſty of them.

* Book II. Canto 12, Stanza 71.

The

THE next ſtanza of POPE repreſents ſome allegorical figures, of which his original was ſo fond.

Hard by a ſty, beneath a roof of thatch
Dwelt OBLOQUY, who in her early days,
Baſkets of fiſh at Billinſgate did watch,
Cod, whiting, oyſter, mackarel, ſprat or plaice:
There learn'd ſhe ſpeech from tongues that never ceaſe.
SLANDER beſide her, like a magpie chatters,
With ENVY (ſpitting cat) dread foe to peace;
Like a curs'd cur, MALICE before her clatters,
And vexing every wight, tears cloaths and all to
tatters.

But theſe perſonages of Obloquy, Slander, Envy and Malice, are not marked with any diſtinct attributes, they are not thoſe living figures *, whoſe attitudes and behaviour

* Mr. Hume is of opinion, that the peruſal of Spenſer becomes tedious to almoſt all his readers. "This effect, ſays he, [Hiſtory of England, pag. 738.] of which every one is conſcious, is uſually aſcribed to the change of manners; but manners have more changed ſince Homer's age, and yet that poet remains ſtill the favourite of every reader of taſte and judgment. Homer copied true natural manners, which, however rough and uncultivated, will always form an agreeable and pleaſing picture; but the pencil of the Engliſh poet was employed in drawing the affectations, and conceits, and fopperies of chivalry, which appear ridiculous as ſoon as they loſe the recommendation of the mode." But they had not ceaſed to be the mode in Spenſer's time.

Spenſer has minutely drawn with ſo much clearneſs and truth, that we behold them with our eyes, as plainly as we do on the cieling of the banquetting-houſe. For in truth the pencil of Spenſer is as powerful as that of Rubens, his brother allegoriſt; which two artiſts reſembled each other in many reſpects, but Spenſer had more grace, and was as warm a colouriſt. Among a multitude of objects delineated with the utmoſt force *, which we might ſelect on

* Whence it came to paſs that Spenſer did not give his poem the due ſimplicity, coherence and unity of a legitimate Epopea, the reader may find in Mr. Hurd's entertaining letter to Mr. Maſon, on the Marks of imitation, pag. 19, and in Obſervations on the Faery Queen, pag. 2, 3, 4. " How happened it, ſays Mr. Hurd, that Sir Philip Sydney in his Arcadia, and afterwards Spenſer in his Faery Queen, obſerved ſo unnatural a conduct in thoſe works; in which the ſtory proceeds as it were by ſnatches, and with continual interruptions? How was the good ſenſe of thoſe writers, ſo converſant beſides in the beſt models of antiquity, ſeduced into this prepoſterous method? The anſwer, no doubt is, that they were copying the deſign, or diſorder rather of Arioſto, the favourite poet of that time." We muſt not try the charming ſallies of Arioſto by the rigid rules of Ariſtotle.

There is a remarkable letter of Bernardo Taſſo, the father of Torquato, in which is this paſſage. " Ne ſò io s'Ariſtotele naſceſſe a queſta età, et vedeſſe il vaghiſſimo poema

on this occaſion, let us ſtop a moment and take one attentive look at the allegorical figures that riſe to our view in the following lines;

By that way's ſide there ſate infernal Pain,
And faſt beſide him ſat tumultuous Strife;
The one, in hand an iron whip did ſtrain,
The other brandiſhed a bloody knife,
And both did gnaſh their teeth, and both did threaten life *.

22.

But gnawing Jealouſie, out of their ſight
Sitting alone his bitter lips did bite;
And trembling Feare ſtill to and fro did flie,
And found no place where ſafe he ſhroud him might.
Lamenting Sorrow did in darkneſſe lie,
And Shame his ugly face did hide from living eye.

To ſhew the richneſs of his fancy, he has given us another picture of Jealouſy, con-

poema dell' Arioſto, conoſcendo la forza de l' uſo, et vedendo che tanto diletta, come l' eſperienza ci dimonſtra, mutaſſe opinione, et conſentiſſe che ſi poteſſe far poema heroico di piu attione: Con la ſua mirabil dottrina, et giudicio, dandogli nova norma, et preſcrivuendogli novi leggi."

Lettere di XIII. Huomini Illuſtri da Tomaſo Porcacchi. In Venetia, 1584. Libro XVII. pag. 422.

* Book II. c. 7. 21.

ceived with equal ſtrength in a ſucceeding book *.

Into that cave he creepes, and thenceforth there
Reſolv'd to build his baleful manſion
In dreary darkneſs, and continual feare
Of that rock's fall; which ever and anon
Threats with huge ruin him to fall upon,
That he dare never ſleep, but that one eye
Still ope he keeps for that occaſion;
Ne ever reſts he in tranquillity,
The roaring billows beat his bowre ſo boiſterouſly †.

Here all is in life and motion; here we behold the true Poet or MAKER; this is creation; it is here, "might we cry out to Spenſer," it is here that you diſplay to us, that you make us feel the ſure effects of genuine poetry, ὁταν ἁ λεγης, ὑπ ενθȣσιασμȣ και παθȣς βλεπειν δοκης, και ὑπ' οψιν τιθης τοις ακȣȣσιν. Longinus ‡.

* Lord Somers was paſſionately fond of the Fairy Queen; it was his favourite work; in the laſt picture which he ſate for to Sir Godfrey Kneller, he deſired to be painted with a Spenſer in his hand.

† Book iii. c. 11.

‡ Περι ὑΨ. Sect. 15.

It

5

It has been faſhionable of late to imitate Spenſer, but the likeneſs of moſt of theſe copies, hath conſiſted rather in uſing a few of his ancient expreſſions, than in catching his real manner. Some however have been executed with happineſs, and with attention to that ſimplicity, that tenderneſs of ſentiment, and thoſe little touches of nature, that conſtitute Spenſer's character. I have a peculiar pleaſure in mentioning two of them *, The School-mistress, by Mr. Shenſtone, and the Education of Achilles, by Mr. Bedingfield †. To theſe muſt be added that exquiſite piece of wild and romantic imagery, Thomſon's Caſtle of Indolence; the firſt canto of which in particular, is marvellouſly pleaſing, and the ſtanzas have a greater flow and freedom than his blank-verſe.

* Dodſley's Miſcellanies, Vol. I. pag. 247, and Vol. III. pag. 119.

† And alſo Dr. Beattie's charming *Minſtrel.*

Pope * has imitated Waller in the third place, and has done it with elegance, eſpecially in the verſes on a fan of his own deſign, for he deſigned with dexterity and taſte. The application of the ſtory of Cephalus and Procris is as ingenious as Waller's Phœbus and Daphne. Waller abounds, perhaps to exceſs, in alluſions to mythology and the ancient claſſics. The French, as may be imagined, complain that he is too learned for the ladies. The following twelve lines contain three alluſions, delicate indeed, but ſome may deem them to be too far-fetched, too much crouded, and not obvious to the Lady to whom they were addreſſed, on her ſinging a ſong of his compoſing.

> Chloris, yourſelf you ſo excell,
> When you vouchſafe to breathe my thought,
> That like a ſpirit with this ſpell
> Of my own teaching I am caught.

* Speaking of his imitations, Pope ſaid to Mr. Spence, " I had once a deſign of giving a taſte of all the Greek poets ; I would have tranſlated a hymn of Homer, an ode of Pindar, an idyllium of Theocritus, &c. ſo that I would have exhibited a general view of their poeſie, throughout its different ages."

That

That eagle's fate and mine are one,
Which on the ſhaft that made him die,
Eſpy'd a feather of his own
Wherewith he wont to ſoar ſo high.
Had Echo with ſo ſweet a grace,
Narciſſus' loud complaints return'd,
Not for *reflexion* of his face,
But of his voice, the boy had burn'd.

Here * is matter enough compreſſed together for Voiture to have ſpun out into fifty lines. If I was to name my favourite among Waller's ſmaller pieces, it ſhould be his apology for having loved before. He begins by ſaying that "they who never had been uſed to the ſurpriſing juice of the grape, render up their reaſon to the firſt delicious cup:" this is ſufficiently gallant, but what he adds has much of the ſublime, and is like a thought of Milton's.

To man that was i' th' evening made,
  Stars gave the firſt delight;
Admiring in the gloomy ſhade,
  Thoſe little drops of light.

* Spenſer and Waller were POPE's great favourites, as he told Mr. Spence, in the order they are named, in his early reading.

Then at Aurora, whoſe fair hand
  Remov'd them from the ſkies,
He gazing tow'rds the Eaſt did ſtand,
  She entertain'd his eyes.
But when the bright ſun did appear,
  All thoſe he 'gan deſpiſe;
His wonder was determin'd there,
  And could no higher riſe.

Which of the French writers has produced any thing at once ſo gallant and ſo lofty? The Engliſh verſification was much ſmoothed by Waller; who uſed to own that he derived the harmony of his numbers from Fairfax's Taſſo, who well-vowelled his lines, though Sandys was a melodious verſifier, and Spenſer has perhaps more variety of muſic than either of them *. A poet who addreſſes his pieces to living characters, and confines himſelf to the ſubjects and anecdotes of his own times, like this courtly author, bids fairer to become popular, than he that is em-

* " Even little poems, ſaid POPE, ſhould be written by a plan. This method is evident in Tibullus, and Ovid's elegies, and almoſt all the pieces of the ancients. A poem on a ſlight ſubject requires the greater care to make it conſiderable enough to be read."

ployed

ployed in the higher ſcenes of poetry and fiction, which are more remote from common manners. It may be remarked laſtly of Waller, that there is no paſſion in his love verſes, and that one elegy of Tibullus, ſo well imitated by Hammond, excels a volume of the moſt refined panegyric.

THE next imitation is of COWLEY, in two pieces, on a garden, and on weeping, in which POPE has properly enough, in conformity to his original, extorted ſome moral, or darted forth ſome witticiſm on every object he mentions: It is not enough to ſay that the laurels ſheltered the fountain from the heat of the day, but this idea muſt be accompanied with a conceit.

—— Daphne, now a tree, as once a maid,
Still from Apollo vindicates her ſhade.

The flowers that grow on the water-ſide could not be ſufficiently deſcribed without ſaying, that

The pale Narciſſus on the bank, in vain,
Transformed, gazes on himſelf again.

In

In the lines on a lady weeping, you might expect a touching picture of beauty in distress; you will be disappointed. Wit on the present occasion is to be preferred to tenderness; the babe in her eye is said to resemble Phaeton so much,

> That heav'n the threat'ned world to spare,
> Thought fit to drown him in her tears:
> Else might th' ambitious nymph aspire,
> To set, like him, the world on fire.

Let not this strained affectation of striving to be witty upon all occasions, be thought exaggerated, or a caricatura of Cowley. It is painful to censure a writer of so amiable a mind, such integrity of manners, and such a sweetness of temper. His fancy was brilliant, strong, and sprightly; but his taste false and unclassical, even though he had much learning. In his latin compositions, his six books on plants, where the subject might have led him to a contrary practice, he imitates Martial rather than Virgil, and has given us more Epigrams than Descriptions. I do not remember

member to have ſeen it enough obſerved, that Cowley had a moſt happy talent of imitating the eaſy manner of Horace's epiſtolary writings; I muſt therefore inſert a ſpecimen of this, his excellence.

Ergo iterum verſus? dices. O Vane! quid ergo
Morbum ejuraſti toties, tibi qui inſidet altis,
Non evellendus, vi vel ratione, medullis?
Numne poetarum (merito dices) ut amantum
Deriſum ridere deum perjuria cenſes?
Parcius hæc, ſodes, neve inclementibus urge
Infelicem hominem dictis; nam fata trahunt me
Magna reluctantem, et nequicquam in vincla mi-
nacem.
Helleborum ſumpſi, fateor, pulchreque videbar
Purgatus morbi; ſed Luna potentior herbis
Inſanire iterum jubet, et ſibi vendicat ægrum.

There is another epiſtle alſo, well worthy peruſal, to his friend Mat. Clifford *, at the end of the ſame volume. POPE †, in

* Settle was aſſiſted in writing the Anti-Achitophel by Clifford, and others the beſt wits of that time, who combined againſt Dryden.

† Another line likewiſe of POPE exactly characteriſes him. The *penſive* Cowley's *moral* lay.———Vol. VI. p. 37. His general preface; his diſcourſe concerning Cromwell; his eſſays on liberty, on obſcurity, on agriculture, on greatneſs, and on himſelf, are full of pleaſing and virtuous ſentiments, expreſſed without any affectation, ſo that he appears to be one of the beſt proſe writers of his time.

one

one of his imitations of Horace, has exhibited the real character of Cowley, with delicacy and candour.

Who now reads Cowley ? if he pleases yet,
His moral pleases, not his pointed wit;
Forgot his epic, nay Pindaric art,
But still I love the language of his heart.

His prose works give us the most amiable idea both of his abilities and his heart. His Pindaric odes cannot be perused with common patience by a lover of antiquity. He that would see Pindar's manner truly imitated, may read Masters's noble and pathetic ode on the Crucifixion; and he that wants to be convinced that these reflections on Cowley are not too severe, may read also his epigrammatic version of it.

Η ουκ οραας ὁλοπορφυρον
Στιλϐοντ' ου φλογι
Σιδονιης αλος, αλ-
-λ, αιματι σαζομενω———

Dost thou not see thy prince in purple clad all o'er,
Not purple brought from the Sidonian shore ?
But made at home with richer gore. COWLEY.

* Ανοιγ', ανοιγε
Πυλας οπωπων·
Και πηγας βλεφαρων
Λυσαι, ψεκαζε, δευε γαιαν.

Open, oh! open wide the fountains of thine eyes,
And let them call
Their ſtock of moiſture forth where e'er it lies,
For this will aſk it all.
'Twould all alas! too little be,
Though thy ſalt tears came from a ſea.

* Compare Cowley's ode on preſenting his book to the Bodleian library, with one of Milton on the ſame ſubject, Ad Johannem Rouſeium, 1646, written in the true ſpirit of the ancient Lyrics, and an excellent imitation of Pindar. One alluſion to Euripides of whom Milton is known to have been ſo fond, I cannot omit.

Æternorum operum cuſtos fidelis,
Quæſtorque gazæ nobilioris,
Quam cui præfuit Ion,
Clarus Erechtheides,
Opulenta dei per templa parentis,
Fulvoſque tripodas, donaque Delphica,
Ion Actea genitus Creuſa.

Nothing can more ſtrongly characterize the different manner and turn of theſe two writers, than the pieces in queſtion. It is remarkable, that Milton ends his ode with a kind of prophecy importing, that however he may be at preſent traduced, yet poſterity will applaud his work.

At ULTIMI Nepotes,
SERIQUE POSTERI,
Judicia rebus ÆQUIORA forſitan
Adhibebunt INTEGRO ſinu,
Tum, livore ſepulto,
Si quid MEREMUR, SERA POSTERITAS ſciet.

COWLEY

COWLEY being early disgusted with the perplexities and vanities of a court life, had a strong desire to enjoy the milder pleasures of solitude and retirement; he therefore escaped from the tumults of London, to a little house at Wandsworth; but finding that place too near the metropolis, he left it for Richmond, and at last settled at Chertsey. He seems to have thought that the swains of Surry had the innocence of those of Sydney's Arcadia; but the perverseness and debauchery of his own workmen soon undeceived him, with whom, it is said, he was sometimes so far provoked, as even to be betrayed into an oath. His income was about three hundred pounds a year. Towards the latter part of his life, he shewed an aversion to the company of women, and would often leave the room if any happened to enter it whilst he was present, but still he retained a sincere affection for Leonora. His death was occasioned by a singular accident *; he

* There is something remarkable in the circumstances that occasioned the deaths of three others of our poets.

OTWAY

he paid a visit on foot with his friend Sprat to a gentleman in the neighbourhood of Chertsey, which they prolonged and feasted too much, till midnight. On their return home they mistook their way, and were obliged to pass the whole night exposed under a hedge, where Cowley caught a severe cold, attended with a fever, that terminated in his death.

THE verses on Silence are a sensible imitation of the Earl of Rochester's on No-

OTWAY had an intimate friend who was murdered in the street. One may guess at his sorrow, who has so feelingly described true affection in his Venice Preserved. He pursued the murderer on foot who fled to France, as far as Dover, where he was seized with a fever, occasioned by the fatigue, which afterwards carried him to his grave in London.

Sir JOHN SUCKLING was robbed by his Valet-de-Chambre; the moment he discovered it, he clapped on his boots in a passionate hurry, and perceived not a large rusty nail that was concealed at the bottom which pierced his heel, and brought on a mortification.

LEE had been some time confined for lunacy, to a very low diet, but one night he escaped from his physician, and drank so immoderately, that he fell down in the Strand, was run over by a hackney-coach, and killed on the spot. These three facts are from Mr. Spence: though OTWAY's death has been differently related.

thing;

thing; which piece, together with his Satire on Man from the fourth of Boileau, and the tenth Satire of Horace, are the only pieces of this profligate nobleman, which modeſty or common ſenſe will allow any man to read. Rocheſter had much energy in his thoughts and diction, and though the ancient ſatiriſts often uſe great liberty in their expreſſions; yet, as the ingenious hiſtorian * obſerves, "their freedom no more reſembles the licence of Rocheſter, than the nakedneſs of an Indian does that of a common proſtitute."

Pope in this imitation has diſcovered a fund of ſolid ſenſe, and juſt obſervation upon vice and folly, that are very remarkable in a perſon ſo extremely young as he was, at the time he compoſed it. I believe on a fair compariſon with Rocheſter's lines, it will be found, that although the turn of the ſatire be copied, yet it is excelled. That Rocheſter ſhould write a ſatire on

* Hume's Hiſtory of Great-Britain. Vol. II. pag. 434.

Man,

Man, I am not ſurprized; it is the buſineſs of the Libertine to degrade his ſpecies, and debaſe the dignity of human nature, and thereby deſtroy the moſt efficacious incitements to lovely and laudable actions: but that a writer of Boileau's purity of manners, ſhould repreſent his kind in the dark and diſagreeable colours he has done, with all the malignity of a diſcontented HOBBIST, is a lamentable perverſion of fine talents, and is a real injury to ſociety. It is a fact worthy the attention of thoſe who ſtudy the hiſtory of learning, that the groſs licentiouſneſs and applauded debauchery of Charles the Second's court, proved almoſt as pernicious to the progreſs of polite literature and the fine arts that began to revive after the Grand Rebellion, as the gloomy ſuperſtition, the abſurd cant, and formal hypocriſy that diſgraced this nation, during the uſurpation of Cromwell *.

ARTEMISIA

* Lord Bolingbroke uſed to relate, that his Great Grandfather Ireton, and Fleetwood, being one day engaged in a private drinking party with Cromwell, and wanting

ARTEMISIA and PHRYNE are two characters in the manner of the Earl of Dorſet, an elegant writer, and amiable man, equally noted for the ſeverity of his ſatire, and the ſweetneſs of his manners, and who gave the faireſt proof that theſe two qualities are by no means incompatible. The greateſt wits, ſays Addiſon, I have ever converſed with, were perſons of the beſt tempers. Dorſet poſſeſſed the rare ſecret of uniting energy with eaſe, in his ſtriking compoſitions. His verſes to Mr. Edward Howard, to Sir Thomas St. Serfe, his epilogue to the Tartuffe, his ſong written at ſea in the firſt Dutch war, his ballad on knotting, and on Lewis XIV. may be named as examples of this happy talent, and as confutations of a ſentiment of the

to uncork a bottle, they could not find their bottle-ſcrew, which was fallen under the table. Juſt at that inſtant, an officer entered to inform the protector, that a deputation from the preſbyterian miniſters attended without. " Tell them, ſays Cromwell, with a countenance inſtantly compoſed, that I am retired, that I cannot be diſturbed, for I am *ſeeking the Lord*," and turning afterwards to his companions, he added, " Theſe ſcoundrels think we are *ſeeking the Lord*, and we are only *looking for our bottle-ſcrew*."

judicious

judicious M. de Monteſquieu, who in his noble chapter on the Engliſh Conſtitution, Book 19, ſpeaks thus of our writers. "As ſociety and the mixing in company, gives to men a quicker ſenſe of ridicule, ſo retirement more diſpoſes men to reflect on the heinouſneſs of vice; the ſatirical writings therefore of ſuch a nation are ſharp and ſevere, and we ſhall find among them many Juvenals, without diſcovering one Horace.

THE DESCRIPTION of the LIFE of a *Country Parſon* is a lively imitation of Swift *, and is full of humour. The point of the likeneſs conſiſts in deſcribing the objects

* See a Pipe of Tobacco, p. 282, vol. 2. Dodſley's Miſcell. where Mr. Hawkins Brown has imitated, from a hint of Dr. John Hoadly, ſix later Engliſh poets with ſucceſs, viz. Swift, POPE, Thomſon, Young, Phillips, Cibber. Some of theſe writers thinking themſelves burleſqued, are ſaid to have been mortified. But POPE obſerved on the occaſion, "Brown is an excellent copyiſt, and thoſe who take his imitations amiſs, are much in the wrong; they are very ſtrongly mannered, and few perhaps could write ſo well if they were not ſo."——In POPE's imitation of the ſixth epiſtle of Horace, there were two remarkable lines, the

objects as they really exist in life, like Hogarth's paintings, without heightening or enlarging them, and without adding any imaginary circumstances. In this way of writing, Swift excelled; witness his description of a morning in the city, of a city shower, of the house of Baucis and Philemon, and the verses on his own death. These are of the same species with the piece before us. In this also consists the chief beauty of Gay's Trivia, a subject Swift desired him to write upon, and for which he furnished him with many hints. The character of Swift has been scrutinized in so many late writings, that it is superfluous to enter upon it, especially as from many materials judiciously melted down and blended together, Dr. Hawksworth

the second of which was thought to contain a heavy anticlimax.

> Grac'd as thou art with all the power of words,
> Known to the Courts, the Commons and the Lords,

The unexpected flatness and familiarity of the last line was thus ridiculed by Mr. Brown with much humour.

> Persuasion tips his tongue whene'er he talks,
> And—*he has chambers in the King's-Bench walks.*

has

has ſet before the public, ſo complete a figure of him. I cannot however forbear to mention a remark of Voltaire, who affirms, "that the famous Tale of a Tub is an imitation of the old ſtory of the three inviſible rings, which a father bequeathed to his three children. Theſe three rings were the Jewiſh, Chriſtian, and Mahometan religions. It is, moreover, an imitation of the hiſtory of Mero and Enegu, by Fontenelle *. Mero was the anagram of Rome, and Enegu of Geneva. Theſe two ſiſters claimed the ſucceſſion to the throne of their fathers. Mero reigned firſt, Fontenelle repreſents her as a ſorcereſs or jugler who could convey away bread, and perform acts of conjuration with dead bodies: This is preciſely the Lord Peter of Swift, who preſents a piece of bread to his two brothers, and ſays to them, 'This, my good friends, is excellent Burgundy, theſe partridges have an admirable flavour.' The

* It was inſerted by *Bayle* in his *Nouvelles*, &c. vol. v. p. 88, as a ſerious narration; ſo happily was the allegory diſguiſed.

ſame Lord Peter in Swift, performs throughout the very part that Mero plays in Fontenelle. Thus all is imitation. The idea of the Perſian Letters is taken from the Turkiſh Spy. Boiardo has imitated Pulci, Arioſto has imitated Boiardo. The geniuſes, apparently moſt original, borrow from each other *.

I SHALL conclude this ſection with a ſtory, which POPE himſelf related, becauſe it is characteriſtical of his old friend, and I ſhall give it in the very words which POPE uſed, when he told it to Mr. Spence.—"Dr. Swift has an odd blunt way that is miſtaken by ſtrangers for ill-nature; it is ſo odd that there is no deſcribing it but by facts †. I'll tell you one, the firſt that comes into my head. One evening Gay and I went to ſee him. On our coming in,

* Oeuvres de Voltaire a Geneve. Tom. 4, pag. 223. 1756.

† The archbiſhop of Armagh Dr. Hoadly, happening to object one day in Swift's company to an expreſſion of POPE, as not being the pureſt Engliſh, Swift anſwered with his uſual roughneſs—"I could never get the blockhead to ſtudy his grammar."

Hey-day,

Hey-day, gentlemen, ſays the Dean, what can be the meaning of this viſit? How came you to leave all the great lords you are ſo fond of, to come hither to ſee a poor ſcurvey Dean?—Becauſe we would rather ſee you than any of them.—Ay, any one that did not know you ſo well as I do, might poſſibly believe you; but ſince you are come I muſt get ſome ſupper for you I ſuppoſe.—No, Doctor, we have ſupped already *.—Supped already, that is impoſſible, why it is not eight o'clock—Indeed we have—That's very ſtrange; but if you had not ſupped, I muſt have got ſomething for you; let me ſee, a couple of lobſters would have done very well, two ſhillings; tarts, a ſhilling: but you will drink a glaſs of wine with me, though you ſupped ſo much before your time only to ſpare my pocket.—No, we had rather talk with you, than drink with you.—But if you had ſupped with me, as in all reaſon you ought to have done, you muſt then have drank

* Tranſcribed from Mr. Spence's anecdotes.

with me.—A bottle of wine two ſhillings—two and two are four, and one is five; juſt two and ſixpence a-piece; there Pope, there's half a crown for you, and there's another for you, Sir; for I won't ſave any thing by you, I am determined. This was all ſaid and done with his uſual ſerіouſneſs on ſuch occaſions: And in ſpite of every thing we could ſay to the contrary, he actually obliged us to take the money."

SECT.

SECT. IX.

Of the ESSAY *on* MAN.

IF it be a true obſervation, that for a poet to write happily and well, he muſt have ſeen and felt what he deſcribes, and muſt draw from living models alone; and if modern times, from their luxury and refinement, afford not manners that will bear to be deſcribed; it will then follow, that thoſe ſpecies of poetry bid faireſt to ſucceed at preſent, which treat of things, not men; which deliver doctrines, not diſplay events. Of this ſort is didactic and deſcriptive poetry. Accordingly the moderns have produced many excellent pieces of this kind. We may mention the Syphilis of Fracaſtorius, the Silk-worms and Cheſs of Vida, the Ambra of Politian, the Agriculture of Alamanni, the Art of Poetry of Boileau, the Gardens of Rapin, the Cyder of Phillips, the Chaſe of Somerville, the Pleaſures of Imagination, the Art of preſerving

ſerving Health, the Fleece, the Religion of Racine the younger, the elegant Latin poem of Brown on the Immortality of the Soul, the Latin poems of STAY and BOSCOVICK, and the philoſophical poem before us; to which, if we may judge from ſome beautiful fragments, we might have added Gray's didactic poem on Education and Government, had he lived to finiſh it. And the Engliſh Garden of Mr. Maſon muſt not be omitted.

THE ESSAY ON MAN is as cloſe a piece of argument, admitting its principles, as perhaps can be found in verſe. POPE informs us in his FIRST preface, "that he choſe this epiſtolary way of writing, notwithſtanding his ſubject was high, and of dignity, becauſe of its being mixed with argument which of its nature approacheth to proſe." He has not wandered into any uſeleſs digreſſions, has employed no fictions, no tale or ſtory, and has relied chiefly on the poetry of his ſtile, for the purpoſe of intereſting his readers. His ſtile is con-

ciſe

ciſe and figurative, forcible and elegant. He has many metaphors and images, artfully interſperſed in the drieſt paſſages, which ſtood moſt in need of ſuch ornaments. Neverthelcſs there are too many lines, in this performance, plain and proſaic. The meaner the ſubject is of a preceptive poem, the more ſtriking appears the art of the poet: It is even of uſe perhaps to chuſe a low ſubject. In this reſpect Virgil had the advantage over Lucretius; the latter, with all his vigour and ſublimity of genius, could hardly ſatisfy and come up to the grandeur of his theme. POPE labours under the ſame difficulty. If any beauty in this Eſſay be uncommonly tranſcendent and peculiar, it is, BREVITY OF DICTION; which, in a few inſtances, and thoſe pardonable, has occaſioned obſcurity. It is hardly to be imagined how much ſenſe, how much thinking, how much obſervation on human life, is condenſed together in a ſmall compaſs. He was ſo accuſtomed to confine his thoughts in rhyme, that he tells us, he could expreſs them more ſhortly this way, than in proſe itſelf. On its firſt publication, POPE did not own it, and it was given by the public to Lord Paget, Dr. Young, Dr. Deſaguliers, and others. Even Swift ſeems to have been deceived: There is a remarkable paſſage in one of his letters. "I confeſs I did never imagine you were ſo deep in morals, or that ſo many new and excellent rules could be produced ſo advantageouſly and agreeably in that ſcience, from any one head. I confeſs in ſome places I was forced to read twice; I believe I told you before what the Duke of D——— ſaid to me on that occaſion; how a judge here who knows you, told him, that on the firſt reading thoſe eſſays, he was much pleaſed, but found ſome lines a little dark: On the ſecond, moſt of them cleared up, and his pleaſure increaſed: On the third, he had no doubt remaining, and then he admired the whole *."

THE ſubject of this Eſſay is a vindication of providence, in which the poet propoſes

* Letters, vol. IX. pag. 140.

to prove, that of all poſſible ſyſtems, infinite wiſdom has formed the beſt: That in ſuch a ſyſtem, coherence, union, ſubordination, are neceſſary; and if ſo, that appearances of evil, both moral and natural, are alſo neceſſary and unavoidable; That the ſeeming defects and blemiſhes in the univerſe, conſpire to its general beauty; That as all parts in an animal are not eyes, and as in a city, comedy, or picture, all ranks, characters, and colours, are not equal or alike; even ſo, exceſſes, and contrary qualities, contribute to the proportion and harmony of the univerſal ſyſtem; That it is not ſtrange, that we ſhould not be able to diſcover perfection and order in every inſtance; becauſe, in an infinity of things mutually relative, a mind which ſees not infinitely, can ſee nothing fully. This doctrine was inculcated by Plato and the Stoics, but more amply and particularly by the later Platoniſts, and by Antoninus and Simplicius. In illuſtrating his ſubject, POPE has been much more deeply indebted to the Theodiceé of Leibnitz, to Archbiſhop

bishop King's Origin of Evil, and to the Moralists of Lord Shaftesbury, than to the philosophers abovementioned. The late Lord Bathurst repeatedly assured me, that he had read the whole scheme of the Essay on Man, in the hand-writing of Bolingbroke, and drawn up in a series of propositions, which POPE was to versify and illustrate. In doing which, our poet, it must be confessed, left several passages so expressed, as to be favourable to fatalism and necessity, notwithstanding all the pains that can be taken, and the turns that can be given to those passages, to place them on the side of religion, and make them coincide with the fundamental doctrines of revelation.

1. Awake *, my St. John! leave all meaner things
To low ambition, and the pride of kings;
Let us (since life can little more supply
Than just to look about us, and to die)
Expatiate free o'er all this scene of man;
A mighty maze! but not without a plan.

EPIST. I. V. 1.

* Ben Jonson begins a poem thus,
Wake! friend, from forth thy lethargy——

THIS

THIS opening is awful, and commands the attention of the reader. The word *awake* has peculiar force, and obliquely alludes to his noble friend's leaving his political, for philoſophical purſuits. May I venture to obſerve, that the metaphors in the ſucceeding lines, drawn from the field ſports of ſetting and ſhooting, ſeem below the dignity of the ſubject; eſpecially,

> EYE nature's walks, SHOOT folly as it flies,
> And CATCH the manners living as they RISE.

2. But vindicate the ways of God to man.

This line is taken from Milton;

> And juſtify the ways of God to man *.

POPE ſeems to have hinted, by this alluſion to the Paradiſe Loſt, that he intended his poem for a defence of providence, as well as Milton: but he took a very different method in purſuing that end; and imagined that the goodneſs and juſtice of the Deity might be defended, *without* hav-

* Paradiſe Loſt, b. i. ver. 26.

ing

ing recourſe to the doctrine of a future ſtate, and of the depraved ſtate of man.

3. But of this frame the bearings, and the ties *,
The ſtrong connections, nice dependencies,
Gradations juſt, has thy pervading ſoul
Look'd thro'? Or can a part contain the whole?

" IMAGINE only ſome perſon entirely a ſtranger to navigation, and ignorant of the nature of the ſea or waters, how great his aſtoniſhment would be, when finding himſelf on board ſome veſſel anchoring at ſea, remote from all land-proſpect, whilſt it was yet a calm, he viewed the ponderous machine firm and motionleſs in the midſt of the ſmooth ocean, and conſidered it's foundations beneath, together with it's cordage, maſts, and ſails above. How eaſily would he ſee the Whole one regular ſtructure, all things depending on one another; the uſes of the rooms below, the lodgements, and the conveniencies of men and ſtores? But being ignorant of the in-

* Τα μερη προς αυτο το ὁλον δει σκοπειν, ει συμφωνα και ἁρμοττοντα εκεινω. Plotinus,

tent

tent or design of all above, would he pronounce the masts and cordage to be useless and cumbersome, and for this reason condemn the frame, and despise the architect? O my friend! let us not thus betray our ignorance; but consider where we are, and in what an universe. Think of the many parts of the vast machine, in which we have so little insight, and of which it is impossible we should know the ends and uses: when instead of seeing to the highest pendants, we see only some lower deck, and are in this dark case of flesh, confined even to the hold and meanest station of the vessel *." I have inserted this passage at length,

* Characteristics, vol. ii. pag, 188. edit. 12mo.—There is a close resemblance in the following lines with another passage of Shaftesbury's Moralists.

What would this man? Now upward will he soar,
And little less than angel, would be more;
Now looking downwards, just as griev'd appears
To want the strength of bulls, the fur of bears.

"Ask not merely, why man is naked, why unhoofed, why slower footed than the beasts: Ask, why he has not wings also for the air, fins for the water, and so on: that he might take possession of each element, and reign in all.

length, becauſe it is a noble and poetical illuſtration of the foregoing lines, as well as of many other paſſages in this Eſſay.

4. Preſumptuous man! the reaſon would'ſt thou find,
Why form'd ſo weak, ſo little and ſo blind?
Firſt if thou can'ſt the harder reaſon gueſs,
Why form'd no weaker, blinder, and no leſs *.

VOLTAIRE, in the late additions to his works, has the following remarkable words. "I own it flatters me to ſee that POPE has fallen upon the very ſame ſentiment which I had entertained many years ago." "Vous vous étonnez que Dieu ait fait l'homme ſi borné, ſi ignorant, ſi peu heureux. Que ne vous étonnez-vous, qu'il ne l'ait pas fait plus borné, plus ignorant, & plus malheureux? Quand un Français & un Anglais

Not ſo, ſaid I, neither; this would be to rate him high indeed! As if he were by nature, lord of all, which is more than I could willingly allow. 'Tis enough, replied he, that this is yielded. For if we allow once, a *ſubordination* in his caſe, if nature herſelf be not for man, but man for nature; then muſt man, by his good leave, ſubmit to the elements of nature, and not the elements to him." Vol. ii. pag. 196, ut ſupra.

Ver. 34.

penſent

penſent de meme; il faut bien qu'ils ayent raiſon *."

5. The lamb thy riot dooms to bleed to-day,
Had he thy reaſon, would he ſkip and play?
Pleas'd to the laſt, he crops the flowery food,
And licks the hand juſt rais'd to ſhed his blood †.

The tenderneſs of this ſtriking image, and particularly the circumſtance in the laſt line, has an artful effect in alleviating the dryneſs in the argumentative parts of the Eſſay, and intereſting the reader.

6. The ſoul uneaſy, and confin'd from home,
Reſts and expatiates in a life to come ‡.

In former editions it uſed to be printed *at home*; but this expreſſion ſeeming to exclude a future exiſtence, as, to ſpeak the plain truth, it was intended to do, it was altered to *from home*, not only with great injury to the harmony of the line, but alſo, to the reaſoning of the context.

* Ouevres de Voltaire. Tom. iv. pag. 227.

† Ver. 81. ‡ Ver. 97.

7. Lo the poor Indian! whoſe untutor'd mind
Sees God in clouds, or hears him in the wind;
His ſoul proud ſcience never taught to ſtray,
Far as the ſolar walk or milky way;
Yet ſimple nature to his hope has giv'n,
Behind the cloud-topp'd hill an humbler heav'n:
Some ſafer world in depth of woods embrac'd,
Some happier iſland in the wat'ry waſte,
Where ſlaves once more their native land behold,
No fiends torment, no Chriſtians thirſt for gold.
To BE content's his natural deſire,
He aſks no angel's wing, no ſeraph's fire;
But thinks, admitted to that equal ſky,
His faithful dog ſhall bear him company *.

POPE has indulged himſelf in but few digreſſions in this piece; this is one of the moſt poetical. Repreſentations of undiſguiſed nature and artleſs innocence always amuſe and delight. The ſimple notions which uncivilized nations entertain of a future ſtate, are many of them beautifully romantic, and ſome of the beſt ſubjects for poetry. It has been queſtioned whether the circumſtance of the dog, although ſtriking at the firſt view, is introduced with propriety, as it is known that this

* Ver. 99.

animal

2

animal is not a native of America. The notion of ſeeing God in clouds, and hearing him in the wind, cannot be enough applauded.

8. From burning ſuns when livid deaths deſcend,
When earthquakes ſwallow, or when tempeſts ſweep
Towns to one grave, whole nations to the deep *.

I quote theſe lines as an example of energy of ſtile, and of POPE's manner of compreſſing together many images, without confuſion, and without ſuperfluous epithets. Subſtantives and verbs are the ſinews of language.

9. If plagues or earthquakes break not heav'n's deſign,
Why then a Borgia or a Catiline † ?

"All ills ariſe from the order of the univerſe, which is abſolutely perfect. Would you wiſh to diſturb ſo divine an order, for the ſake of your own particular intereſt? What if the ills I ſuffer ariſe from malice or oppreſſion? But the vices and imper-

* Ver. 142. † Ver. 156.

fections of men are alſo comprehended in the order of the univerſe,

If plagues, &c.

Let this be allowed, and my own vices will be alſo a part of the ſame order."—— Such is the commentary of the academiſt on theſe famous lines *.

10. The general order, *ſince the whole began*,
Is kept in nature, and is kept in man †.

How this opinion is any way reconcileable with the orthodox doctrine of the lapſed condition of man, the chief foundation of the chriſtian revelation, it is difficult to ſay.

11. Why has not man a microſcopic eye?
For this plain reaſon, man is not a fly.
Say what the uſe, were finer optics giv'n,
T' inſpect a mite, not comprehend the heav'n?
Or touch, if tremblingly alive all o'er,
To ſmart and agonize at ev'ry pore ‡?

"If by the help of ſuch microſcopical eyes, if I may ſo call them, a man could pene-

* Hume's Eſſays, quarto, pag. 106.

† Ver. 171. ‡ Ver. 193.

trate

trate farther than ordinary into the ſecret compoſition and radical texture of bodies, he would not make any great advantage by the change; if ſuch an acute ſight would not ſerve to conduct him to the market and exchange, if he could not ſee things he was to avoid at a convenient diſtance, nor diſtinguiſh things he had to do with by thoſe ſenſible qualities others do *."

12. If nature thunder'd in his opening ears,
And ſtunn'd him with the muſic of the ſpheres,
How would he wiſh that heav'n had left him ſtill
The whiſpering zephyr, and the purling rill † ?

It is juſtly objected, that the argument required an inſtance drawn from real ſound, and not from the imaginary muſic of the ſpheres. Locke's illuſtration of this doctrine, is not only proper but poetical ‡. "If our ſenſe of hearing were but one thouſand times quicker than it is, how would a perpetual noiſe diſtract us; and we

* Locke's Eſſay on Human Underſtanding, vol. I. pag. 256.

† Ver. 201.

‡ Eſſay on Human Underſtanding, vol. I. pag. 255.

ſhould in the quieteſt retirement, be leſs able to ſleep or meditate, than in the middle of a ſea-fight."

13. From the *green* myriads in the *peopled* graſs—
The mole's *dim* curtain, and the lynx's beam;
Of ſmell the *headlong* lioneſs between,
And hound ſagacious on the *tainted* green:
The ſpider's touch how exquiſitely fine,
Feels at each thread, and lives along the line *.

THESE lines are ſelected as admirable patterns of forcible diction. The peculiar and diſcriminating expreſſiveneſs of the epithets diſtinguiſhed above by italics will be particularly regarded. Perhaps we have no image in the language, more lively than that of the laſt verſe. "To live along the line" is equally bold and beautiful. In this part of this Epiſtle the poet ſeems to have remarkably laboured his ſtyle, which abounds in various figures, and is much elevated. POPE has practiſed the great ſecret of Virgil's art, which was to diſcover the very ſingle epithet that preciſely ſuited each occaſion.

* Ver. 210.

14. Without

14. Without this juſt gradation, could they be
Subjected, theſe to thoſe, or all to thee?
The pow'rs of all ſubdu'd by thee alone,
Is not thy reaſon all theſe pow'rs in one *?

"Such then is the admirable diſtribution of nature, her adapting and adjuſting not only the ſtuff or matter to the ſhape and form, and even the ſhape itſelf and form, to the circumſtance, place, element, or region; but alſo the affections, appetites, ſenſations, mutually to each other, as well as the matter, form, action, and all beſides; all managed for the beſt, with perfect frugality and juſt reſerve: profuſe to none, but bountiful to all: never employing in one thing more than enough; but with exact œconomy retrenching the ſuperfluous, and adding force to what is principal in every thing. And is not thought and reaſon principal in man? Would we have no reſerve for theſe? No ſaving for this part of his engine †?"

* Ver. 229.

† The Moraliſts, vol. ii. pag. 199.

15. Above,

15. Above, how high, progreffive life may go!
Around, how wide! how deep extend below!
Vaft chain of being! which from God began,
Natures ætherial, human, angel, man,
Beaft, bird, fifh, infect, what no eye can fee,
No glafs can reach; from infinite to thee,
From thee to nothing *.

"THAT there fhould be more fpecies of intelligent creatures above us, than there are of fenfible and material below us, is probable to me from hence; that in all the vifible corporeal world, we fee no chafms, or gaps. All quite down from us, the defcent is by eafy fteps, and a continued feries of things, that in each remove differ very little from one another.—And when we confider the infinite power and wifdom of the maker, we have reafon to think, that it is fuitable to the magnificent harmony of the univerfe, and the great defign and infinite goodnefs of the architect, that the fpecies of creatures fhould alfo, by gentle degrees, defcend to us downwards: which if it be probable, we have reafon then to

* Ver. 235.

be perſuaded, that there are far more ſpecies of creatures above us, than there are beneath; we being in degrees of perfection, much more remote from the infinite being of God, than we are from the loweſt ſtate of being, and that which approaches neareſt to nothing *."

16. From nature's chain whatever link you ſtrike,
Tenth, or ten thouſandth, breaks the chain alike †.

THIS doctrine is preciſely the ſame with that of the philoſophical emperor ‡.

17. Juſt as abſurd, to mourn the taſks or pains,
The great directing MIND of ALL ordains §.

Here again we muſt inſert another noble ſentiment of the ſame lofty writer.

* Locke's Eſſay on Human Underſtanding, vol. ii. pag. 49.

† Ver. 245.

‡ Πηρȣται γαρ το ὁλοκληρον, εαν και ὁτι ȣν διακοψης της συναφειας και συνεχειας, ὡσπερ των μοριων, ȣτω δε και των αιτιων· διακοπτεις δε ὁσον επι σοι ὁταν δυσαρεϛης, και τροπον τινα αναιρης. M. Antoninus, Lib. v. S. 8.

§ Ver. 265.

As, when it is ſaid, that, Æſculapius hath preſcribed to one a courſe of riding, or the cold bath, or walking bare-footed; ſo it may be ſaid, that the nature preſiding in the whole, hath preſcribed to one a diſeaſe, a maim, a loſs of a child, or ſuch like. The word preſcribed, in the former caſe, imports that he enjoined it as conducing to health; and in the latter too, whatever befals any one, is appointed as conducive to the purpoſes of fate or providence. Now there is one grand harmonious compoſition of all things. M. Antoninus, B. 5.

18. All are but parts of one ſtupendous whole,
Whoſe body nature is and God the ſoul;
That chang'd thro' all, and yet in all the ſame;
Great in the earth, as in th' ætherial frame;
Warms in the ſun, refreſhes in the breeze,
Glows in the ſtars, and bloſſoms in the trees;
Lives thro' all life, extends thro' all extent,
Spreads undivided, operates unſpent;
Breathes in our ſoul, informs our mortal part,
As full as perfect in a hair as heart;
As full as perfect in vile man that mourns,
As the rapt ſeraph that adores and burns:
To him no high, no low, no great, no ſmall;
He fills, he bounds, connects, and equals all *.

* Ver. 267.

WHILST

WHILST I am tranſcribing this exalted deſcription of the omnipreſence of the Deity, I feel myſelf almoſt tempted to retract an aſſertion in the beginning of this work, that there is nothing tranſcendently ſublime in POPE. Theſe lines have all the energy and harmony that can be given to rhyme. They bear ſo marvellous a ſimilitude to the old Orphic verſes quoted in the valuable treatiſe Περι Κοσμου, that I cannot forbear introducing them, as they are curious and ſublime.

Ζευς πρωτος γενετο, Ζευς ὕστατος αρκικεραυνος·
Ζευς κεφαλη, Ζευς μεσσα· Διος δ' εκ παντα τετυκται.
Ζευς πυθμην γαιης τε και ουρανου αστεροεντος·
Ζευς αρσην γενετο, Ζευς αμβροτος επλετο νυμφη.
Ζευς πνοιη παντων, Ζευς ακαματου πυρος ορμη·
Ζευς ποντου ριζα, Ζευς ἥλιος, ηδε σεληνη·
Ζευς βασιλευς, Ζευς αρχος ἁπαντων αρχικεραυνος.
Παντας γαρ κρυψας αυτις φαος ες πολυγηθες
Εξ ἱερης κραδιης ανενεγκατο μερμερα ρεζων*.

NOR have we a leſs example of ſublimity in the three preceding lines, which deſcribe the univerſal confuſion that muſt enſue, upon

* Αριστοτελης Περι Κοσμου, pag. 378. edit. Lugduni. fol. 1590.

upon any alteration made in the entire and coherent plan of the creation.

> Let earth unbalanced from her orbit fly,
> Planets and suns rush lawless thro' the sky;
> Let ruling angels from their spheres be hurl'd,
> Being on being wreck'd, and world on world;
> Heav'n's whole foundations to their centre nod,
> And nature tremble to the throne of God *.

It is very observable that these noble lines were added after the first edition. It is a pleasing amusement to trace out the alterations that a great writer gradually makes in his works. Many other parts of this epistle have been judiciously amended and improved. At first it ran,

> How instinct varies! what a hog may want
> Compar'd with thine, half-reas'ning elephant.

And again;

> What the advantage, if his finer eyes
> Study a mite, not comprehend the skies,

Which lines at present stand thus,

> How instinct varies in the grovling swine,
> Compar'd, half-reas'ning elephant, with thine.

* Ver. 251.

Say

Say what the uſe, were finer optics giv'n,
T' inſpect a mite, not comprehend the heav'n.

Formerly it ſtood,

No ſelf-confounding faculties to ſhare;
No ſenſes ſtronger than his brain can bear.

At preſent,

No pow'rs of body or of ſoul to ſhare,
But what his nature and his ſtate can bear.

It appeared at firſt,

Expatiate free o'er all this ſcene of man,
A mighty maze! of walks without a plan.

We read at preſent,

A mighty maze! but not without a plan.

19. Submit.——In this, or any other ſphere,
Secure to be as bleſt as thou canſt bear:
Safe in the hand of one diſpoſing pow'r
Or in the natal, or the mortal hour *.

I cannot reſiſt the pleaſure of illuſtrating this ſentiment in the words of a writer, whoſe friendſhip I eſteem to be no ſmall happineſs and honour. "Teach us each to regard himſelf, but as a part of this

* Ver. 285.

great

great whole; a part which for its welfare we are as patiently to resign, as we resign a single limb for the welfare of our whole body. Let our life be a continued scene of acquiescence and of gratitude; of gratitude, for what we enjoy; of acquiescence, in what we suffer; as both can only be referable to that concatenated order of events, which cannot but be best, as being by thee approved and chosen *."

20. All nature is but art, unknown to thee;
All chance, direction which thou canst not see;
All discord, harmony not understood;
All partial evil, universal good †.

This is the doctrine that reigns throughout the lofty hymn of Cleanthes the Stoic, particularly in these beautiful and masculine verses.

Ουδε τι γιγνεται εργον επι χθονι σου διχα Δαιμων,
Ουδε κατ' αιθεριον θειον πολον, ουτ' επι ποντω,
Πλην ὁποσα ρεζουσι κακοι σφετερησιν ανοιαις,
Αλλα συ και τα περισσα επισιασαι αρτια θειναι,
Και κοσμειν τα ακοσμα· και ου φιλα σοι φιλα εστιν.

* Three Treatises by James Harris, Esq; pag. 231.

† Ver. 289.

Ω δε γαρ εις ἑν ἁπαντα συνηρμοκας εσθλα κακοισιν,
Ωσθ᾽ ἑνα γιγνεσθαι παντων λογον αιεν εοντων *.

Thus tranſlated by Mr. Weſt;

For nor in earth, nor earth-encircling floods,
Nor yon æthereal pole, the ſeat of gods,
Is aught performed without thy aid divine,
Strength, wiſdom, virtue, mighty Jove, are thine!
Vice is the act of man, by paſſion toſt,
And in the ſhoreleſs ſea of folly loſt;
But thou, what vice diſorders, canſt compoſe,
And profit by the malice of thy foes;
So blending good with evil, fair with foul,
As thence to model one harmonious WHOLE.

21. Chaos of thought and paſſion, all confus'd;
Still by himſelf abus'd, or diſabus'd;
Created half to riſe, and half to fall;
Great lord of all things, yet a prey to all;
Sole judge of truth, in endleſs error hurl'd:
The glory, jeſt and riddle of the world †!

IT was remarked long ago in the Adventurer ‡, that theſe reflexions were minutely copied from Paſcal, who ſays;

* Hymn. apud Hen. Steph. pag. 49.
See to this purpoſe a fine paſſage in Plutarch de Animi Tranquillit. in vol. ii. pag. 473, 474. fol. Francfourti, 1620. Particularly the paſſage of Euripides there quoted.

† Epiſt. ii. v. 13. ‡ No. 63.

"What a chimera then is man! what a confuſed chaos! what a ſubject of contradiction! a profeſſed judge of all things, and yet a feeble worm of the earth! The great depoſitary and guardian of truth, and yet a mere huddle of uncertainty! the glory and the ſcandal of the univerſe."

22. Superior beings when of late they ſaw
A mortal man unfold all nature's law,
Admir'd ſuch wiſdom in an earthly ſhape,
And ſhew'd a Newton as we ſhew an ape *.

The author of the letter on the Marks of imitation, is induced to think, from the ſingularity of this ſentiment, that the great poet had his eye on Plato; *ὅτι ανθρωπων ὁ σοφωτατος προς θεον πιθηκος φαινεται*. But I am more inclined to think that Pope borrowed it from a paſſage in the zodiac of Palingenius, which the abovementioned Adventurer has alſo quoted, and which Pope, who was a reader of the poets of Palingenius's age, ſome of whom he publiſhed, was more likely to fall upon, than on this thought of Plato.

* Ver. 34.

Simia

Simia cœlicolûm riſuſque jocuſque deorum eſt;
Tunc homo, quum temerè ingenio confidit, et audet
Abdita naturæ ſcrutari, arcanaque divûm.

23. Trace ſcience then, with modeſty thy guide;
First ſtrip off all her equipage of pride;
Deduct what is but vanity, or dreſs,
Or learning's luxury, or idleneſs;
Or tricks to ſhew the ſtretch of human brain,
Mere curious pleaſure, or ingenious pain;
Expunge the whole, or lop th' excreſcent parts,
Of all our vices have created arts *.

THE abuſes of learning are enumerated with brevity and elegance, in theſe few lines. It was a favourite ſubject with our author; and it is ſaid, he intended to have written four epiſtles on it, wherein he would have treated of the extent and limits of human reaſon, of arts and ſciences uſeful and attainable, of the different capacities of different men, of the knowledge of the world, and of wit. Such cenſures, even of the moſt unimportant parts of literature, ſhould not, however, be carried too far; and a ſenſible writer obſerves, that there

* Ver. 43. There is ſome obſcurity in this line, occaſioned by omitting the *relative*.

is not indeed any part of knowledge which can be called entirely useless. "The most abstracted parts of mathematics, and the knowledge of mythological history, or antient allegories, have their own pleasures not inferior to the more gay entertainments of painting, music, or architecture; and it is for the advantage of mankind that some are found, who have a taste for these studies. The only fault lies, in letting any of those inferior tastes, engross the whole man to the exclusion of the nobler pursuits of virtue and humanity *." We may here apply an elegant observation of Tully, who says in his Brutus, "Credo, sed Atheniensium quoque plus interfuit firma tecta in domiciliis habere, quam Minervæ signum ex ebore pulcherrimum: tamen ego me Phidiam esse mallem quam vel optimum fabrum lignarium; quare non quantum quisque prosit, sed quanti quisque sit, ponderandum est: præsertim cum pauci pingere egregiè possint aut fingere, operarii autem aut bajuli deesse non possint."

* Hutcheson's Nature and Conduct of the Passions, pag. 174.

24. Passions,

24. Paſſions, tho' ſelfiſh, if their means be fair,
Liſt under reaſon and deſerve her care;
Thoſe, *that imparted*, court a nobler aim,
Exalt their kind, and take ſome virtue's name *.

We find an † obſcurity in theſe lines, ariſing from the uſe of the participle *imparted*; a mode of ſpeaking of which Pope was fond, ſtudious as he was of brevity, and which often betrayed him into the ſame fault: *Paſſions, that court an aim*, is ſurely a ſtrange expreſſion.

25. In lazy apathy let Stoics boaſt
Their virtue fix'd! 'tis fix'd as in a froſt;
Contracted all, retiring to the breaſt;
The ſtrength of mind is exerciſe, not reſt ‡.

* Ver. 97.

† When I am writing, ſays Fontenelle, I often ſtop and aſk; "Do I myſelf underſtand this ſentence?" And yet, Fontenelle, whom the French accuſe of introducing the abrupt, affected ſtyle, is frequently obſcure. "Non minus autem cavenda erit, ſays Quintilian, quæ nimium corripientes omnia ſequitur, obſcuritas: ſatiuſque eſt aliquid narrationi ſupereſſe, quam deeſſe. Nam cum ſupervacua cum tædio dicuntur, neceſſaria cum periculo ſubtrahuntur."
Inſtitut. Orat. Lib. iv. C. 2.

Happy is he who can unite brevity with perſpicuity.—— It is but of one writer that Quintilian ſays, Idem lætus ac preſſus, tum copiâ, tum brevitate mirabilis. Lib. x. C. 1.

‡ Ver. 101.

Perhaps a ſtronger example cannot be found, of taking notions upon truſt without any examination, than the univerſal cenſure that has been paſſed upon the Stoics, as if they ſtrenuouſly inculcated a total inſenſibility with reſpect to paſſion. He that would be convinced that this trite accuſation is ill-grounded, may conſult the notes Mr. Harris has added to his third treatiſe *. There he will find the genuine doctrines of the Stoics examined with accuracy and ſagacity, in a learned deduction of paſſages, from all the beſt writers of that ſchool; the ſum of which quotations, in the nervous language of that critic, appears to be this; " That the Stoics, in their character of their virtuous man, included rational deſire, averſion, and exultation; included love, and parental affection; friendſhip, and a general charity or benevolence to all mankind: that they conſidered it as a duty, ariſing from our very nature, not to neglect the welfare of pub-

* From note pag. 325 to pag. 331.

lic ſociety, but to be ever ready, according to our rank, to act either the magiſtrate or the private citizen: that their apathy was no more than a freedom from perturbation, from irrational and exceſſive agitations of the ſoul: and conſequently that the ſtrange apathy, commonly laid to their charge, and in the demoliſhing of which there have been ſo many triumphs, was an imaginary apathy, for which they were no way accountable."

26. LOVE, HOPE, and JOY, fair PLEASURE's ſmiling train,
HATE, FEAR, and GRIEF, the family of PAIN.

THIS beautiful group of allegorical perſonages, ſo ſtrongly contraſted, how do they act? The proſopopeia is unfortunately dropped, and the metaphor changed immediately in the ſucceeding lines.

Theſe mix'd with art, and to due bounds confin'd,
Make, and maintain the balance of the mind *.

27. On different ſenſes different objects ſtrike †.

A didactic poet who has happily indulged himſelf in bolder flights of enthu-

* Ver. 120.

† Ver. 127.

ſiaſm, ſupported by a more figurative ſtile, than our author uſed, has thus nobly illuſtrated this very doctrine.

——— Diff'rent minds
Incline to diff'rent objects: one purſues,
The vaſt alone, the wonderful, the wild;
Another ſighs for harmony, and grace,
And gentleſt beauty. Hence when lightning fires
The arch of heav'n, and thunders rock the ground;
When furious whirlwinds rend the howling air,
And ocean groaning from the loweſt bed,
Heaves his tempeſtuous billows to the ſky;
Amid the mighty uproar, while below
The nations tremble, Shakeſpear looks abroad
From ſome high cliff, ſuperior, and enjoys
The elemental war. But Waller longs
All on the margin of ſome flow'ry ſtream
To ſpread his careleſs limbs, amid the cool
Of plantane ſhades.———

We have here a ſtriking example of that poetic ſpirit, that harmonious, and varied verſification, and that ſtrength of imagery, which conſpire to excite our admiration of this beautiful poem *.

28. Proud of an eaſy conqueſt all along,
She but removes weak paſſions for the ſtrong †.

* The Pleaſures of Imagination, Book iii. v. 546.
† Ver. 157.

THIS

This is from the Duke de la Rochefoucault. Whenever we get the better of our paſſions it is more owing to their weakneſs than our own ſtrength. And again, there is in the heart of man a perpetual ſucceſſion of paſſions, inſomuch that the ruin of one is always the riſe of another *.

29. Let pow'r, or knowledge, gold or glory, pleaſe,
Or oft more ſtrong than all, the love of eaſe †.

An acute obſervation plainly taken from La Rochefoucault. " 'Tis a miſtake to believe that none but the violent paſſions, ſuch as ambition and love, are able to triumph over the other paſſions. Lazineſs, as languid as it is, often gets the maſtery of them all, uſurps over all the deſigns and actions of life, and inſenſibly conſumes, and deſtroys both paſſions and virtues ‡."

30. Virtuous and vicious ev'ry man muſt be,
Few in th' extreme, but all in the degree:
The rogue and fool by fits is fair and wiſe;
And ev'n the beſt, by fits, what they deſpiſe §.

* Max. x.

† Ver. 170.

‡ Max. CCLXVI.

§ Ver. 233.

A fine

A fine reflection, and calculated to ſubdue that petulant contempt and unmerited averſion which men too generally entertain againſt each other, and which diminiſh and deſtroy the ſocial affections. Our emulation, ſays one of the beſt-natured philoſophers, our jealouſy or envy, ſhould be reſtrained in a great meaſure, by a conſtant reſolution of bearing always in our minds the lovely ſide of every character *. The compleatly evil are as rare as the perfectly virtuous, there is ſomething amiable almoſt in every one, as Plato obſerves in his Phædon.

This charitable doctrine of putting candid conſtructions on thoſe actions that ap-

* Hutcheſon's Nature and Conduct of the Paſſions, p. 190.

Ὁ ουν αδελφος εαν αδικῃ εντευθεν αυτο ου λαμβανης, ὅτι αδικει· αυτη γαρ λαβη εστιν αυτου ου φορητη· αλλ' εκειθεν μαλλον, ὅτι αδελφος, ὅτι συντροφος.

See Epicteti Enchiridion, alſo.

Many leſſons on this uſeful ſpecies of humanity, tending to ſoften the diſguſt that ariſes from a proſpect of the abſurdity and wickedneſs of human nature, are to be found in Marcus Antoninus; and many noble Precepts in the New Teſtament rightly underſtood have the ſame tendency, but are delivered with more dignity and force, and demand certainly a deeper attention and more implicit regard.

pear

pear moſt blameable, nay, moſt deteſtable and moſt deformed, is illuſtrated and enforced with great ſtrength of argument and benevolence by KING, in his fifth chapter on the origin of evil *; where he endeavours to evince the prevalence of moral good in the world, and teaches us to make due allowances for mens follies and vices.

31. What crops of wit, and honeſty appear,
From ſpleen, from obſtinacy, hate or fear † ?

Au Cid perſecuté Cinna doit ſa naiſſance,
Et peut-eſtre ta plume aux Cenſeurs de Pyrrhus
Doit les plus nobles traits dont tu peignis Burrhus ‡.

32. Heav'n forming each on other to depend,
A maſter, or a ſervant, or a friend,
Bids each on other for aſſiſtance call,
'Till one man's weakneſs grows the ſtrength of all.
Wants, frailties, paſſions, cloſer ſtill ally
The common intereſt, or endear the tie.
To theſe we owe true friendſhip, love ſincere,
Each home-felt joy that life inherits here §.

IT

* See alſo to this purpoſe a ſenſible paſſage in Hutcheſon's Conduct of the Paſſions, pag. 183.

† Ver. 185.

‡ Boileau, Epiſtre vii. a M. Racine, pag. 57

§ " In rerum ſyſtemate vel optimè conſtituto, debent eſſe diverſa animantium genera ſuperiora, et inferiora, ut

locus

It was an objection conſtantly urged by the ancient Epicureans, that man could not be the creature of a benevolent being, as he was formed in a ſtate ſo helpleſs and infirm: Montagne took it and urged it alſo. They never conſidered or perceived that this very infirmity and helpleſſneſs were the

locus ſit præclaris animi virtutibus ubi ſe exerceant: excluderentur enim commiſeratio, beneficentia, liberalitas, fortitudo, æquanimitas, patientia, lenitas, et officia omnia gratuita et immerita, quorum ſenſus longe eſt omnium lætiſſimus, et memoria jucundiſſima; ſi nulla eſſet imbecillitas, nulla indigentia, nulla hominum vitia et errores."

Hutcheſon. Metaphyſicæ Synopſis, cap. ii. pag. 81. This reſembles the doctrine of the old Stoic Chryſippus as he is quoted by Aulus Gellius, lib. vi. cap. 1. "Nullum adeo contrarium ſine contrario altero. Quo enim pacto juſtitiæ ſenſus eſſe poſſet niſi eſſent injuriæ? Aut quid aliud juſtitia eſt quam injuſtitiæ privatio? Quid item fortitudo intelligi poſſet niſi ex ignaviæ oppoſitione? Quid continentia niſi ex intemperantia? Quo item modo prudentia eſſet, niſi foret ex contrario imprudentia?"——"To this purpoſe the elegant lyric poet.

Who ſounds in diſcord, beauty's reign,
Converts to pleaſure ev'ry pain,
Subdues the hoſtile forms to reſt,
And bids the univerſe be bleſt."

"This is that magic divine, which by an efficacy paſt comprehenſion, can transform every appearance, the moſt hideous, into beauty, and exhibit all things fair and good to thee! Eſſence Increate! who art of purer eyes than to behold iniquity." Three Treatiſes, by J. H. pag. 234.

cauſe

cause and cement of society; that if men had been perfect and self-sufficient, and had stood in no need of each others assistance, there would have been no occasion for the invention of the arts, and no opportunity for the exertion of the affections. The lines therefore in which Lucretius proposes this objection, are as unphilosophical and inconclusive, as they are highly pathetic and poetical.

Tum porrò puer, ut sævis projectus ab undis
Navita, nudus humi jacet, infans, indigus omni
Vitali auxilio, cum primum in luminis oras
Nixibus ex alvo matris natura profudit;
Vagituque locum lugubri complet, ut æquum est,
Cui tantum in vitâ restat transire malorum *.

THERE is a passage in the Moralists which I cannot forbear thinking POPE had in his eye, and which I must not therefore omit, as it serves to illustrate and confirm so many parts of the Essay on Man; I shall therefore give it at length without apology.

* Lib. v. ver. 223.

"THE young of moſt other kinds, are inſtantly helpful to themſelves, ſenſible, vigorous, know how to ſhun danger, and ſeek their good: A human infant is of all the moſt helpleſs, weak, infirm. And wherefore ſhould it not have been ſo ordered? Where is the loſs in ſuch a ſpecies? Or what is man the worſe for that defect, amidſt ſuch large ſupplies? Does not this defect engage him the more ſtrongly to ſociety *, and force him to own that he is *purpoſely*, and *not by accident*, made rational and ſociable; and can no otherwiſe increaſe or ſubſiſt, than in that ſocial intercourſe and community which is his natural ſtate? Is not both conjugal affection, and natural affection to parents, duty to magiſtrates, love of a common city, community, or country, with the other duties and ſocial parts of life, deduced from hence,

* A longer care man's helpleſs kind demands;
That longer care contracts more laſting bands.
Ep. iii. v. 131.

And again;
And ſtill new needs, new helps, new habits riſe,
That graft benevolence on charities. Ep. iii. v. 137.

and

and founded in these very wants? What can be happier than such a deficiency, as it is the occasion of so much good? What better than a want so abundantly made up, and answered by so many enjoyments? Now if there are still to be found among mankind, such as even in the midst of these wants seem not ashamed to affect a right of independency, and deny themselves to be by nature sociable; where would their shame have been, had nature otherwise supplied these wants? What duty or obligation had been ever thought of? What respect or reverence of parents, magistrates, their country, or their kind? Would not their full and self-sufficient state more strongly have determined them to throw off nature, and deny the ends and author of their creation * ?"

31. And pride bestow'd on all a common friend †.

THE observation is from La Rochefoucault; " Nature, who so wisely has fitted

* The Moralists, pag. 201. † Ver. 272.

the

the organs of our body to make us happy, ſeems likewiſe to have beſtowed pride on us, on purpoſe, as it were, to ſave us the pain of knowing our imperfections *."

Un ſot en ecrivant fait tout avec plaiſir.
Il n' a point en ſes vers l' embarras de choiſir,
Et toujours amoreux de ce qu' il vient d' ecrire,
Ravi d' etonnement en ſoi-meme il s' admire.
Mais un eſprit ſublime en vain veut s' elever,
A ce degré parfait qu' il tache de trouver;
Et toujours mecontent de ce qu' il vient de faire
Il plaiſt a tout le monde, & ne ſcauroit ſe plaire.

When Boileau read theſe words to his friend Moliere to whom they are addreſſed, the latter, ſqueezing his hand with earneſtneſs, ſaid——" This is one of the beſt truths you have ever uttered. I am not one of thoſe ſublime geniuſes of whom you ſpeak; but ſuch as I am, I muſt declare I have never wrote any thing in my life, with which I have been thoroughly ſatisfied †."

34. See matter next, with various life endu'd,
Preſs to one centre ſtill, the gen'ral good.

* Maxim 36.

† Sat. 2. 85.

See

See dying vegetables life ſuſtain,
See life diſſolving vegetate again:
All forms that periſh other forms ſupply,
(By turns we catch the vital breath and die)
Like bubbles on the ſea of matter born,
They riſe, they break, and to that ſea return *.

POPE has again copied Shafteſbury ſo cloſely in this paſſage, as to uſe almoſt his very words. "Thus in the ſeveral orders of terreſtrial forms, a reſignation is required, a ſacrifice and mutual yielding of natures one to another. The vegetables by their death, ſuſtain the animals; and the animal bodies diſſolved, enrich the earth, and raiſe again the vegetable world. The numerous inſects are reduced by the ſuperior kinds of birds and beaſts: And theſe again are checked by man; who in his turn ſubmits to other natures, and reſigns his form a ſacrifice in common to the reſt of things. And if in natures ſo little exalted or pre-eminent above each other, the ſacrifice of intereſt can appear ſo juſt; how much more reaſonably may all inferior na-

* Ep. 3. v. 13.

tures be ſubjected to the ſuperior nature of the world * !"

35. Has God, thou fool! work'd ſolely for thy good,
Thy joy, thy paſtime, thy attire, thy food?
Who for thy table feeds the wanton fawn,
For him as kindly ſpread the flowery lawn:
Is it for thee the lark aſcends and ſings?
Joy tunes his voice, joy elevates his wings †.

THE poetry of theſe lines is as beautiful, as the philoſophy is ſolid. " They who imagine that all things in this world were made for the immediate uſe of man alone, run themſelves into inextricable difficulties. Man indeed is the head of this lower part of the creation, and perhaps it was deſigned to be abſolutely under his command. But that all things here tend directly to his own uſe, is, I think, neither eaſy nor neceſſary to be proved. Some manifeſtly ſerve for

* The Moraliſts, pag. 130. After borrowing ſo largely from this treatiſe, our author ſhould not methinks have ridiculed it, as he does, in the Fourth Book of the Dunciad; ver. 417.

Or that bright image to our fancy draw,
Which Theocles in raptur'd viſion ſaw.

† Ver. 27.

the

the food and ſupport of others, whoſe ſouls may be neceſſary to prepare and preſerve their bodies for that purpoſe, and may at the ſame time be happy in a conſciouſneſs of their own exiſtence. 'Tis probable they are intended to promote each others good reciprocally: Nay, man himſelf contributes to the happineſs *, and betters the condition of the brutes in ſeveral reſpects, by cultivating and improving the ground, by watching the ſeaſons, by protecting and providing for them, when they are unable to protect and provide for themſelves." Theſe are the words of Dr. Law, in his learned Commentary on King's Origin of Evil, firſt publiſhed in Latin, 1701, a work of penetration and cloſe reaſoning; which, it is remarkable, Bayle had never read, but only ſome extracts from it, when he firſt wrote his famous article of the Paulicians, in his

* That very life his learned hunger craves,
He ſaves from famine, from the ſavage ſaves;
Nay, feaſts the animal he dooms his feaſt,
And till he ends the being makes it bleſt.
Ep. iii. v. 63.

Dictionary, where he has artfully employed all that force and acuteness of argument, which he certainly possessed, in promoting the gloomy and uncomfortable scheme of Scepticism or Manicheism.

36. And reason raise o'er instinct as you can,
In this 'tis God directs, in that 'tis man *.

THERE is a fine observation of Montesquieu †, concerning the condition of brutes. They are deprived of the high advantages we enjoy; but they have some which we want. They have not our hopes, but then they are without our fears; they are subject like us to death, but it is without knowing it; most of them are even

* Ep. iii. 97.

† We ought not to be blind to the faults of this fine writer, whatever applause he deserves in general. But it must be confessed, that his style is too short, abrupt, and epigrammatic; he tells us himself, he was fond of Lucius Florus; and he believed too credulously, and laid too great a stress upon, the relations of voyage-writers and travellers; as indeed did Locke, for which he is ridiculed by Shaftesbury, vol. i. p. 344, of the Characteristics. If Shaftesbury, said the great Bishop *Butler*, had lived to see the candor and moderation of the present times, in discussing religious subjects, he would have been a good christian.

more

more attentive than we are to ſelf-preſervation; and they do not make ſo bad a uſe of their paſſions. B. i. c. 1.

37. Who taught the nations of the field and wood
To ſhun their poiſon, and to chuſe their food?
Preſcient, the tides or tempeſts to withſtand,
Build on the wave, or arch beneath the ſand *?

THIS paſſage is highly finiſhed; ſuch objects are more ſuited to the nature of poetry than abſtract ideas. Every verb and epithet has here a deſcriptive force. We find more imagery from theſe lines to the end of the epiſtle, than in any other parts of this Eſſay. The origin of the connexions in ſocial life, the account of the ſtate of nature, the riſe and effects of ſuperſtition and tyranny, and the reſtoration of true religion and juſt government, all theſe ought to be mentioned as paſſages that deſerve high applauſe, nay as ſome of the moſt exalted pieces of Engliſh poetry.

38. Man walk'd with beaſt, joint tenant of the ſhade †.

* Ver. 99. † Ver. 152.

Lucretius, agreeably to his uncomfortable ſyſtem, has preſented us with a different, and more horrid picture of this ſtate of nature. The calamitous condition of man is exhibited by images of much energy, and wildneſs of fancy.

——— Sæcla ferarum
Infeſtam miſeris faciebant ſæpe quietem :
Ejectique domo fugiebant ſaxea tecta
Setigeri ſuis adventu, validque Leonis,
Atque intempeſtâ cedebant nocte paventes
Hoſpitibus ſævis inſtrata cubilia fronde.

He repreſents afterwards ſome of theſe wretched mortals mangled by wild beaſts, and running diſtracted with pain through the woods, with their wounds undreſſed and putrifying:

At quos effugium ſervârat, corpore adeſo,
Poſterius tremulas ſuper ulcera tetra tenentes
Palmas, horriferis accibant vocibus Orcum ;
Donicum eos vita privârunt vermina ſæva,
Expertes opis, ignaros quid volnera vellent *.

Pain is forcibly expreſſed by the action deſcribed in the ſecond line, and by the epithet *tremulas*.

* Lib. v. ver. 991.

39. The

39. The ſhrine with gore unſtain'd, with gold undreſt,
Unbrib'd, *unbloody*, ſtood the blameleſs prieſt *.

The effect of alliteration is here felt by the reader. But at what period of time could this be juſtly ſaid, if we conſider the very early inſtitution of ſacrifice, according to the ſcripture-account of this venerable rite?

40. Ah! how unlike the man of times to come!
Of half that live the butcher and the tomb;
Who, foe to nature, hears the gen'ral groan,
Murders their ſpecies, and betrays his own †.

Ovid, on the ſame topic, has nothing ſo manly and emphatical. "Hears the general groan," is nobly expreſſed, and the circumſtance of *betraying* his own ſpecies, is an unexpected and ſtriking addition to the foregoing ſentiment. Thomſon has enlarged on this doctrine, with that tenderneſs and humanity for which he was ſo juſtly beloved, in his Spring, at verſe three hundred and thirty. Our poet aſcribes the violence of the paſſions to the uſe of animal food.

* Ep. iii. 156. † Ep. iii. 161.

But juſt diſeaſe to luxury ſucceeds,
And every death its own avenger breeds *.

41. Thus then to man the voice of nature ſpake,
"Go from the creatures thy inſtructions take;
"Learn from the birds what food the thickets yield;
"Learn from the beaſts the phyſic of the field †."

THE proſopopœia is magnificent, and the occaſion important, no leſs than the origin of the arts of life. NATURE is perſonified alſo by Lucretius, and introduced ſpeaking with ſuitable majeſty and elevation; ſhe is chiding her fooliſh and ungrateful children for their vain and impious diſcontent.

Quid tibi tantopere 'ſt, mortalis, quod nimis ægris
Luctibus indulges? quid mortem congemis, ac fles?—
Aufer abhinc lacrymas, barathro et compeſce querelas.

THERE is an authoritative air in the brevity of this ſentence, as alſo in the concluding line of her ſpeech; and particularly in the very laſt word. "Æquo animoque, agedum, jam aliis concede:—neceſſe 'ſt ‡."

* Ver. 165. † Ep. iii. ver. 171. ‡ Lib. iii. ver. 975.

42. Thy

42. Thy arts of building from the bee receive,
Learn of the mole to plow, the worm to weave *.

THE Romans have left us ſcarcely any piece of poetry ſo ſtriking and original, as the beginning and progreſs of arts at the end of the fifth book of Lucretius †. I ſhall at preſent confine myſelf to tranſcribe his beautiful account of the riſe of muſic.

At liquidas avium voces imitarier ore
Ante fuit multo, quam lævia carmina cantu
Concelebrare homines poſſent, aureiſque juvare.
Et zephyri cava per calamorum ſibila primum
Agreſtes docuere cavas inflare cicutas.
Inde minutatim dulceis didicere querelas,
Tibia quas fundit digitis pulſata canentum,
Avia per nemora, ac ſylvas ſaltuſque reperta,
Per loca paſtorum deſerta, atque otia dia ‡.

43. He from the wond'ring furrow call'd the food,
Taught to command the fire, controul the flood,
Draw forth the monſters of th' abyſs profound,
Or fetch the aerial eagle to the ground §.

* Ver. 175.

† The Perſians, it is ſaid, diſtinguiſh the different degrees of the ſtrength of fancy in different poets, by calling them, *painters* or *ſculptors*. Lucretius, from the force of his images, ſhould be ranked among the latter. He is, in truth, a SCULPTOR-POET. His images have a bold relief.

‡ Lib. v. ver. 1378.

§ Ver. 219.

A FINER

A FINER example can perhaps ſcarce be given of a compact and comprehenſive ſtile *. The manner in which the four elements were ſubdued is compriſed in theſe four lines alone. POPE is here, as Quintilian ſays of another, denſus et brevis et inſtans ſibi. There is not an uſeleſs word in this paſſage; there are but three epithets, *wondering*, *profound*, *aerial*; and they are placed preciſely with the very ſubſtantive that is of moſt conſequence: if there had been epithets joined with the other ſubſtantives, it would have weakened the nervouſneſs of the ſentence. This was a ſecret of verſification POPE well underſtood, and hath often practiſed with peculiar ſucceſs.

44. Who firſt taught ſouls enſlav'd, and realms undone,
Th' ENORMOUS faith of many made for one †.

" QUAND les ſauvages de la Louiſiane veulent avoir du fruit, ils coupent l' arbre

* We have here what Dionyſius ſays of Alcæus, ἡδυ μετα δεινοτητος, " Sweetneſs with ſtrength." Edit. Sylburg, p. 69. tom. ii.

† Ver. 241.

au

au piè & cueillent le fruit. Voilà le Gouvernement despotique." A sentiment worthy of the free spirit of Demosthenes, and an image worthy of the genius of Homer*.

45. Such is the world's great harmony, that springs
From order, union, full consent of things †.

THERE is no where to be found so perfect an illustration of this doctrine, that the beauty and concord of the universe arise from contrarieties, as in the short treatise of Aristotle, περι κοσμȢ, which, notwithstanding the different form of its composition, ought to be ascribed to this philo-

* Chapit. 13, De L'Esprit des Loix. These few words are the whole chapter. Woe be to the liberty and science of that country, where this noble and original work is prohibited to be read. Can that author be suspected of irreligion, who in the sixth chapter of his twenty-fourth book has entirely demolished one of the most subtle objections against Christianity, and that too urged by one of the ablest adversaries to our holy religion, M. Bayle; who asserts, in his Thoughts on the Comet, that a society of men practising the rules of Christianity, in their full rigour, could not long subsist.

† Ver. 295.

sopher:

ſopher *: I ſhall inſert it at length in its ſublime original, it being, as it were, a ſummary or compendium of the philoſophy of the poem before us. "Και τοι γε τις εθαυμασε, πως ποτε ει εκ των εναντιων αρχων συνεστηκεν ὁ κοσμος, λεγω δη ξηρων τε και ὑγρων, ψυχρων τε και θερμων, ου παλαι διεφθαρται και απολωλεν· ὡς καν ει πολιν τινες θαυμαζοιεν, ὁπως διαμενη, συνεστηκυιαν εκ των εναντιων εθνων· Πενητων λεγω, και πλουσιων· νεων, και γεροντων, ασθενων, ισχυρων· πονηρων, χρηστων. Αγνοουσι δε, ὁτι τουτ' ην πολιτικης ὁμονοιας το θαυμασιωτατον· λεγω δε, ὁτι εκ πολλων μιαν, και ὁμοιαν εξ ανομοιων, αποτελει

* The learned have been divided in their opinions concerning this piece. Muretus, both the Scaligers, Caſaubon, Heinſius, Menage, Voſſius, Naude, Alcyonius, and others, will not aſcribe it to Ariſtotle, and lay great ſtreſs on a paſſage of Proclus in his fifth book on the Timæus. On the other hand, Demetrius Phalereus, Stobæus, Apuleius, Juſtin Martyr, Beſſarion, Bradwardin, and our own truly learned Biſhop Berkley, unanimouſly give it to Ariſtotle. This opinion is confirmed by a ſenſible diſcourſe on the ſubject, cap. 19. Petiti Miſcell. Obſervation. Lib. 2. One of his obſervations I will not omit. "Scriptus quippe ad Alexandrum Regem, ut Titulus indicat, ideoque faciliore, quam alii, ſtilo, et aperto orationis plauſibilique filo: ut decet Regibus ſcribentem, ut illi univerſæ naturalis ſcientiæ compendium eſſet. Quo pacto et objectionem a ſtili diſcrepantiâ ductam removeo."

διαθεσιν,

διαθεσιν, ὑποδεχομενη και πασαν φυσιν, και τυχην· ισως δε και των εναντιων η φυσις γλιχεται, και εκ τουτων αποτελειν το συμφωνον, ουκ εκ των ὁμοιων· ὡσπερ αμελει το αῤῥεν συνηγαγε προς το θηλυ, και ουχ ἑκατερον προς το ὁμοφυλον, και την πρωτην ὁμονοιαν δια των εναντιων συνηψεν, ου δια των ὁμοιων· εοικε δε και ἡ τεχνη την φυσιν μιμουμενη, τουτο ποιειν· ζωγραφια μεν γαρ, λευκων τε και μελανων, ωχρων τε και ερυθρων χρωματων ἐγκερασαμενη φυσεις, τας εικονας τοις προηγουμενοις απετελεσε συμφωνους· μουσικη δε, οξεις ἁμα και βαρεις φθογγους μιξασα, εν διαφοροις φωναις μιαν απετελεσεν ἁρμονιαν· γραμματικη δε, εκ φωνεντων και αφωνων γραμματων κρασιν ποιησαμενη, την ὁλην τεχνην απ᾽ αυτων συνεστησατο· ταυτο δε τουτο ην και το παρα τω σκοτεινω λεγομενον Ηρακλειτω· συναψειας ουλα, και ουχι ουλα· συμφερομενον, και διαφερομενον· συναδον, και διαδον· και εκ παντων ἑν και εξ ἑνος παντα." It is to be lamented that the present ſtate of literature in this kingdom, has rendered it neceſſary, to ſubjoin a Latin tranſlation of this beautiful and exalted paſſage, which to be able to read in its original is no vulgar happineſs.

Take

Take it therefore in the words of Budæus. "Tametsi extiterunt, qui sese admirari addubitabundi dicerent, qui fieri tandem posset, si e principiis contrariis mundus constitit, siccis dico et humidis, frigidis et calidis, ut jam dici non dissolutus fuerit atque interierit. Perinde quasi mirari quisquam debeat, quonam pacto civitas incolumis perduret, quæ e gentibus contrariis composita sit, egenis inquam et divitibus, juvenibus et senio confectis, infirmis et valentibus, pravis atque innocentibus. Ignorantia est ista utique hominum, hoc esse in concordia civili non videntium, longe admirabilissimum, quod ex multis ipsa unum efficit affectum, et e dissimilibus similem, omnis illa quidem naturæ susceptrix et fortunæ. Atque haud scio an etiam contrariorum appetens sit natura: ex eisque consona, non item e similibus conficiat. Sic certe ipsa marem cum fœmina conjunxit, non etiam cum suo horum utrumque sexu. Quin primam etiam concordiam per contraria, non per similia devinxit. Adde quod ars naturæ æmulatrix

hoc

hoc idem facit. Siquidem pictura, alborum nigrorumque colorum, luteorumque et rubrorum naturas inter se attemperans, effigies rerum efficit consonas exemplaribus. Musica acutis et gravibus sonis, longisque et brevibus una permixtis in diversis vocibus unum ex illis concentum absolutum reddidit. Grammatica, ex elementis vocalibus et mutis inventa temperatura artem omnem literaturæ ex illis compositam reliquit. Hocque nimirum illud est, quod apud Heraclitum legitur (Scotinum ab obscuritate dictum) crispa, inquit, et minime crispa unà vinxeris, consentiens et dissentiens, consonans et dissonans, unum etiam ex omnibus, omniaque ex uno."

46. O Happiness! our being's end and aim!
Good, Pleasure, Ease, Content, whate'er thy name *.

He begins his address to Happiness after the manner of the ancient hymns †, by

* Ep. iv. ver. 1.

† Παρα μεν τη Σαπφω και τω Αλκμανι πολλαχου ευρισκομεν. Την μεν γαρ Αρτεμιν εκ μυριων ορεων, μυριων δε πολεων, ετι δε ποταμων ανακαλει. Την δε Αφροδιτην εκ Κυπρου, Κνιδου, Συριας, και πολλαχοθεν αλλαχοθεν ανακαλει. Menander Rhetor. de Hymnis.

enumerating

enumerating the titles and various places of abode of this goddefs. He has undoubtedly perfonified her at the beginning, but he feems to have dropped that idea in the feventh line, where the deity is fuddenly transformed into a plant; from thence this metaphor of a vegetable is carried on diftinctly through the eleven fucceeding lines, till he fuddenly returns to confider Happinefs again as a perfon, in the eighteenth line,

And fled from monarchs, St. John, dwells with thee.

For to *fly* and to *dwell*, cannot juftly be predicated of the fame fubject, that immediately before was defcribed as twining with laurels, and being reaped in harvefts.

Of the numberlefs treatifes that have been written on Happinefs, one of the moft fenfible is that of Fontenelle, in the third volume of his works. Our author's leading principle is, that Happinefs is attainable by all men;

For mourn our various portions as we pleafe,
Equal is common Senfe, and common Eafe.

So

So Horace alſo in Epiſt. 18. B. i.

Æquum mî animum ipſe parabo.

" But Horace (ſays a penetrating obſerver on human life) was groſsly miſtaken: the thing for which he thought he ſtood in no need of Jupiter's aſſiſtance, was what he could leaſt expect from his own ability. It is much more eaſy to get even riches and honours by one's induſtry, than a quiet and contented mind. If it be ſaid, that riches and honours depend on a thouſand things which we cannot diſpoſe of at pleaſure, and that therefore it is neceſſary to pray to God that he would turn them to our advantage; I anſwer, that the ſilence of the paſſions, and the tranquillity and eaſe of the mind, depend upon a thouſand things that are not under our juriſdiction. The ſtomach, the ſpleen, the lymphatic veſſels, the fibres of the brain, and a hundred other organs, whoſe ſeat and figure are yet unknown to the anatomiſts, produce in us many uneaſineſſes, jealouſies, and vexations. Can we alter thoſe organs? Are they in our own power?"

47. When nature ſicken'd, and each gale was death *.

This is a verſe of a marvellous comprehenſion and expreſſiveneſs. The direfulneſs of this peſtilence is more emphatically ſet forth in theſe few words, than in forty ſuch odes as Sprat's on the plague at Athens †.

48. What makes all phyſical or moral ill?—
There deviates Nature, and here wanders Will ‡.

Pope here accounts for the introduction of moral evil from the abuſe of man's free will. This is the ſolid and ſcriptural ſolution of that grand and difficult queſtion, which in vain hath puzzled and bewildered the ſpeculatiſts of ſo many ages, *ποθεν το κακον*. Milton, in one of his ſmaller and neglected poems, has left us a ſublime paſſage founded on the Chriſtian doctrine of the Fall, and of the preceding harmony of all things.

* Ver. 108.

† *Ταυθ' ὁτι μεν ἐστιν ισχυρα, και στιβαρα, και αξιωματικα*. He elſewhere commends a writer, on account of his, *πυκνοτητος, και σεμνοτητος*. Dionyſ. Halicarnaſſ. *περι συνθεσεως. τμ. κβ.*

‡ Ver. 111.

That

That we on earth with undiſcording voice
May rightly anſwer that melodious noiſe;
As once we did, till diſproportion'd ſin
Jarr'd againſt Nature's chime, and with harſh din
Broke the fair muſic that all creatures made
To their great Lord, whoſe love their motion ſway'd
In perfect diapaſon, whilſt they ſtood
In firſt obedience, and their ſtate of good *.

49. ——— A better wou'd you fix?
Then give Humility a coach and ſix †.

Worth makes the man, and want of it the fellow;
The reſt is all but leather or prunella ‡.

Not one looks backward, onward ſtill he goes,
Yet ne'er looks forward further than his noſe §.

To ſigh for ribbands if thou art ſo ſilly,
Mark how they grace Lord Umbra or Sir Billy ||.

In a work of ſo ſerious and ſevere a caſt, in a work of reaſoning, in a work of theology, deſigned to explain the moſt intereſting ſubject that can employ the mind of man, ſurely ſuch ſtrokes of levity, of ſatire, of ridicule, however poignant and witty, are ill placed and diſguſting, are vio-

* At a Solemn Muſic, vol. ii. pag. 38.
† Ver. 17. ‡ Ver. 204.
§ Ver. 223. || Ver. 276.

 lations

lations of that propriety which Pope in general so strictly observed. Lucretius preserves throughout, the dignity he at first assumed; even his sarcasms and irony on the superstitious, have something august, and a noble haughtiness in them; as in particular where he asks how it comes to pass that Jupiter sometimes strikes his own temples with his thunderbolts; whether he employs himself in casting them in the deserts for the sake of exercising his arm; and why he hurls them in places where he cannot strike the guilty.

——Tum fulmina mittat; et ædes
Sæpe suas disturbet, et in deserta recedens
Sæviat, exercens telum, quod sæpe nocentes
Præterit, exanimatque indignos, inque merentes *.

He has turned the insult into a magnificent image.

50. Heroes are much the same, the point's agreed,
From Macedonia's madman to the Swede.

The modern Alexander has been thus characterized by the British Juvenal, in

* Lib. ii. ver. 1100.

lines

lines as nervous and energetic as are to be found in any part of our author.

A frame of adamant, a ſoul of fire,
No dangers fright him, and no labours tire;
O'er Love, o'er Fear, extends his wide domain,
Unconquer'd Lord of Pleaſure and of Pain.

And afterwards of his unexpected death.

Did rival monarchs give the fatal wound?
Or hoſtile millions preſs him to the ground?
His fall was deſtin'd to a barren ſtrand,
A petty fortreſs and a dubious hand;
He left a name, at which the world grew pale,
To point a moral, or adorn a tale *.

Two ſucceeding paſſages, in this fourth epiſtle, the firſt, at line 237, on the emptineſs of Fame; the ſecond, at line 259, on the inconveniences that attend ſuperior parts and talents, are replete with ſtrong ſenſe, and a penetrating knowledge of men and things, expreſſed with vigour and conciſeneſs.

51. Self-love but ſerves the virtuous mind to wake,
As the ſmall pebble ſtirs the peaceful lake †.

* Dodſley's Miſcellanies, vol. iv. The Vanity of Human Wiſhes, by Mr. Johnſon. † Ver. 363.

It is obſervable that this ſimilitude, which is to be found in Silius Italicus, l. xiii. v. 24, and alſo in Du Bartas, and in Shakeſpear's Henry VI. hath been uſed twice more in the writings of our poet; in the Temple of Fame in the four hundred and thirty-ſixth line, and in the Dunciad at the four hundred and fifth. This Eſſay is not decorated with many compariſons; two however ought to be mentioned, on account of their aptneſs and propriety. The firſt is, where he compares man to the vine, that gains its ſtrength from the embrace it gives: the ſecond is conceived with peculiar felicity; all Nature does not perhaps afford ſo fit and cloſe an application. It is indeed equally new, philoſophical, and poetical.

> On their own axis as the planets run,
> Yet make at once their circle round the ſun;
> So two conſiſtent motions * *act* the ſoul;
> And one regards itſelf, and one the whole †.

* Should it not be *actuate*, or *act upon?* He has uſed this expreſſion again, Illiad xv. v. 487,

> That fix'd as fate, this *acted* by a God.

† Ep. iii. ver. 301.

52. Come

52. Come then, my Friend! my Genius! come along;
Oh maſter of the poet and the ſong * !

In this concluding addreſs of our author to Lord Bolingbroke †, one is at a loſs which to admire moſt, the warmth of his friendſhip, or the warmth of his genius. Pope indeed idolized him: when in company with him, he appeared with all the deference and ſubmiſſion of an affectionate ſcholar. He uſed to ſpeak of him as a being of a ſuperior order, that had condeſcended to viſit this lower world; in particular, when the laſt comet appeared and approached near the earth, he told ſome of his acquaintance, "it was ſent only to convey Lord Bolingbroke HOME AGAIN; juſt as a ſtage-coach ſtops at your door to take up a paſſenger." A graceful perſon,

* Ver. 373.

† Thoſe paſſages in Bolingbroke's poſthumous works, that bear the cloſeſt reſemblance to the tenets of this Eſſay are the following. Vol. iv. octavo edition, p. 223 & p. 324; p. 94 of vol. 5; p. 388 of vol. iv. & 389; and p. 49 of vol. iv. p. 5 & 6 of vol. v. p. 17 of vol. v. p. 316 of vol. iv. p. 36 of vol. v. p. 51 of vol. v. p. 328 of vol. iv. and more particularly than all, p. 326 of vol. iv.

a flow of nervous eloquence, a vivid imagination, were the lot of this accomplished nobleman; but his ambitious views being frustrated in the early part of his life, his disappointments embittered his temper, and he seems to have * been disgusted with all religions and all governments. I have been informed from an eye-witness of one his last interviews with POPE, who was then given over by the physicians, that Bolingbroke, standing behind POPE's chair, looked earnestly down upon him, and repeated several times, interrupted with sobs, "O Great God, what is man! I never knew a person that had so tender a heart for his particular friends, or a warmer benevolence for all mankind." It is to be hoped that Bolingbroke † profited by those remarkable

* His manner of reasoning and philosophising has been so happily caught in a piece entitled *A Vindication of Natural Society*; that many, even acute readers, mistook it for a genuine discourse of the author whom it was intended to expose; it is indeed a master-piece of irony.—No writings that raised so mighty an expectation in the public as those of Bolingbroke, ever perished so soon and sunk into oblivion.

† It is asserted on good authority, that Bolingbroke was accustomed to ridicule POPE as not understanding the drift of

remarkable words that POPE ſpoke in his laſt illneſs to the ſame gentleman who communicated the foregoing anecdote;—— "I am ſo certain of the ſoul's being immortal,

of his own principles in their full extent: It is plain from many of our author's letters, vol. ix. p. 324, that he was pleaſed to find ſuch an interpretation could be given to this poem as was conſiſtent with the fundamental principles of religion. *This alſo* farther appears from ſome curious letters that paſſed in the year one thouſand ſeven hundred and forty-two, between Ramſay, Racine the younger, and our author. The former addreſſed a vindication of the principles of the Eſſay on Man to Racine, who had charged it with Spinoziſm and irreligion. This produced a letter from POPE to Racine, which concludes with theſe remarkable words. "I declare therefore loudly and with the greateſt ſincerity, that my ſentiments are diametrically oppoſite to thoſe of Spinoza, and even of Leibnitz. They are in truth perfectly agreeable to the tenets of Paſcal, and the Archbiſhop of Cambray: and I ſhall think it an honour to imitate the moderation and docility of the latter, in always ſubmitting all my private opinions to the deciſion of the church." London, Sept. 1, 1742.

There is a circumſtance in the letter of Ramſay abovementioned, too remarkable to be omitted; and which perhaps ſome may be almoſt tempted to doubt the truth of. In a caſe of ſo delicate a nature I chuſe to quote the original. "M. le Chevalier Newton, grand Géometre & nullement Métaphyſicien, étoit perſuadé de la vérité de la Religion: mais il voulut rafiner ſur d' anciennes erreurs Orientales, & renouvella l'Arianiſme par l' organe de ſon fameux diſciple & intreprete M. Clarke; qui m' avoua quelque tems avant que de mourir après pluſieurs conférences que j' avois eues avec lui, combien il ſe repentoit d' avoir ſait imprimer ſon Ouvrage:

mortal, that I ſeem even to feel it within me, as it were by intuition." After ſuch a declaration, and after writing ſo fervent and elevated a piece of devotion, as the univerſal

Ouvrage: je fus témoin il y a douze ans, à Londres, des derniers ſentimens de ce modeſte & vertueux Docteur."

Œuvres de Racine, tom. i. p. 233.

The manner in which Ramſay endeavours to explain the doctrine of the Eſſay is as follows. "Pope is far from aſſerting that the preſent ſtate of man is his *primitive* ſtate, (*but ſee above, pag.* 70) and is conformable to order. His deſign is to ſhew that, *ſince the Fall*, all is proportioned with weight, meaſure, and harmony, to the condition of a *degraded* being, who ſuffers, and who deſerves to ſuffer, and who cannot be reſtored but by ſufferings; that phyſical evils are deſigned to cure moral evil; that the paſſions and the crimes of the moſt abandoned men are confined, directed, and governed by infinite wiſdom, in ſuch a manner, as to make order emerge out of confuſion, light out of darkneſs, and to call out innumerable advantages from the tranſitory inconveniences of this life; that this ſo gracious Providence conducts all things to its own ends, without ever hurting the liberty of intelligent beings, and without either cauſing or approving the effects of their deliberate malice; that All is *ordained* in the phyſical order, as All is *free* in the moral; that theſe two orders are connected cloſely without fatality, and are not ſubject to that neceſſity which renders us virtuous without merit, and vicious without crime; that, we ſee at preſent but a ſingle wheel of the magnificent machine of the univerſe; but a ſmall link of the great chain; and but an inſignificant part of that immenſe plan which will one day be unfolded. Then will God fully juſtify all the incomprehenſible proceedings of his wiſdom and goodneſs;

and

universal prayer, would it not be injustice to accuse our author of libertinism and irreligion? Especially, as I am told he had inserted an address to Jesus Christ, in the Essay

and will vindicate himself, as Milton speaks, from the rash judgment of mortals."

Lettre De M. De Ramsay,
A Pontoise le 28 April, 1742.

It will be proper to subjoin Bolingbroke's own account of this Essay, given in a letter to Swift, August 2, 1731.

" Does POPE talk to you of the noble work, which, at my instigation, he has begun in such a manner, that he must be convinced, by this time, I judged better of his talents than he did.—The first epistle, which considers man, and the habitation of man, relatively to the whole system of universal being.—The second, which considers him in his own habitation, in himself, and relatively to his own particular system.—And the third, which shews how an universal cause works to one end, but works by various laws: how man, and beast, and vegetable, are linked in a mutual dependency: parts necessary to each other, and necessary to the Whole: how human societies were formed; from what spring true religion and true policy are derived; how God has made our greatest interests and our plainest duty indivisibly the same. These three epistles, I say, are finished. The fourth he is now intent upon. It is a noble subject: he pleads the cause of God. I use Seneca's expression against that famous charge which atheists in all ages have brought, the supposed unequal dispensations of Providence; a charge which I cannot heartily forgive your divines for admitting. You admit it indeed for an extreme good purpose, and you build on this admission the necessity of a future state of rewards and punishments; but if you should find, that this future

Eſſay on Man, which he omitted at the inſtance of Biſhop Berkley, becauſe the Chriſtian diſpenſation did not come within the compaſs of his plan. Not that ſo pious and worthy a prelate could imagine, that this Platonic ſcheme, of OPTIMISM, or the BEST, ſufficiently accounts for the introduction of moral and phyſical evil into the world; which in truth nothing but revelation can explain, and nothing but a future ſtate can compenſate *.

future ſtate will not account for God's juſtice in the preſent ſtate, which you give up, in oppoſition to the atheiſt; would it not have been better to defend God's juſtice in this world, againſt theſe daring men, by irrefragable reaſons, and to have reſted the other point on revelation? I do not like conceſſions made againſt demonſtration, repair or ſupply them how you will. The epiſtles I have mentioned will compoſe a firſt book; the plan of the ſecond is ſettled. You will not underſtand by what I have ſaid, that POPE will *go ſo deep* into the argument, or *carry* it ſo far as I have hinted.

* The Eſſay on Man was elegantly, but unfaithfully, tranſlated into French verſe by M. Du Reſnel. It was more accurately rendered into French proſe by M. De Silhouete. Which tranſlation has been often printed; at Paris 1736; at London 1741, in Quarto; at the Hague 1742. He has ſubjoined a defence of the doctrines of the Eſſay from Warburton's Letters: and has added a tranſlation alſo, with a large commentary, of the four ſucceeding epiſtles of POPE.

Marmontel,

Marmontel, in his *Poetique Françoise*, has paſſed a ſevere ſentence on the obſcurity and inconcluſiveneſs of POPE's reaſoning. Vol. ii. p. 536.

In the very laſt edition of biſhop Law's tranſlation of the Origin of Evil, p. 17, is the following remarkable paſſage: "I had now the ſatisfaction of ſeeing that thoſe very principles which had been maintained by archbiſhop *King*, were adopted by Mr. *Pope*, in his Eſſay on Man; this I uſed to recollect, and ſometimes relate, with pleaſure, conceiving that ſuch an account did no leſs honour to the Poet, than to our Philoſopher; but was ſoon made to underſtand that any thing of that kind was taken highly amiſs, by one (*i. e.* Biſhop *Warburton*) who had once held the doctrine of that ſame Eſſay to be rank atheiſm, but afterwards turned a warm advocate for it, and thought proper to deny the account abovementioned, with heavy menaces againſt thoſe who preſumed to inſinuate that POPE borrowed any thing from any man whatſoever."

SECT.

SECT. X.

Of the Moral ESSAYS *in five* EPISTLES *to ſeveral Perſons.*

THE patrons and admirers of French literature, uſually extol thoſe authors of that nation who have treated of life and manners: and five of them particularly are eſteemed to be unrivalled; namely, MONTAIGNE, CHARRON, LA ROCHFOUCAULT, LA BRUYERE, and PASCAL. Theſe are ſuppoſed to have penetrated deeply into the moſt ſecret receſſes of the human heart, and to have diſcovered the various vices and vanities that lurk in it. I know not why the Engliſh ſhould in this reſpect yield to their polite neighbours, more than in any other. BACON in his Eſſays and Advancement of Learning, HOBBES and HUME in their Treatiſes, PRIOR in his elegant and witty Alma, RICHARDSON in his Clariſſa, and FIELDING in his Tom Jones, (comic writers

writers are not here included) have ſhewn a profound knowledge of man; and many pourtraits of ADDISON may be compared with the moſt finiſhed touches of LA BRUYERE. But the Epiſtles we are now entering upon will place the matter beyond a diſpute; for the French can boaſt of no author who has ſo much exhauſted the ſcience of morals, as POPE has in theſe five Epiſtles. They indeed contain all that is ſolid and valuable in the above-mentioned French writers, of whom our author was remarkably fond: But whatever obſervations he has borrowed from them, he has made his own by the dexterity of his application.

1. Men may be read, as well as books, too much *.

"STUDY life;" cry the unlettered men of the world: but that world cannot be known merely by that ſtudy alone. The dread of pedantry is a characteriſtic folly of the preſent age. We adopted it from the French, without conſidering the reaſons that give riſe to it among that people: the

* Ep. i. ver. 10.

religious,

religious, and particularly the Jesuits, perceiving that a taste for learning began widely to diffuse itself among the laity, could find no surer method of repressing it, than by treating the learned character as ridiculous. This ridicule was carried so far, that, to mention one instance out of ten thousand, the publisher of La Rochfoucault's maxims makes a grave apology in form, for quoting Seneca in Latin.

2. At half mankind, when gen'rous Manly raves,
All know 'tis virtue, for he thinks them knaves *.

The character alluded to is the principal one in the Plain Dealer of Wycherly, a comedy taken from the Misanthrope of Moliere, but much inferior to the original. Alcestes has not that bitterness of spirit, and has much more humanity and honour than Manly. Writers transfuse their own characters into their works: Wycherly was a vain and profligate libertine; Moliere was beloved for his candour, sweetness of temper and integrity. It is re-

* Ver. 57.

markable that the French did not relish this incomparable comedy for the three first representations. The strokes of its satire were too subtle and delicate to be felt by the generality of the audience, who expected only the gross diversion of laughing; so that at the fourth time of its being acted, the author was forced to add to it one of his coarsest farces; but Boileau in the mean time affirmed that it was the capital work of their stage, and that the people would one time be induced to think so.

3. Unthought-of frailties cheat us in the wise *.

For who could imagine that Locke was fond of romances; that Newton once studied astrology; that Roger Ascham and Dr. Whitby were devoted lovers of cock-fighting; that Dr. Clarke valued himself for his agility, and frequently amused himself in a private room of his house in leaping over the tables and chairs: and that our author himself was a great

* Ver. 69.

epicure? When he ſpent a ſummer with a certain nobleman, he was accuſtomed to lie whole days in bed on account of his head-achs, but would at any time riſe with alacrity, when his ſervant informed him there were ſtewed lampreys for dinner. On the eve of an important battle, the Duke of MARLBOROUGH was heard chiding his ſervant for having been ſo extravagant as to light four candles in his tent, when Prince Eugene came to confer with him. ELIZABETH was a coquet, and BACON received a bribe. Dr. BUSBY had a violent paſſion for the ſtage; it was excited in him by the applauſes he received in acting the Royal Slave before the King at Chriſt-Church; and he declared, that if the rebellion had not broke out, he had certainly engaged himſelf as an actor. LUTHER was ſo immoderately paſſionate, that he ſometimes boxed MELANCTHON's ears; and MELANCTHON himſelf was a believer in judicial aſtrology, and an interpreter of dreams. RICHLIEU and MAZARIN were ſo ſuperſtitious as to employ and penſion

MORIN,

MORIN, a pretender to aſtrology, who caſt the nativities of theſe two able politicians. Nor was TACITUS himſelf, who generally appears ſuperior to ſuperſtition, untainted with this folly, as may appear from the twenty-ſecond chapter of the ſixth book of his annals. Men of great genius have been ſomewhere compared to the pillar of fire that conducted the Iſraelites, which frequently turned a cloudy ſide towards the ſpectator.

4. See the ſame man, in vigour, in the gout;
Alone, in company, in place, or out;
Early at buſineſs, and at hazard late;
Mad at a fox-chaſe, wiſe at a debate;
Drunk at a borough, civil at a ball;
Friendly at Hackney, faithleſs at Whitehall *.

THE unexpected inequalities of our minds and tempers are here exhibited in a lively manner, and with a perfect knowledge of nature. I cannot forbear placing before the reader Tully's pourtrait of Cataline, whoſe inconſiſtencies and varieties of conduct are thus enumerated; "Ute-

* Ver. 71.

batur hominibus improbis multis, et quidem optimis ſe viris deditum eſſe ſimulabat; erant apud illum illecebræ libidinum multæ: erant etiam induſtriæ quidam ſtimuli ac laboris; flagrabant libidinis vitia apud illum: vigebant etiam ſtudia rei militaris: neque ego unquam fuiſſe tale monſtrum in terris ullum puto, tam ex contrariis diverſiſque inter ſe pugnantibus naturæ ſtudiis, cupiditatibus que conflatum. Quis clarioribus viris quodam tempore jucundior? Quis turpioribus conjunctior? Quis civis meliorum partium aliquando? Quis tetrior hoſtis huic civitati? Quis in voluptatibus inquinatior? Quis in laboribus patientior? Quis in rapacitate avarior? Quis in largitione effuſior *?"

5. What made, ſay, Montagne, or more ſage Charron †.

One of the reaſons that makes Montagne ſo agreeable a writer is, that he gives ſo ſtrong a picture of the way of life of a country gentleman in the reign of Henry the Third. The deſcriptions of his caſtle,

* Orat. pro M. Cælio. Sect. 3. † Ver. 87.

of his library, of his travels, of his entertainments, of his diet and dreſs, are particularly pleaſing. Malebranche and Paſcal have ſeverely and juſtly cenſured his ſcepticiſm. Peter Charron contracted a very ſtrict friendſhip with him, inſomuch that Montagne permitted him by his will to bear his arms: in his book of Wiſdom which was publiſhed at Bourdeaux, in the year one thouſand ſix hundred and one, he has inſerted a great number of Montagne's ſentiments; this treatiſe has been loudly blamed for its freedom by many writers of France, and particularly GARASSE the Jeſuit. Our Stanhope, though eſteemed an orthodox Divine, tranſlated it. BAYLE has remarked in oppoſition to theſe cenſurers, that of a hundred thouſand readers, there are hardly three to be found in any age, who are well qualified to judge of a book, wherein the ideas of an exact and metaphyſical reaſoning are ſet in oppoſition to the moſt common opinions. POPE has borrowed many remarks from Charron, of which ſenſible writer Bolingbroke was particularly fond.

6. A godless regent tremble at a star *.

The duke of Orleans, here pointed at, was an infidel and libertine, and at the same time, as well as Boulanvilliers and Cardan who calculated the nativity of Jesus Christ, was a bigotted believer in judicial astrology; he was said to be the author, which however has been doubted, of many of those flimsy songs, nugæ canoræ, to which the language and the manners of France seem to be peculiarly adapted. He knew mankind. "Quiconque est sans honneur & sans humeur, said he frequently, est un courtisan parfaite." Crebillon the father, a writer far superior to his son, during this profligate and debauched regent's administration, wrote a set of odes against him, of wonderful energy and keenness, and almost in the spirit of Alceus; if it be not a kind of profanation to speak thus, of any production of a poet that writes under a despotic government.

* Ver. 90.

7. Alas

7. Alas in truth the man but chang'd his mind,
Perhaps was ſick, in love, or had not din'd *.

For the deſtruction of a kingdom, ſaid a man of wit, nothing more is ſometimes requiſite than a bad digeſtion of the prime miniſter. The Grand Seignior offered to aſſiſt Henry IV. againſt his rebellious ſubjects, not for any deep political reaſon, but only becauſe he hated the word, *League*. It is a fault in Davila, as well as Tacitus, never to aſcribe great events, to whim, caprice, private paſſions, and petty cauſes.

8. Judge we by nature? Habit can efface,
Intereſt o'ercome, or policy take place:
By actions? thoſe uncertainty divides:
By paſſions? theſe diſſimulation hides;
Opinions? they ſtill take a wider range:
Find if you can in what you cannot change.
Manners with fortunes, humours turn with climes,
Tenets with books, and principles with times †.

We find here in the compaſs of eight lines, an anatomy of human nature; more ſenſe and obſervation cannot well be compreſſed and concluded in a narrower ſpace.

* Ver. 127. † Ver 182.

This paſſage might be drawn out into a voluminous commentary, and be worked up into a ſyſtem concerning the knowledge of the world: There ſeems to be an inaccuracy in the uſe of the laſt verb; the natural temperament is by no means ſuddenly changed, or *turned* with a change of climate, though undoubtedly the humours are originally formed by it: *influenced by*, would be a more proper expreſſion than *turn with*, if the metre would admit it.

9. His paſſion ſtill, to covet gen'ral praiſe,
His life, to forfeit it a thouſand ways;
A conſtant bounty which no friend has made;
An angel tongue which no man can perſuade;
A fool with more of wit than half mankind,
Too raſh for thought, for action too refin'd:
A tyrant to the wife his heart approves;
A rebel to the very king he loves;
He dies an out-caſt of each church and ſtate,
And harder ſtill flagitious yet not great *.

THIS character of the Duke of Wharton is finiſhed with much force and expreſſiveneſs †; the contradictions that were in it

* Ver. 205.

† Compare it with that of Zimri, the Duke of Buckingham, in Abſalom and Achitopel: in which Dryden has excelled our author.

are

are ſtrongly contraſted. In an entertaining work lately publiſhed, which it is hoped will diffuſe a reliſh for biography, we have a remarkable anecdote relating to this nobleman's ſpeech in favour of the biſhop of Rocheſter. His Grace, then in oppoſition to Court, went to Chelſea the day before the laſt debate on that prelate's affair, where acting contrition, he profeſſed being determined to work out his pardon at Court by ſpeaking againſt the biſhop, in order to which he begged ſome hints. The miniſter was deceived, and went through the whole cauſe with him, pointing out where the ſtrength of the argument lay, and where it's weakneſs. The Duke was very thankful, returned to town, paſſed the night in drinking, and without going to bed, went to the Houſe of Lords, where he ſpoke FOR the biſhop, recapitulating in the moſt maſterly manner, and anſwering all that had been urged againſt him *.

10. When Cataline by rapine ſwell'd his ſtore;
When Cæſar made a noble dame a whore;

* Catalogue of the Royal and Noble Authors of England, vol. ii. p. 133.

In

In this the lust, in that the avarice
Were means, not ends; ambition was the vice *.

The same passion excited Richlieu to throw up the dyke at Rochelle, and to dispute the prize of poetry with Corneille; whom to traduce was the surest method of gaining the affection of this ambitious minister, who aspired equally to excel in all things; nay, who formed a design to be canonized as a saint. A perfect contrast to the character of Cardinal Fleury, who shewed that it was possible to govern a great state with moderate abilities, and a mild temper. His ministry is impartially represented by Voltaire in the age of Louis XIV.

11. Lucullus, when frugality could charm,
Had roasted turnips in the Sabin farm †.

Few writers of his country have displayed a greater energy of sentiment than Crebillon ‡; in his Cataline we have a noble

* Ver. 214.

† Ver. 218. See Considerations on Lucullus, in the second vol. of L' Abbé de St. Real, p. 1.

‡ The creditors of Crebillon would have stopped the profits of this tragedy, but the spirited old bard appealed to

noble one that may illuſtrate this doctrine of POPE; " If, ſays this fierce and inflexible conſpirator, I had only Lentulus's of my party, and if it was filled only with men of virtue, I ſhould eaſily aſſume that character alſo, and be more virtuous than any of them."

Et s' il n' étoit rempli que d' hommes vertueux,
Je n' aurois pas de peine à l' être encor plus qu' eux.

12. In this one paſſion man can ſtrength enjoy,
As fits give vigour, juſt when they deſtroy *.

THE ſtrength and continuance of what our author calls the ruling paſſion, is ſtrongly exemplified in EIGHT characters; namely, the POLITICIAN, the DEBAUCHEE, the GLUTTON, the OECONOMIST, the COQUET, the COURTIER, the MISER, and the PATRIOT. Of theſe characters, the moſt lively, becauſe the moſt dramatic,

to the king in council, and procured an honourable decree in his favour, ſetting forth, that works of genius ſhould not be deemed Effects that were capable of being ſeized. This writer's works were lately printed in a magnificent manner at the Louvre, in two volumes, quarto, at the expence of Madam Pompadour.

* Ver. 22.

are

are the fifth and ſeventh. There is true humour alſo in the circumſtance of the frugal crone who blows out one of the conſecrated tapers in order to prevent it's waſting. Shall I venture to inſert another example or two? An old uſurer lying in his laſt agonies was preſented by the prieſt with the crucifix. He opened his eyes a moment before he expired, attentively gazed on it, and cried out, "Theſe jewels are counterfeit, I cannot lend more than ten piſtoles upon ſo wretched a pledge." To reform the language of his country was the ruling paſſion of Malherbe. The prieſt who attended him in his laſt moments, aſked him if he was not affected with the deſcription he gave him of the joys of heaven? By no means, anſwered the incorrigible bard, I deſire to hear no more of them, if you cannot deſcribe them in a purer ſtyle. Both theſe ſtories would have ſhone under the hands of Pope.

This doctrine of our author may be farther illuſtrated by the following paſſage of of Bacon. " It is no leſs worthy to obſerve, how little alteration, in good ſpirits, the approaches of death make; for they appear to be the ſame men, till the laſt inſtant. Auguſtus Cæſar died in a compliment; Livia, conjugii noſtri memor, vive et vale. Tiberius in diſſimulation; as Tacitus ſaith of him: Jam Tiberium vires et corpus, non diſſimulatio deſerebant. Veſpaſian, in a jeſt, Ut puto Deus fio. Galba with a ſentence; Feri, ſi ex re ſit populi Romani; holding forth his neck. Septimius Severus, in diſpatch; Adeſte, ſi quid mihi reſtat agendum *."

THIS epiſtle concludes with a ſtroke of art worthy admiration. The poet ſuddenly ſtops the vein of ridicule with which he was flowing, and addreſſes his friend in a moſt delicate compliment, concealed under the appearance of ſatire.

And you! brave Cobham, to the lateſt breath
Shall feel your ruling paſſion ſtrong in death:

* Bacon's Eſſays. Eſſay ii. which were much read by POPE.

Such

Such in those moments as in all the past,
"Oh save my country, heav'n, shall be your last."

13. Narcissa's nature, tolerably mild,
To make a wash, would hardly stew a child;
Has ev'n been prov'd to grant a lover's pray'r;
And paid a tradesman once to make him stare;
Gave alms at Easter, in a Christian trim,
And made a widow happy for a whim *.

The epistle on the characters of women, from whence this truly witty character is taken, is highly finished, and full of the most delicate satire. Bolingbroke, a judge of the subject, thought it the master-piece of Pope. But the bitterness of the satire is not always concealed in a laugh. The characters are lively, though uncommon. I scarcely remember one of them in our comic writers of the best order. The ridicule is heightened by many such strokes of humour, carried even to the borders of extravagance, as that in the second line, here quoted. The female foibles have been the subject of perhaps more wit, in every language, than any other topic that can be

* Epist. ii. v. 53.

named.

named. The ſixth ſatire of Juvenal, though deteſtable for its obſcenity, is undoubtedly the moſt witty of all his ſixteen; and is curious for the picture it exhibits of the private lives of the Roman ladies. POPE confines himſelf to paint thoſe inconſiſtencies of conduct, to which a volatile fancy is thought to incline the ſex. And this he exemplifies in the contrarieties that may be diſcovered in the characters of the AFFECTED, the SOFT-NATURED, the WHIMSICAL, the LEWD and VICIOUS, the WITTY and REFINED. In this comprehenſive view is perhaps included each ſpecies of female folly and abſurdity, which is the proper object of ridicule. If this Epiſtle yields, in any reſpect, to the tenth ſatire of Boileau on the ſame ſubject, it is in the delicacy and variety of the tranſitions, by which the French writer paſſes from one character to another, always connecting each with the foregoing. It was a common ſaying of Boileau, ſpeaking of La Bruyere, that one of the moſt difficult parts of compoſition, was the art of tranſition. That

we

we may see how happily POPE has caught the manner of Boileau, let us survey one of his pourtraits: it shall be that of his learned lady.

Qui s'offrira d'abord? c'est cette Scavante,
Qu'estime Roberval, & que Sauveur frequente.
D'ou vient qu'elle a l' œil trouble, & le teint si terni?
C'est que sur le calcal, dit-on, de Cassini,
Un Astrolabe en main, elle a dans sa goûtiere
Il suivre Jupiter passé le nuit entiere:
Gardons de la troubler. Sa science, se croy,
Aura par s'occuper ce jour plus d'un employ.
D'un nouveau microscope ou doit en sa présence
Tantost chez Dalancé faire l'experience;
Puis d'une femme morte avec son embryon,
Il faut chez Du Vernay voir la dissection *.

14. No thought advances, but her eddy brain
Whisks it about, and down it goes again.
Full sixty years the world has been her trade,
The wisest fool much time has ever made.
From loveless youth to unrespected age,
No passion gratify'd, except her rage.

* Which last line is a little gross and offensive: as it must be confessed are some of POPE. There is not a single stroke of this sort in Young's Satires on Women. I wish the delicacy and reservedness of four or five Ladies now living, who have real learning and taste, would permit me to insert their names in this place, as a contrast to this affected character in Boileau.

So

So much the fury ſtill outran the wit,
The pleaſure miſs'd her, and the ſcandal hit *.

THESE ſpirited lines are part of a character deſigned for the famous Dutcheſs of Marlborough; whom SWIFT had alſo ſeverely ſatirized in the *Examiner*. Her beauty, her abilities, her political intrigues, are ſufficiently known †. The violence of her temper frequently broke out into wonderful and ridiculous indecencies. In the laſt illneſs of the great Duke her huſband, when Dr. Mead left his chamber, the

* Ver. 125. Epiſt. ii.

† See the account of her own conduct, drawn up under her own eye and direction, by Mr. HOOKE, author of the Roman Hiſtory, of the life of Fenelon, and of the tranſlation of the travels of Cyrus. Dr. KING, of St. Mary Hall, in Oxford, informed me, that this elegant tranſlation was made at Dr. Cheyne's houſe at Bath, and that he himſelf had often been Hooke's Amanuenſis on this occaſion, who dictated his tranſlation to him with uncommon facility and rapidity. The Dutcheſs rewarded Hooke with 5,000*l.* for his trouble; but quarrelled with him afterwards, becauſe, as ſhe affirmed, he attempted to convert her to Popery. Hooke was a Myſtic, and a Quietiſt, and a warm diſciple of Fenelon. It was he who brought a Catholic prieſt to take our author's confeſſion on his death-bed. The prieſt had ſcarce departed, when Bolingbroke, coming over from Batterſea, flew into a great fit of paſſion and indignation on the occaſion.

Dutchefs, difliking his advice, followed him down ftairs, *fwore* at him bitterly, and was going to tear off his perriwig. Her friend Dr. Hoadly, bifhop of Winchefter, was prefent at this fcene. Thefe lines were fhewn to her Grace as if they were intended for the portrait of the Dutchefs of Buckingham, but fhe foon ftopped the perfon that was reading them to her, and called out aloud—" I cannot be fo impofed upon—I fee plainly enough for whom they are defigned;" and abufed POPE moft plentifully on the fubject; though fhe was afterwards reconciled to, and courted him. This character, together with thofe of PHILOMEDE and CLOE, were firft publifhed in this edition of POPE. They are all animated with the moft poignant wit. That of Cloe is particularly juft and happy, who is reprefented as content merely and only to *dwell in decencies*, and fatisfied to avoid giving offence; and is one of thofe many infignificant and ufelefs beings,

> Who want, as thro' blank life they dream along,
> Senfe to be right, and paffion to be wrong;

as

5

as says the ingenious author of the *Universal Passion*; a work that abounds in wit, observation on life, pleasantry, delicacy, urbanity, and the most well-bred raillery, without a single mark of spleen and ill-nature. These were the first *characteristical* satires in our language, and are written with an ease and familiarity of style, very different from this author's other works. The four first were published in folio, in the year 1725 *; and the fifth and sixth, incomparably the best, on the characters of women, in the year 1727, that is, eight years before this epistle of

* In these, the characters of *Clarinda*, of *Zantippe* the *violent* lady, of *Delia* the chariot-driver, of *Master* Betty the huntress, of *Daphne* the critic, of *Lemira* the sick lady, of the female *Philosopher*, of the *Theologist*, of the *languid* lady, of *Thalestris* the *swearer*, of *Lyce* the old beauty, of *Lavinia*, of a *nymph* of *spirit*, of *Julia* the *manager*, of *Alicia* the *sloven*, of Clio the *slanderer*, of the *affected Asturia*, of the female *Atheist*, and of the female *Gamester*; are all of them drawn with truth and spirit. And the introductions to these two satires, particularly the address to the incomparable Lady Betty Germain, are perhaps as elegant as any thing in our language. After reading these pieces, so full of a knowledge of the world, one is at a loss to know what Mr. POPE could mean by saying, that though *Young* was a man of genius, yet that *he wanted common sense*.

POPE. Dr. Young was one of the moſt amiable and benevolent of men; moſt exemplary in his life, and ſincere in his religion*. Nobody ever ſaid more brilliant things in converſation. The late Lord MELCOMBE informed me, that when he and Voltaire were on a viſit to his Lordſhip at Eaſtbury, the Engliſh poet was far ſuperior to the French, in the variety and the novelty of his bon mots and repartees; and Lord Melcombe was himſelf a good judge of wit and humour, of which he himſelf had a great portion. If the friendſhip with which Dr. Young honoured me does not miſlead me, I think I may venture to affirm, that many high ſtrokes of character in his *Zanga*; many ſentiments and

* Mr. Walter Harte aſſured me, he had ſeen the preſſing letter that Dr. Young wrote to Mr. POPE, urging him to write ſomething on the ſide of Revelation, in order to take off the impreſſions of thoſe doctrines which the Eſſay on Man were ſuppoſed to convey. He alluded to this in the concluſion of his firſt Night-thought.

O had he preſs'd his theme, purſu'd the track
Which opens out of darkneſs into day!
O had he mounted on his wing of fire,
Soar'd where I ſink, and ſung *immortal* man!
How had he bleſt mankind and reſcu'd me!

images

images in his *Night-thoughts*; and many ſtrong and forcible deſcriptions in his paraphraſe on *Job*, mark him for a ſublime and original genius. Though at the ſame time I am ready to confeſs, that he is not a correct and equal writer *, and was too often turgid and hyperbolical.

15. See how the world its veterans rewards,
A youth of frolics, an old age of cards;
Fair to no purpoſe, artful to no end,
Young without lovers, old without a friend;
A fop their paſſion, but their prize a ſot,
Alive, ridiculous; and dead, forgot †.

The antitheſis, ſo remarkably ſtrong in theſe lines, was a very favourite figure with our poet: he has indeed uſed it but in too

* So little ſenſible are we of our own imperfections, that the very laſt time I ſaw Dr. Young, he was ſeverely cenſuring and ridiculing the falſe pomp of fuſtian writers, and the nauſeouſneſs of *bombaſt*. I remember he ſaid, that ſuch torrents of eloquence were *muddy* as well as *noiſy*; and that theſe *violent* and *tumultuous* authors, put him in mind of a paſſage in Milton, B. ii. v. 539.

Others, with vaſt Typhæan rage more fell,
Rend up both rocks and hills, and ride the air
In whirlwind. Hell ſcarce holds the wild uproar.

† Ver. 243.

many parts of his works; nay, even in his translation of the Iliad *; where it ought not to have been admitted: and which Dryden has but rarely uſed in his Virgil. Our author ſeldom writes many lines together without an antitheſis. It muſt be allowed ſometimes to add ſtrength to a ſentiment, by an oppoſition of images;

* Voltaire ſpeaks thus of La Motte: ſo popular and acute a critic may, perhaps, be attended to.——Au-lieu d'échauffer ſon génie en tâchant de copier les ſublimes peintures d'Homére, il voulut lui donner de l'eſprit; c'eſt la Manie de la plûpart des François; une eſpéce de pointe qu'ils appellent un trait, une petite antithéſe, un lèger contraſte de mots leur ſuffit.—The following lines are inſtances:

On offenſe les dieux, mais par des ſacrifices
De ces dieux irrités on fait des dieux propices.

And again——

Tout le camp s'écria dans une joie extrême,
Que ne vaincra-t-il point, il s'eſt vaincu lui meme.

I muſt only juſt add, that La Motte, in all the famous diſpute about the ancients, never ſaid a thing ſo ill-founded, and ſo void of taſte, as the following words of the ſame Voltaire: "Homere n' a jamais fait répandre de pleurs." *Affectus* quidem vel illos *mites* vel hos *concitatos*, nemo erit *tam indoctus* qui non in ſuâ poteſtate hunc auctorem habuiſſe fateatur. Quintilian, lib. 10. cap. 1. Had Voltaire ever read Quintilian? or rather, had he ever read Homer—in the original? If Boileau, ſaid the Prince of Conti, does not write againſt Perrault, I will go myſelf to the Academy, and I will write upon his ſeat, *Brutus, you are aſleep*.

but,

but, too frequently repeated, it becomes tiresome, and disgusting. Rhyme has almost a natural tendency to betray a writer into it. But the purest authors have despised it, as an ornament pert, and puerile, and epigrammatic. Seneca, Pliny, Tacitus, and later authors, abound in it. Quintilian has sometimes used it, with much success; as when he speaks of style; magna, non nimia; sublimis, non abrupta; severa, non tristis; læta, non luxuriosa; plena, non tumida. And sometimes Tully; as, vicit pudorem libido, timorem audacia, rationem amentia. But these writers fall into this mode of speaking but seldom, and do not make it their *constant* and *general manner*. Those moderns who have not acquired a true taste for the simplicity of the best ancients *, have generally run into a frequent use of *point*, *opposition*, and *contrast*. They who begin to study painting, are struck at first with the pieces of the most vivid colouring; they are almost

* See what Dionysius says of Isocrates, p. 99, v. 2. Edit. Sylb. There are no antitheses in Demosthenes.

ashamed to own, that they do not relish and feel the modest and reserved beauties of Raphael. The exact proportion of St. Peter's at Rome, occasions it not to appear so great as it really is. 'Tis the same in writing; but, by degrees, we find that Lucan, Martial, Juvenal, Q. Curtius, and Florus, and others of that stamp, who abound in figures that contribute to the false florid, in luxuriant metaphors, in pointed conceits, in lively antitheses, unexpectedly darted forth, are contemptible for the very causes which once excited our admiration. 'Tis then we relish Terence, Cæsar, and Xenophon.

16. Kept dross for Duchesses, *the world shall know it*,
To you gave sense, good-humour, and a poet *.

The world shall know it—is an unmeaning expression, and a poor expletive, into which our poet was forced by the rhyme †.

* Ver. 291.

† La Rime gêne plus qu'elle n' orne les vers. Elle les charge d'Epithétes; elle rend souvent la diction forcée, & pleine d' une vaine parure. En allongant les discours, elle les affoiblit. Souvent on a recours à un vers inutile; pour en amener un bon. FENELON to M. DE LA MOTTE. Lettres, p. 62. A Cambray, 26 Janvier 1719.

Maudit

Maudit ſoit le premier, dont la verve inſenſée,
Dans les bornes d' un vers renferma ſa penſée,
Et donnant à ſes mots une étroite priſon,
Voulut avec la rime enchaîner la raiſon *.

RHYME alſo could alone be the occaſion of the following faulty expreſſions; taken too from ſome of his moſt finiſhed pieces.

Not Cæſar's Empreſs would *I deign to prove*—
If Queenberry to ſtrip *there's no compelling*—
Rapt into future times the *bard begun*—
Know all the noiſe the buſy *world can keep*—
If true, a woful likeneſs, and *if lyes*—
Nothing ſo true as what you once *let fall*—
For virtue's ſelf may too much *zeal be had*—
———can no *wants endure*—
Nay half in heav'n *except what's mighty odd*—
——— can have no *flaw*—
——— on ſuch a world *we fall*—
——— take ſcandal *at a ſpark*—
——— do *the knack*, and——do *the feat*—

And more inſtances might be added, if it were not diſagreeable to obſerve theſe ſtraws in amber. But if rhyme occaſions ſuch inconveniences and improprieties in ſo exact a writer as our author, what can be

* Boileau, Sat. 2. v. 53.

expected

expected from inferior versifiers *? It is not my intention to enter into a trite and tedious discussion of the several merits of rhyme and blank verse. Perhaps rhyme may be properest for shorter pieces; for lyric, elegiac, and satiric poems; for pieces where closeness of expression, and smartness of style, are expected; but for subjects of a higher order, where any enthusiasm or emotion is to be expressed, or for poems of a greater length, blank verse is undoubtedly preferable. An epic poem in rhyme appears to be such a sort of thing, as the Æneid would have been if it had been written, like Ovid's Fasti, in hexameter and pentameter verses; and the reading it would have been as tedious as

* Our author told Mr. HARTE, that, in order to disguise his being the author of the second epistle of the Essay on Man, he made, in the first edition, the following bad rhyme:

A cheat! a whore! who starts not at the *name*,
In all the inns of court, or Drury-*Lane* *?

And HARTE remembered to have often heard it urged, in enquiries about the author, whilst he was unknown, that it was impossible it could be POPE's, on account of this very passage. POPE inserted many good lines in *Harte*'s Essay on *Reason*.

* V. 205.

the

the travelling through that one long, ſtrait, avenue of firs, that leads from *Moſcow* to *Peterſburg*. I will give the reader Mr. POPE's own opinion on this ſubject, and in his own words, as delivered to Mr. Spence. "I have *nothing* to ſay for rhyme *; but that I doubt if a poem can *ſupport* itſelf without it in our language, unleſs it be ſtiffned with ſuch ſtrange words, as are likely to deſtroy our language itſelf. The high ſtyle that is

* Boileau, whoſe practice it was to make the ſecond line of a couplet before the firſt, having written (in his ſecond ſatire) this line,

Dans mes vers recouſus mettre en pieces Malherbe,

it was thought impoſſible by La Fontaine and Moliere, and other critical friends, for him to find a proper rhyme for the word Malherbe: at laſt he hit upon the following;

Et tranſpoſant cent fois & le nom & le verbe.

Upon ſhewing which line to La Fontaine, he cried out—"Ah! how happy have you been, my friend! I would give the very beſt of all my Tales to have made ſuch a diſcovery." So important in the eyes of French poets is a lucky rhyme! *Voltaire* gives us the following anecdote. Queſtions ſur l'Encycloped. Partie 5, 255 page. "Je me ſouviendrai toûjours que je demandai au célébre POPE, pourquoi Milton n'avait pas rimé ſon Paradis perdu; & qu'il me répondit, *Becauſe he could not*; parce qu'il ne le pouvait pas."——But the moſt harmonious of rhymers has ſaid—"What rhyme adds to ſweetneſs, it takes away from ſenſe." DRYDEN.—The rhymes in *L'Allegro* and *Il Penſeroſo* are juſt and correct.

affected

affected ſo much in blank verſe, would not have been ſupported even in Milton, had not his ſubject turned ſo much on ſuch *ſtrange* and *out of the world* things as it does*."—May we not, however, venture to obſerve, that more of that true harmony which will beſt *ſupport* a poem, will reſult from a *variety* of pauſes, and from an intermixture of thoſe different *feet* (iambic and trochaïc particularly) into which our language naturally falls, than from the uniformity of *ſimilar terminations*. "*There can be no muſic*," ſays COWLEY, "*with only one note*."

17. Bleſt paper-credit! laſt and beſt ſupply!
That lends corruption lighter wings to fly!
Gold, imp'd by thee, can compaſs hardeſt things,
Can pocket States, can fetch or carry Kings;
A ſingle leaf ſhall waft an army o'er,
Or ſhip off Senates to a diſtant ſhore;
A leaf, like Sybils', ſcatter to and fro
Our fates and fortunes, as the winds ſhall blow;

* But there are many paſſages in Milton of the moſt flowing ſoftneſs and ſmoothneſs; without any marks of this high ſtyle, any hard or antiquated words, or harſh inverſions; which are by no means eſſential to blank verſe.

Pregnant

Pregnant with thousands * flits the scrap unseen,
And silent sells a King, or buys a Queen †.

"NOT one of my works" (said POPE to Mr. Spence) was more laboured than my epistle on the Use of Riches." It does indeed abound in knowledge of life, and in the justest satire. The lines above quoted have also the additional merit of touching on a subject that never occurred to former satirists. And though it was difficult to say any thing new about avarice, "a vice that has been so pelted (says COWLEY) with good sentences," yet has our author done it so successfully, that this epistle, together with Lord BACON's thirty-third *Essay*, contains almost all that can be said on the use and abuse of riches, and the absurd extremes of avarice and profusion. But our poet has enlivened his precepts with so many various characters, pictures, and images, as may entitle him to claim the preference over all that have

* The word *flits* heightens the satire, by giving us the strong idea of an obscene and ill-omened bird.

† Of the use of Riches, v. 39.

treated

treated on this tempting ſubject, down from the time of the Plutus of Ariſtophanes. That very lively and amiable old nobleman, the late Lord BATHURST, told me, "that he was much ſurprized to ſee what he had with repeated pleaſure ſo often read as an *epiſtle* addreſſed to himſelf, in this edition converted into a *dialogue*; in which," ſaid he, "I perceive I really make but a ſhabby and indifferent figure, and contribute very little to the ſpirit of the *dialogue*, if it *muſt be* a *dialogue*; and I hope I had generally more to ſay for myſelf in the many charming converſations I uſed to hold with POPE and Swift, and my old poetical friends."

18. A Stateſman's ſlumbers how this ſpeech would ſpoil!
"Sir, Spain has ſent a thouſand jars of oil;
Huge bales of Britiſh cloth blockade the door;
A hundred oxen at your levee roar *."

NOTHING can exceed this ridicule of the many inconveniences that would have *encumbered villainy*, by bribing and by paying *in kind*. The following examples

* Ver. 55.

carry

carry the ſatire ſtill higher, and can hardly be thought to be excelled by any ſtrokes of irony and humour in the beſt parts of Horace, Juvenal, or Boileau.

His Grace will game; to White's a bull be led,
With * ſpurning heels, and with a butting head.
To White's be carry'd, as to ancient † games,
Fair courſers, vaſes, and alluring dames.
Shall then Uxorio, if the ſtakes he ſweep,
Bear home ſix whores, and make his lady weep?
Or ſoft Adonis, ſo perfum'd and fine,
Drive to St. James's a whole herd of ſwine ‡?

WE can only lament that our author did not live long enough to be a witneſs of the midnight (or morning) *orgies* of the gameſters at BROOKS's. What a ſubject for the ſeverity of his ſatire! Perhaps we might have ſeen men,

Safe from the bar, the pulpit, and the throne,
Yet touch'd and ſham'd by *ridicule* alone!

* As a conſecrated beaſt to a ſacrifice; and alluding to Virgil, with much pleaſantry,

Jam cornu petat, & pedibus qui ſpargat arenam.

† Alluding to the prizes that Achilles beſtows in the games of Homer. Iliad. 23. b.

‡ Ver. 67.

For

For ſurely that vice deſerves the keeneſt invective, which, more than any other, has a natural and invincible tendency to narrow and to harden the heart, by *impreſſing* and *keeping* up *habits of ſelfiſhneſs.* "I foreſee, (ſaid MONTESQUIEU to a friend viſiting him at *La Brede*) that *gaming* will, one day, be the ruin of Europe. During play, the body is in a ſtate of indolence, and the mind in a ſtate of vicious activity."

19. Damn'd to the mines, an equal fate betides
The ſlave that digs it, and the ſlave that hides *.

† THIS is plainly taken from the cauſes of the *decay* of *Chriſtian Piety.* "It has always been held, ſays this excellent writer, the ſevereſt treatment of ſlaves and malefactors, damnare ad metalla, to force them to dig in the mines: now this is the covetous man's lot, from which he is never to expect a releaſe." And the character of Helluo the glutton, who exclaimed even

* Ver. 109.

† See the Adventurer, N° 63, publiſhed 1753. The reflection with which CHARTRES's epitaph, in this epiſtle, concludes, is from LA BRUYERE.

in his laſt agonies (at the end of the firſt of theſe epiſtles)

—— then bring the jowl!

is clearly borrowed from the concluſion of one of the tales of LA FONTAINE:

Puis qu'il faut que je meure
Sans faire tant de façon,
Qu' on m' apporte tout à l' heure
Le reſte de mon poiſſon.

So true is that candid acknowledgment which our author makes in his ſenſible preface, " I fairly confeſs that I have ſerved myſelf all I could by reading." But the noble paſſage I ſhall next quote, he has not borrowed from any writer. It is intended to illuſtrate the uſefulneſs, in the hands of a gracious Providence, that reſults from the extremes of avarice and profuſion; and it recurs to the leading principle of our author's philoſophy, namely, that contrarieties and varieties, and exceſſes, in the moral as well as the natural world, by counter-poizing and counter-working each other, contribute ultimately to the *benefit* and *beauty* of the *whole*.

Hear then the truth; "'tis Heav'n each paſſion ſends,
And different men directs to different ends;
Extremes in nature equal good produce,
Extremes in man concur to gen'ral uſe.
Aſk we what makes one keep, and one beſtow?
That Pow'r who bids the ocean ebb and flow;
Bids ſeed-time, harveſt, equal courſe maintain,
Thro' reconcil'd extremes of drought and rain;
Builds life on death, on change duration founds,
And gives th' eternal wheels to know their rounds."

VOLTAIRE has, in many parts of his works, beſides his *Candide*, and his *Philoſophical Dictionary*, exerted the utmoſt efforts of his wit and argument to depreciate and deſtroy the doctrine of *Optimiſm*, and the idea that,

Th' eternal art educes good from ill.

HE imagines, abſurdly enough, that the only ſolid method of accounting for the origin of evil, conſiſtently with the other attributes of God, is not to allow his *omnipotence* *. Sa puiſſance eſt très grande; mais

* See alſo *Hume*'s Dialogues concerning Natural Religion, 8vo. 1779.

mais qui nous a dit qu'elle eſt infinie, quand ſes ouvrages nous montrent le contraire? Quand la ſeule reſſource qui nous reſte pour le diſculper eſt d' avouer que ſon pouvoir n' a pu triompher du mal phyſique & moral? Certes, j'aime mieux l'adorer borné que mechant. Peutêtre dans la vaſte machine de la nature, le bien l' a-t-il emporté neceſſairement ſur le mal, & l'eternel artiſan a été forcé dans ſes moyens, en feſant encore (malgré tant de maux) ce qu'il avait de mieux *.

VOLTAIRE, after having run the full career of infidelity and ſcepticiſm, ſeems to have ſunk at laſt into abſolute fataliſm. The ſentiments are indeed put into the mouth of MEMMIUS, the friend and patron of LUCRETIUS, and addreſſed to CICERO: this being the method the French philoſopher took to acquaint us with his own thoughts.

* Queſtions ſur l'Encyclopedie, 9 partie, p. 348. So inconcluſive and unphiloſophical an aſſertion, deſerves no ſerious confutation.

Je ſuis donc ramené malgré moi à cette ancienne idée que je vois étre la baſe de tous les ſyſtémes, dans laquelle tous les philoſophes retombent aprés mille détours, & qui m'eſt démontrée par toutes les actions des hommes, par les miennes, par tous les événemens que j'ai lus, que j'ai vus, & auxquels j'ai eu part; c'eſt le fataliſme, c'eſt la néceſſité dont je vous ai déjà parlé*.

20. Like ſome *lone* Chartreux ſtands the good old hall,
Silence without, and faſts within the wall;
No *rafter'd* roofs with dance and tabor ſound,
No *noontide* bell invites the country round:
Tenants with ſighs the *ſmoakleſs* tow'rs ſurvey,
And turn th' unwilling ſteeds another way:
Benighted wanderers, the foreſt o'er,
Curs'd the *ſav'd candle*, and *unop'ning* door;
While the *gaunt* maſtiff *growling* at the gate,
Affrights the beggar, whom he longs to eat †.

In the worſt inn's worſt room, with *mat half*-hung,
The floors of *plaiſter*, and the *walls of dung*,
On once a *flock*-bed, but repair'd with *ſtraw*,
With *tape-ty'd* curtains, never meant to draw,

* "He muſt have a very good ſtomach (ſays Mr. Gray) that can digeſt the *Crambe recocta* of Voltaire. Atheiſm is a vile diſh, though all the cooks of France combine to make new ſauces for it." Letters, quarto, page 385.

† Ver. 187.

The

The *George* and *Garter dangling* from that bed
Where *tawdry yellow* ſtrove with *dirty red*,
Great Villers lies *.——

THE uſe, the force, and the excellence of language, certainly conſiſts in raiſing, *clear*, *complete*, and *circumſtantial* images, and in turning *readers* into *ſpectators*. I have quoted the two preceding paſſages as eminent examples of this excellence, of all others the moſt eſſential in poetry. Every epithet, here uſed, *paints* its object, and *paints* it *diſtinctly*. After having paſſed over the moat full of creſſes, do you not *actually* find yourſelf in the middle court of this forlorn and ſolitary manſion, overgrown with docks and nettles? And do you not hear the dog that is going to aſſault you?—Among the other fortunate circumſtances that attended Homer, it was not one of the leaſt, that he wrote before *general* and *abſtract* terms were invented. Hence his Muſe (like his own Helen ſtanding on the walls of Troy) points out every *perſon*, and *thing*, *accurately* and *forcibly*. All the views

* Ver. 399.

and profpects he lays before us, appear as *fully* and *perfectly* to the *eye*, as that which engaged the attention of Neptune, when he was fitting (Iliad, b. 13. v. 12.)

> Ὑψου̃ ἐπ' ακροτατης κορυφης Σαμου ὑληεσσης,
> Θρηικιης· ενθεν γαρ εφαινετο πασα μεν Ιδη,
> Φαινετο δε Πριαμοιο πολις, και νηες Αχαιω̃ν.

Those who are fond of *generalities*, may think the number of *natural*, *little* circumftances, introduced in the beautiful narration of the expedition of Dolon and Diomed (Book the 10th) too *particular* and *trifling*, and below the dignity of Epic poetry. But every reader of a juft tafte will always admire the *minute* defcription of the helmet and creft, at verfe the 257th; the clapping of the wings of the Heron which they could not fee; the *fquatting* down among the dead bodies till Dolon had paffed; Ulyffes *hiffing* to Diomed as a fignal; the ftriking the horfes with his bow, becaufe *he had forgotten* to bring his whip with him; and the innumerable circumftances which make this narration fo *lively*,

fo

ſo *dramatic*, and ſo *intereſting*. Half the Iliad and the Odyſſey might be quoted as examples of this way of writing. So different from the unfiniſhed, half-formed figures, preſented to us by many modern writers. How much is the pathetic heightened by Sophocles, when, ſpeaking of Deianira determined to deſtroy herſelf, and taking leave of her palace, he adds, a circumſtance that *Voltaire* would have diſdained!

—— Κλαιε δ' οργανων οτε
Ψαυσειεν, οις εχρητο δειλαια παρος*.

Among the Roman poets, *Lucretius* will furniſh many inſtances of this ſort of ſtrong painting. Witneſs his portrait of a jealous man; Book the 4th, v. 1130.

Aut quod in ambiguo *verbum jaculata* reliquit;
Aut nimium *jactare* oculos, aliumve *tueri*
Quod putat, in vultûque videt *veſtigia* riſûs.

Of Iphigenia going to be ſacrificed, at the moment, when,

—— mæſtum ante aras aſtare parentem
Senſit, & hunc propter ferrum *celare* miniſtros †.

* Trachiniæ, v. 922. † Book i. v. 21.

Of Fear, in Book iii. v. 155.

> Sudorem itaque & *pallorem* exiſtere toto
> Corpore; & *infringi* linguam; vocemque aboriri;
> *Caligare* oculos; *ſonere* aures; *ſuccidere* artus.

WITHOUT ſpecifying the various *ſtrokes* of nature, with which Virgil has deſcribed the prognoſtics of the weather in his firſt Georgic, let us only conſider with what energy he has *enumerated* and *particularized* the geſtures and attitudes of his dying Dido. No five verſes ever contained more images, or images more *diſtinctly* expreſſed.

> Illa *graves oculos* conata *attollere*, rurſus
> *Deficit*; infixum *ſtridet* ſub pectore vulnus:
> *Ter* ſeſe *attollens*, *cubitoque innixa* levavit,
> *Ter revoluta toro* eſt; *oculiſque errantibus*, alto
> Quæſivit cælo lucem, *ingemuitque* repertâ *.

The *words* of *Virgil* have here painted the *dying* Dido, as *powerfully* as the *pencil* of *Reynolds* has done, when ſhe is juſt *dead*.

BUT none of the Roman writers has diſplayed a greater force and vigour of imagination than TACITUS; who was in truth

* Æn. iv. 688.

*a great poet**. With what an aſſemblage of maſterly ſtrokes has he exhibited the diſtreſs of the Roman army under *Cæcina*, in the firſt book of the Annals! Nox per diverſa inquies; cum barbari feſtis epulis, *læto cantu*, aut *truci* ſonore, ſubjecta vallium ac reſultantes ſaltus, complerent. Apud Romanos, *invalidi* ignes, *interruptæ* voces, atque ipſi paſſim *adjacerent* vallo, *oberrarent* tentoriis, inſomnes magis quam pervigiles, ducemque terruit *dira quies*. And what a ſpectre he then immediately calls up, in the ſtyle of MICHAEL ANGELO! Nam Quintilium Varum, *ſanguine oblitum*, & paludibus *emerſum*, *cernere* & *audire* viſus eſt, velut *vocantem*, non tamen *obſecutus*, & *manum intendentis* repuliſſe.

A CELEBRATED foreigner, the Count Algarotti, has paſſed the following cenſure on our poetry, as deficient in this reſpect.

* "The *Cyropædia* of Xenophon is vague and languid: the *Anabaſis* circumſtantial and animated;" ſays the learned and ingenious Hiſtorian of the Decline and Fall of the Roman Empire. Vol. ii. p. 467.

"LA

"La poesia dei populi *settentrionali* pare a me, che, generalménte parlando, consista più di *pensieri*, che d' *immagini*, si compiaccia delle riflessione equalmente che dei sentimenti: non sia cosi *particolareggiata*, e *pittoresca* come e la nostra. Virgilio a cagione d'esempio rappresentando Didone quando esce alla caccia fa una tal descrizione del suo vestimento, che tutti i ritrattisti, leggendo quel passo, la vestirebbono a un modo:

Tandem progreditur, magnâ stipante caterva,
Sidoniam picto chlamydem circumdata limbo;
Cui pharetra ex auro, crines nodantur in aurum,
Aurea purpuream subnectit fibuli vestem.

Non cosi il Miltono quando descrive la nuda bellezza di Eva:

Grace was in all her steps, heav'n in her eye,
In every gesture, dignity and love.

Con quella parole generale, e *astratte* idee di grazia, cielo, amore, e maestà non pare a lei che ognuno si formi in mente una Eva a posta sua * ?"

* See his works. Livorno. t. 8.

It muſt indeed be granted, that this paſſage gives no diſtinct and particular idea of the perſon of Eve; but in how many others has Milton drawn his *figures*, and expreſſed his *images*, with *energy* and *diſtinctneſs*?

Under a coronet his flowing hair
In curls on either cheek play'd; wings he wore
Of many a colour'd plume ſprinkled with gold;
His habit fit for ſpeed ſuccinct, and held
Before his decent ſteps a ſilver wand *.

Dire was the toſſing, deep the groans; DESPAIR
Tended the ſick, buſieſt from couch to couch;
And over them triumphant Death his dart
Shook, but delay'd to ſtrike †.

From his ſlack hand the garland, wreath'd for Eve,
Down dropt, and all the faded roſes ſhed;
Speechleſs he ſtood, and pale ‡!

And SPENCER, the maſter of MILTON, ſo much abounds in portraits peculiarly marked, and ſtrongly created, that it is difficult to know which to ſelect from this copious magazine of the moſt lively painting. The ſame may be ſaid of SHAKESPEARE; whoſe

* Par. Loſt, b. iii. v. 640.
† B. xi. v. 489.
‡ B. ix. v. 892.

little

little touches of nature it is no wonder VOLTAIRE could not relish, who affords no example of this beauty in his *Henriade*, and gives no proofs of a *picturesque fancy*, in a work that abounds more in *declamation*, in moral and political reflections, than in poetic images; in which there is little *character* and less *nature*, and in which the author himself *appears throughout the piece, and is himself the hero of his poem* *.

I HAVE dwelt the longer on this subject, because I think I can perceive many symptoms, even among writers of eminence, of departing from these *true* and *lively*, and *minute*, representations of Nature, and of *dwelling in generalities*. To these I oppose the testimony of, perhaps, the most judicious and elegant critic among the ancients. Proculdubio qui dicit *expugnatam* esse civitatem, complectitur omnia quæcunque talis fortuna recipit: sed in affectus minus pene-

* As much as the author has ventured to censure the epic poem of Voltaire, yet he greatly admires many of his tragedies.

trat brevis hic velut nuntius. At ſi *aperias* hæc quæ verbo uno incluſa erant, *apparebunt* effuſæ per domos ac templa *flammæ*, & *ruentium* tectorum fragor, & ex diverſis clamoribus unus quidam ſonus; *aliorum* fuga incerta; *alii* in extremo *complexû* ſuorum cohærentes, & infantium fæminarumque ploratus, & malè uſque in illum diem ſervati fato ſenes; tum illa profanorum ſacrorumque *direptio*, *efferentium* prædas, *repetentiumque* diſcurſus, & *acti* ante ſuum quiſque prædonem *catenati*, & conata *retinere infantem* ſuum *mater*, & ſicubi majus lucrum eſt, pugna inter victores. Licet enim hæc omnia, ut dixi, complectatur *everſio*, MINUS EST TAMEN TOTUM DICERE, QUAM OMNIA *.

21. Who hung with woods yon mountain's ſultry brow?
From the dry rock who bade the waters flow?
Not to the † ſkies in uſeleſs columns toſt,
Or in proud falls magnificently loſt;

But

* QUINTILIAN, lib. viii. cap. 3. And ſee alſo a paſſage of exquiſite taſte in DEMETRIUS PHALEREUS. Pag. 122 and 123. Oxon. 1676.

† Has not the learned commentator, in his note on this paſſage, given an illuſtration rather hard and far-ſought, in the following words?

" The

But clear and artleſs, pouring thro' the plain,
Health to the ſick, and ſolace to the ſwain.
Whoſe cauſeway parts the vale with ſhady rows?
Whoſe ſeats the weary traveller repoſe?
Who taught that heav'n-directed ſpire to riſe?
"The MAN of ROSS," each liſping babe replies.
Behold the market-place with poor o'erſpread!
The Man of Roſs divides the weekly bread.
He feeds yon alms-houſe, neat, but void of ſtate,
Where AGE and WANT ſit ſmiling at the gate:
Him portion'd maids, apprentic'd orphans bleſt,
The young who labour, and the old who reſt *.

THESE lines, which are eminently beautiful, particularly one of the three laſt,

" The *intimation* in the firſt line well ridicules the *madneſs* of faſhionable magnificence; theſe columns aſpiring to prop the ſkies, in a very different ſenſe from the heaven-directed ſpire in the verſe that follows; as the *expreſſion* in the ſecond line expoſes the *meanneſs* of it, in *falling proudly*, to no purpoſe."—Perhaps the ſame may be ſaid of a note that follows, on verſe 333.

" Cutler and Brutus, dying, both exclaim,
Virtue and wealth! what are ye but a name!"

There is a greater beauty in this compariſon than the common reader is aware of. Brutus was, in morals at leaſt, a *Stoic*, like his uncle.—Now *Stoical virtue* was, as our author truly tells us, not *exerciſe* but *apathy*. Contracted all, retiring to the breaſt. In a word, like Sir J. Cutler's *purſe*, nothing for uſe, but kept cloſe ſhut, and centered all within himſelf. Now *virtue* and *wealth*, thus circumſtanced, are indeed no other than mere names."

* Ver. 253.

containing

containing a fine proſopopœia, have conferred immortality on a plain, worthy, and uſeful citizen of Herefordſhire, Mr. John Kyrle, who ſpent his long life in advancing and contriving plans of public utility. The HOWARD of his time: who deſerves to be celebrated more than all the heroes of PINDAR. The particular reaſon for which I quoted them, was to obſerve the pleaſing effect that the uſe of common and familiar words and objects, judiciouſly managed, produce in poetry. Such as are here the words, *cauſeway*, *ſeats*, *ſpire*, *market-place*, *alms-houſe*, *apprentic'd*. A faſtidious delicacy, and a falſe refinement, in order to avoid meanneſs, have deterred our writers from the introduction of ſuch words; but DRYDEN often hazarded it, and gave by it a ſecret charm, and a natural air to his verſes, well knowing of what conſequence it was ſometimes to ſoften and ſubdue his tints, and not to paint and adorn every object he touched, with perpetual pomp and unremitted ſplendor.

22. Sir Balaam now, he lives like other folks,
He takes his chirping pint, and cracks his jokes:

"Live

"Live like yourſelf," was ſoon my Lady's word;
And lo! two puddings ſmok'd upon the board*.

This tale of Sir Balaam, his progreſs and change of manners, from being a plodding, ſober, plain, and punctual citizen, to his becoming a debauched and diſſolute courtier and ſenator, abounds in much knowledge of life, and many ſtrokes of true humour, and will bear to be compared with the exquiſite hiſtory of Eugenio and Coruſodes, in one of Swift's Intelligencers.

Lord Bathurst, Lord Lyttelton, Spence, Harte, and other of his friends, have aſſured me, that among intimates Pope had an admirable talent for telling a ſtory. In great companies he avoided ſpeaking much. And in his examination before the Houſe of Lords, in Atterbury's trial, he faultered ſo much as to be hardly intelligible.

23. You ſhow us, Rome was glorious, not profuſe,
And pompous buildings once were things of uſe:

* Ver. 357.

Yet

Yet ſhall (my Lord) your juſt, your noble rules,
Fill half the land with imitating-fools *.

THUS our author addreſſes the EARL of BURLINGTON, who was then publiſhing the deſigns of Inigo Jones, and the Antiquities of Rome by Palladio. "Never was protection and great wealth † (ſays an able judge of the ſubject) more generouſly and judiciouſly diffuſed, than by this great perſon, who had every quality of a genius and artiſt, except envy. Though his own deſigns were more chaſte and claſſic than Kent's, he entertained him in his houſe till his death, and was more ſtudious to extend his friend's fame than his own. As we have few ſamples of architecture more antique and impoſing than the colonnade within the court of his houſe in Piccadilly, I cannot help mentioning the effect it had on myſelf. I had not only never ſeen it, but had never heard of it, at leaſt with any attention, when, ſoon after my return from Italy, I was invited to

* Ver. 25.

† Mr. Walpole, p. 108. Anecdotes of Painting, vol. iv.

to a ball at Burlington-houſe. As I paſſed under the gate by night, it could not ſtrike me. At day-break, looking out of the window to ſee the ſun riſe, I was ſurprized with the viſion of the colonnade that fronted me. It ſeemed one of thoſe edifices in Fairy Tales, that are raiſed by genii in a night's time."—POPE having appeared an excellent *moraliſt* in the foregoing epiſtles, in this appears to be as excellent a *connoiſſeur* *, and has given not only ſome of our *firſt*, but our *beſt* rules and obſervations on *architecture* and *gardening*, but particularly on the latter of theſe uſeful and entertaining arts, on which he has dwelt more largely, and with rather more knowledge of the ſubject. The following is copied verbatim from a little paper which he gave to Mr. SPENCE †. "Arts are taken from nature, and, after a thouſand

* Though he always thought highly of *Addiſon's* Letter from Italy, yet he ſaid the poet had ſpoken in terms too general of the fineſt buildings and paintings, and without much diſcrimination of taſte.

† "Who had both taſte and zeal for the preſent ſtyle," ſays Mr. Walpole, p. 134.

thousand vain efforts for improvements, are best when they return to their first simplicity. A sketch or analysis of the first principles of each art, with their first consequences, might be a thing of most excellent service. Thus, for instance, all the rules of architecture * might be reducible to three or four heads; the justness of the openings; bearings upon bearings; the regularity of the pillars, &c. That which is not just in buildings is disagreeable to the eye (as a greater upon a lesser, &c.) and this may be called the *reasoning* † *of the eye.* In laying out a garden, the first and chief thing to be considered is the genius of the place. Thus at Riskins, now called Peircy Lodge, Lord * * * should

* Our author was so delighted with Grævius, that he drew up a little Latin treatise on the chief buildings of Rome, collected from this antiquarian. Mr. Gray had also an exquisite taste in architecture, joined to the knowledge of an accurate antiquarian. See the introduction to Bentham's History of Ely Cathedral, supposed to be drawn up by Gray, or under his eye.

† To see all the beauties that a place was susceptible of, was to possess, as Mr. Pitt expressed it, "*The prophetic eye of taste.*"

have raiſed two or three mounts, becauſe his ſituation is all a plain, and nothing can pleaſe without variety."

Mr. Walpole, in his elegant and entertaining Hiſtory of *Modern Gardening*, has clearly proved that *Kent* was the artiſt to whom the Engliſh nation was chiefly indebted for diffuſing a taſte in laying out grounds, of which the French and Italians have no idea. But he adds, much to the credit of our author, that Pope undoubtedly contributed to form Kent's taſte. The deſign of the Prince of Wales's garden at Carlton Houſe, was evidently borrowed from the Poet's at Twickenham. There was a little affected modeſty in the latter, when he ſaid of all his works he was moſt proud of his garden. And yet it was a ſingular effort of art and taſte to impreſs ſo much variety and ſcenery on a ſpot of five acres. The paſſing through the gloom from the grotto to the opening day, the retiring and again aſſembling ſhades, the duſky groves, the larger lawn, and the ſolemnity

ſolemnity of the termination at the cypreſſes that lead up to his mother's tomb, are managed with exquiſite judgment; and though Lord Peterborough * aſſiſted him,

To form his quincunx and to rank his vines;

thoſe were not the moſt pleaſing ingredients of his little perſpective. I do not know whether the diſpoſition of the garden at Rouſham, laid out for General Dormer, and in my opinion the moſt engaging of all Kent's works, was not planned on the model of Mr. Pope's, at leaſt in the opening and retiring "ſhades of Venus's Vale."

It ought to be obſerved, that many years before this epiſtle was written, and before Kent was employed as an improver of grounds, even ſo early as the year 1713,

* I cannot forbear adding, in this place, the following anecdote from Pope to Mr. Spence; which I give in his own words:—"Lord Peterborough, after a viſit to Fenelon, Archbiſhop of Cambray, ſaid to me—Fenelon is a man that was caſt in a particular mould, that was never made uſe of for any body elſe. He's a delicious creature! But I was forced to get from him as ſoon as I poſſibly could, for elſe he would have made me *pious*."

POPE ſeems to have been the very firſt perſon that cenſured and ridiculed the formal, French, Dutch, falſe and unnatural, mode in gardening, by a paper in the Guardian, Number 173, levelled againſt capricious operations of art, and every ſpecies of *verdant* ſculpture, and *inverted* nature; which paper abounds with *wit* as well as *taſte*, and ends with a ridiculous catalogue of various figures cut in ever-greens. Neither do I think that theſe four lines in this epiſtle,

> Here Amphitrite ſails thro' myrtle bow'rs;
> There gladiators fight, or die in flow'rs:
> Un-water'd ſee the drooping ſea-horſe mourn,
> And ſwallows rooſt in Nilus' duſty urn *,

do at all excel the following paſſage in his Guardian:

"A citizen is no ſooner proprietor of a couple of yews, but he entertains thoughts of erecting them into giants, like thoſe of Guildhall. I know an eminent Cook, who beautified his country ſeat with a coronation dinner in greens, where you ſee the

* Ver. 123.

champion

champion flouriſhing on horſeback at one end of the table, and the queen in perpetual youth at the other."

But it was the vigorous and creative imagination of Milton, ſuperior to the prejudices of his times *, that exhibited in his Eden, the firſt hints and outlines of what a beautiful garden ſhould be; for even his beloved Ariosto and Tasso, in their luxuriant pictures of the gardens of Alcina and Armida, ſhewed they were not free from the unnatural and *narrow* taſte of their countrymen; and even his maſter, Spencer, has an *artificial fountain* in the midſt of his *bowre of bliſs*.

I cannot forbear taking occaſion to remark in this place, that, in the ſacred drama, intitled, *L'Adamo*, written and publiſhed at Milan, in the year 1617, by Gio. Battista Andreini, a Florentine,

* How aſtoniſhing, that his ſpirit could not be diminiſhed or cruſhed, by poverty, danger, blindneſs, diſgrace, ſolitude, and old age!

which Milton certainly had read, (and of which Voltaire has given ſo falſe and ſo imperfect an account, in his Eſſay on the Epic Poets) the prints that are to repreſent *Paradiſe* are full of clipt hedges, ſquare parterres, ſtrait walks, trees uniformly lopt, regular knots and carpets of flowers, groves nodding at groves, marble fountains, and water-works. And yet theſe prints were deſigned by CARLO ANTONIO PROCCACHINI, a celebrated landſchape painter of his time, and of the ſchool of the CARRACHES: many of thoſe works are ſtill admired at Milan. To every ſcene of this drama is prefixed a print of this artiſt's deſigning. And, as the book is very curious and uncommon, I intend to give a ſpecimen and analyſis of it in the Appendix to this volume.

IT hence appears, that this enchanting art of modern gardening, in which this kingdom claims a preference * over every

* In CASTELL's Villa's of the Ancients illuſtated, folio, London, 1728, may be ſeen how much the celebrated Tuſcan villa reſembled our gardens, as they were planned a few years ago. Pliny's villa was like his genius.

nation

nation in Europe, chiefly owes its origin and its improvements to two great poets, MILTON and POPE. May I be ſuffered to add, in behalf of a favourite author, and who would have been a firſt-rate poet, if his ſtyle had been equal to his conceptions, that the Seaſons of THOMSON have been very inſtrumental in diffuſing a general * taſte for the beauties of *nature* and *landſchape*.

24. To build, to plant, whatever you intend,
To rear the column, or the arch to bend,
To ſwell the terrace, or to ſink the grot;
In all, let Nature never be forgot.
But treat the Goddeſs like a modeſt Fair,
Nor over-dreſs, nor leave her wholly bare;
Let not each beauty ev'ry where be ſpy'd,
When half the ſkill is decently to hide.
He gains all points who pleaſingly confounds,
Surpriſes, varies, and conceals the bounds †.

The beſt comments that have ever been given on theſe ſenſible and ſtriking pre-

* It is only within a few years that the pictureſque ſcenes of our own country, our lakes, mountains, caſcades, caverns, and caſtles, have been viſited and deſcribed.

† Ver. 47.

cepts,

cepts, are, *Painſhill*, *Hagley*, the *Leaſowes*, *Perſefield*, *Woborn*, *Stourhead*, and *Blenheim*; all of them exquiſite ſcenes in different ſtyles, and fine examples of *practical* poetry.

25. Conſult the GENIUS * of the place in all,
That tells the waters, or to riſe or fall;
Or helps th' ambitious hill the heav'ns to ſcale,
Or ſcoops in circling theatres the vale;
Calls in the country, catches op'ning glades,
Joins willing woods, and varies ſhades from ſhades,
Now breaks, or now directs th' intending lines,
Paints as you plant, and as you work deſigns †.

Would it not give life and vigour to this noble *proſopopœia*, if we were to venture to

* Dr. Warburton's diſcoveries of ſome latent beauties in this paſſage, ſeem to be fanciful and groundleſs, and never thought of by the author. "First, the *Genius* of the place (ſays this commentator) *tells the waters*, or ſimply gives directions: then, *he helps* th' ambitious hill, or is a fellow-labourer: then again, he *ſcoops* the *circling theatre*, or *works alone*, and in *chief*. Afterwards, riſing faſt in our idea of dignity, he *calls in the country*, alluding to the orders of princes in their progreſs, when accuſtomed to diſplay all their ſtate and magnificence: his character then *grows ſacred*, he *joins willing woods*, a metaphor taken from one of the offices of the prieſthood; till, at length, he becomes a divinity, and *creates* and *preſides* over the whole.

Now breaks, or now directs——&c."

† Ver. 57.

alter

alter only one word, and read, in the ſecond line,

> HE tells the waters—

inſtead of

> *That* tells— ?

OUR author is never happier than in his alluſions to painting, an art he ſo much admired and underſtood: So below, at verſe 81,

> The wood *ſupports* the plain, the parts *unite*,
> And *ſtrength* of *ſhade contends* with *ſtrength* of *light.*

Indeed, the two arts in queſtion differ only in the materials which they employ. And it is neither exaggeration or affectation to call MR. BROWN a great *painter*; for he has realized

> Whate'er LORRAIN light-touch'd with ſoftening hue,
> Or ſavage ROSA daſh'd, or learned POUSSIN drew *.

26. Still follow ſenſe, of ev'ry art the ſoul,
Parts anſwering parts ſhall ſlide into a whole;
Spontaneous beauties all around advance,
Start ev'n from difficulty, ſtrike from chance;
Nature ſhall join you; Time ſhall make it grow,
A work to wonder at—perhaps a STOW †.

* Caſtle of Indolence, ſt. 38.

† Ver. 65.

I MUST

I MUST confess (says the Earl of Peterborough, Letter 34, vol. viii.) that in going to Lord Cobham's I was not led by curiosity: I went thither to see what I had seen, and what I was sure to like. I had the idea of those gardens so fixed in my imagination by many descriptions, that nothing surprized me; Immensity and Van Brugh appear in the whole, and in every part. Your joining in your letter animal and vegetable beauty, makes me use this expression: "I confess the stately SACHARISSA at Stow, but am content with my little AMORET." (meaning Bevis Mount, near Southampton.) It is plain, therefore, that Lord P. was not pleased with these gardens; but they have, since his time, received many capital alterations and additions; of which the ingenious author of *Observations* on *Modern Gardening* has given an accurate account, and a minute analysis, in page 213 of his entertaining work; and he concludes his description in the following words: "Magnificence and splendor are the characteristics of Stow; it is like one of those places celebrated in antiquity,

antiquity, which were devoted to the purposes of religion, and filled with sacred groves, hallowed fountains, and temples dedicated to several deities; the resort of distant nations, and the object of veneration to half the heathen world; this pomp is, at STOW, blended with beauty; and the place is equally distinguished by its amenity and grandeur."

27. And Nero's terraces desert their walls *.

This line is obscure; it is difficult to know what is meant by the terraces deserting their walls. In line 172, below, is another obscurity;—" *his* hard heart denies"—it does not immediately occur *whose* heart, the word is so far separated from the person intended.

28. Ev'n in an ornament it's place remark,
Nor in an hermitage set DR. CLARKE †.

THESE lines are as ill-placed, and as injudicious, as the busto which they were

* Ver. 72. † Ver. 77.

designed

designed to censure. POPE caught an aversion to this excellent man from BOLINGBROKE, who hated CLARKE, not only because he had written a book, which this declamatory philosopher could not confute, but because he was a favourite of Queen CAROLINE. In our author's manuscripts were two other lines upon this writer:

Let CLARKE live half his days the poor's support,
But let him pass the other half at Court.

His *Attributes*, and his *Sermons*, will be read and admired by all lovers of good reasoning, as long as this Epistle by all lovers of good poetry.

29. At Timon's villa let us pass a day,
Where all cry out, "What sums are thrown away*!"

THE whole gang of malignant and dirty scribblers, who envied the success and superior merit of POPE, was in arms at this description, which they applied to the Duke of Chandos, and his house at Canons.

* Ver. 99.

Welsted

Welſted publiſhed in folio a moſt abuſive libel, entitled, *Of Dulneſs and Scandal, occaſioned by the Character of Lord Timon*, &c. And Lady Wortley Montague joined in the accuſation, in her *Verſes* addreſſed *to the Imitator of Horace* *. The Duke, though at firſt alarmed, was, it is ſaid, afterwards convinced of our author's innocence. I have thought it not improper to inſert at length the following letter, as it contains the moſt direct and poſitive denial of this fact; as it was written at the very time, to a private friend, and expreſſed all Pope's feelings on the ſubject; and as it is not to be found in this edition of his works. It is addreſſed to Aaron Hill, Eſq; an affected and fuſtian writer †, but who, by

* Theſe are the lines. Page 5, folio. London, for A. Dodd.

But if thou ſee'ſt a great and generous heart,
Thy bow is doubly bent to force a dart.
Nor only juſtice vainly we demand,
But even benefits can't rein thy hand;
To this, or that, alike in vain we truſt,
Nor find thee leſs ungrateful than unjuſt.

† See his Athelwood—and his tranſlation of that fine play Merope, which I have frequently reproached Mr. Garrick

by ſome means or other, gained our author's confidence and friendſhip.

Twickenham, Dec. 22, 1731.

DEAR SIR,

I THANK you for your Tragedy Athelwood, which I have read over a *ſixth* time, and of which I not only preſerve, but increaſe, my eſteem. You have been kind to this age, in not telling the next, in your preface, the ill taſte of the town;

rick for acting—his Poem on Acting—his poem in praiſe of Blank Verſe, which begins thus; and which one would think was burleſque:

Up, from Rhyme's poppied vale! and ride the ſtorm
That thunders in blank verſe!———

See his works throughout, in 4 vols. octavo; from which the treatiſe on the Bathos might have been much enriched with many truly ridiculous examples, viz.

Some black-ſoul'd Fiend, ſome Fury ris'n from hell
Has darken'd all diſcernment. MEROPE.

————— Thro' night's eye
Saw the pale murderer ſtalk! Ibid.

Some hint's officious reach had touch'd her ear.

One is ſurprized that ſuch a writer could be an intimate friend of Bolingbroke, Pope, and Thomſon. He had however the merit of being one of the very firſt perſons who took notice of Thomſon, on the publication of Winter, on which he wrote a complimentary copy of verſes. See a letter of Thomſon's to Hill, dated Goodman's Coffee-houſe, 1726.

of

of which the reception you describe it to have given of your play—worse, indeed, than I had heard, or could have imagined—is a more flagrant instance than any of *those trifles* mentioned in *my Epistle*; which yet, I hear, the sore vanity of our pretenders to taste flinches at extremely. The *title* you mention had been properer to that Epistle.—I have heard no criticisms about it, nor do I listen after them. Nos hæc novimus esse nihil. (I mean, I think the verses to be so:) But as you are a man of tender sentiments of honour, I know it will grieve you to hear another undeservedly charged with a crime his heart is free from; for, if there is truth in the world, I declare to you, I never imagined the least application of what I said of Timon could be made to the D— of Ch——s, than whom there is scarce a more blameless, worthy, and generous, beneficent character, among all our nobility: And if I have not lost my senses, the town has lost 'em, by what I heard so late as but two days ago, of the uproar on this head. I am certain,

 if

if you calmly read every particular of that deſcription, you'll find almoſt all of 'em point-blank the reverſe of that perſon's villa. It's an aukward thing for a man to print, in defence of his own work, againſt a chimæra: you know not who, or what, you fight againſt; the objections ſtart up in a new ſhape, like the armies and phantoms of magicians, and no weapon can cut a miſt or a ſhadow. Yet it would have been a pleaſure to me, to have found ſome friend ſaying a word in my juſtification, againſt a malicious falſhood. I ſpeak of ſuch, as have known by their own experience, theſe twenty years, that I always took up their defence, when any ſtream of calumny ran upon them. If it gives the Duke one moment's uneaſineſs, I ſhould think myſelf ill paid, if the whole earth admir'd the poetry; and, believe me, would rather never have written a verſe in my life, than any one of 'em ſhould trouble a truly good man. It was once my caſe before, but happily reconciled; and, among generous minds, nothing ſo indears friends,

as

5

as the having offended one another. I lament the malice of the age, that ſtudies to ſee its own likeneſs in every thing; I lament the dulneſs of it, that cannot ſee an excellence: The firſt is my unhappineſs, the ſecond your's; I look upon the fate of your piece, like that of a great treaſure, which is bury'd as ſoon as brought to light; but it is ſure to be dug up the next age, and enrich poſterity."

30. His ſtudy! with what authors is it ſtor'd?
In Books, not Authors, curious is my Lord;
To all their dated backs he turns you round;
Theſe Aldus printed, theſe Du Sueil has bound:
Lo! ſome are vellum, and the reſt as good,
For all his Lordſhip knows; but they are wood *.

THERE is a flatneſs and inſipidity in the laſt couplet, much below the uſual manner of our author. YOUNG has been more ſprightly and poignant on the ſame ſubject.

With what, O Codrus! is thy fancy ſmit?
The flower of learning, and the bloom of wit.
Thy gaudy ſhelves with crimſon bindings glow,
And EPICTETUS is a perfect beau;

* Ver. 133.

How fit for thee! bound up in crimſon too,
Gilt, and like them, devoted to the view.
Thy books are *furniture.* Methinks 'tis hard
That Science ſhould be purchas'd by the yard;
And TONSON, turn'd upholſterer, ſend home
The gilded leather to *fit up* thy room *.

31. Where *ſprawl* † the Saints of VERRIO and LAGUERRE ‡.

ONE ſingle verb has marked with felicity and force the diſtorted attitudes, the indecent ſubjects, the want of nature and grace, ſo viſible in the pieces of theſe two artiſts, employed to adorn § our royal palaces and chapels. "I cannot help thinking (ſays POPE to Mr. Allen, in Letter 89, vol. ix.) and I know you will join with me, who have been making an altar-piece, that the zeal of the firſt reformers was ill-

* Univerſal Paſſion, Sat. 2.

† He is not ſo happy in the uſe of another verb below, at verſe 153.

The rich buffet well-coloured ſerpents *grace.*

‡ Ver. 146.

§ Strange as it may ſeem, yet I believe we may venture to aſſert, that there is not a painted cieling or ſtair-caſe in this kingdom, that we ſhould not be aſhamed to ſhew to an intelligent foreigner.

placed,

placed, in removing *pictures* (that is to ſay, *examples*) out of churches *; and yet ſuffering *epitaphs* (that is to ſay, flatteries and falſe hiſtory) to be a burthen to church-walls, and the ſhame as well as deriſion of all honeſt men."—This is the ſentiment, it may be ſaid, of a *papiſtical* poet; and yet I cannot forbear thinking it is founded on good ſenſe, and religion well-underſtood. Notwithſtanding the illiberal and ill-grounded rage which has lately been excited againſt Popery, yet I hope we may ſtill, one day, ſee our places of worſhip beautified with proper ornaments, and the generoſity and talents of our living artiſts perpetuated on the naked walls of St. Paul's.

32. To reſt the cuſhion and ſoft Dean invite,
Who never mentions hell to ears polite †.

THIS it ſeems was a fact concerning a certain ſmooth, and ſupple, and inoffenſive

* The chapel of New College in Oxford will ſoon receive a ſingular and invaluable ornament: A window, the glaſs of which is ſtained by Mr. JERVIS, from that exquiſite picture of the Nativity by Sir Joſhua Reynolds.

† Ver. 149.

Divine, one, we may imagine, that held the doctrines which Dr. *Young* ſo agreeably laughs at in his ſixth ſatire;

"Shall pleaſures of a ſhort duration chain
A *Lady*'s ſoul in everlaſting pain?
Will the great Author us poor worms deſtroy,
For now and then a *ſip* of tranſient joy?"
No, he's for ever in a ſmiling mood,
He's like themſelves; or how could he be good?
And they blaſpheme, who blacker ſchemes ſuppoſe.—
Devoutly thus, Jehovah they depoſe,
The pure, the juſt! and ſet up in his ſtead,
A deity, that's perfectly *well-bred!*

33. Yet hence the poor are cloath'd, the hungry fed;
Health to himſelf, and to his infants bread
The lab'rer bears * ———

A FINE turned and moral reflection, which illuſtrates the doctrines of his Eſſay, in the ſecond epiſtle, when he ſays, at line 237,

Each individual ſeeks a ſev'ral goal;
But Heav'n's great view is One, and that the whole;
That counterworks each folly and caprice;
That diſappoints th' effect of ev'ry vice;—

* Ver. 169.

That

That *Virtue's* end from *Vanity* can raiſe,
Which ſeeks no intereſt, no reward but praiſe;
And builds on wants, and on defects of mind,
The joy, the peace, the glory of mankind.

THAT Providence ſhould extract good from evil, and alter its natural biaſs and malignity, is a doctrine widely different from the looſe and flagitious principles of MANDEVILLE, who has endeavoured to prove that *Private Vices* are *Public* Benefits.

34. You too proceed! make falling arts your care,
Erect new wonders, and the old repair;
Jones and Palladio to themſelves reſtore,
And be whate'er Vitruvius was before *.

THIS is not fulſome adulation, but only ſuch honeſt praiſe as the noble Lord whom he addreſſed ſtrictly deſerved: who inherited all that love of ſcience and uſeful knowledge for which his family has been ſo famous. The name of BOYLE is, indeed, auſpicious to literature. That ſublime genius and good man, Biſhop BERK-

* Ver. 192.

LEY, owed his preferment chiefly to this accompliſhed peer. For it was he that recommended him to the Duke of Grafton, in the year 1721, who took him over with him to Ireland when he was Lord Lieutenant, and promoted him to the deanery of Derry in the year 1724 *. Berkley gained the patronage and friendſhip of Lord Burlington, not only by his true politeneſs and the peculiar charms of his converſation, which was exquiſite, but by his profound and perfect ſkill in architecture; an art which he had very particularly and accurately ſtudied in Italy, when he went and continued abroad four years †, with Mr. Aſhe,

* ATTERBURY was deſirous of ſeeing Berkley; to whom he was introduced by the Earl of Berkley. After he had left the room, What does your Lordſhip think of my couſin, ſaid the Earl, does he anſwer your Lordſhip's expectations? The Biſhop, lifting up his hands in aſtoniſhment, replied, "So much underſtanding, ſo much knowledge, ſo much innocence, and ſo much humility, I did not think had been the portion of any but angels, till I ſaw this gentleman."
——Duncombe's Letters.

† In this journey he paid a viſit to Father Malebranche. The converſation turned on our author's celebrated ſyſtem of the non-exiſtence of matter. Malebranche, who had an inflammation in his lungs, and whom he found preparing a medicine

Ashe, son of the Bishop of Clogher. With an insatiable and philosophic attention, Berkley surveyed and examined every object of curiosity. He not only made the usual tour, but went over *Apulia* and *Calabria*, and even travelled on foot through *Sicily*, and drew up an account of that very classical ground; which was lost in a voyage to NAPLES, and cannot be sufficiently regretted. His generous project for erecting an University at Bermudas, the effort of a mind truly active, benevolent, and patriotic, is sufficiently known.

35. Bid harbours open, public ways extend,
Bid temples worthier of the God ascend;

medicine in his cell, and cooking it in a small pipkin, for his disorder, exerted his voice and lungs so violently in the heat of their dispute, that he increased his disorder, which carried him off a few days after. See Biogr. Britannica, vol. ii. p. 251, as it is highly improved by the candid and learned Dr. Kippis.—Many a vulgar critic hath sneered at the SIRIS of Berkley, for beginning with *Tar* and ending with the *Trinity*; incapable of observing the great art with which the transitions in that book are finely made, where each paragraph depends on and arises out of the preceding, and gradually and imperceptibly leads on the reader, from common objects to more remote, from matter to spirit, from earth to heaven.

Bid

Bid the broad arch the dangerous flood contain,
The mole projected break the roaring main;
Back to his bounds their subject sea command,
And roll obedient rivers through the land *.

No country has been enriched and adorned, within a period of thirty or forty years, with so many works of public spirit, as Great Britain has been; witness our many extensive roads, our inland navigations (some of which excel the boasted canal of *Languedoc*) the lighting and the paving and beautifying our cities, and our various and magnificent edifices. A general good taste has been diffused in planting, gardening, and building. The ruins of Palmyra, the Antiquities of Athens and Spalatro, and the Ionian antiquities, by WOOD, STUART, ADAM, and CHANDLER, are such magnificent monuments of learned curiosity as no country in Europe can equal. Let it be remembered, that these fine lines of POPE were written when we had no WYATT or BROWN, BRINDLEY or REYNOLDS; no Westminster-bridge, no Pan-

* Ver. 197.

theon,

theon, no Royal Academy, no King that is at once a judge and a patron of all thoſe fine arts, which ought to be employed in raiſing and beautifying a palace equal to his dignity and his taſte.

36. See the wild waſte of all-devouring years,
How Rome her own ſad ſepulchre appears.

THIS is the opening of the epiſtle to Mr. *Addiſon* *, upon his treatiſe on medals, written in that pleaſing form of compoſition ſo unſucceſsfully attempted by many modern authors, DIALOGUE. In no one ſpecies of writing have the ancients ſo indiſputable a ſuperiority over us. The dialogues of Plato and Cicero, eſpecially the former, are perfect dramas; where the characters are ſupported with conſiſtency and nature, and the reaſoning ſuited to the characters.

* FICORINI, the celebrated virtuoſo, ſaid to Mr. Spence, at Florence:—"Addiſon did not go any great depth in the ſtudy of medals: all the knowledge he had of that kind, I believe he received of me: and I did not give him above twenty leſſons on that ſubject."

"THERE

"THERE are in English *Three* dialogues, and but three" (says a learned and ingenious author *, who has himself practised this way of writing with success) "that deserve commendation; namely, the *Moralists* of Lord SHAFTESBURY; Mr. ADDISON's Treatise on Medals; and the Minute Philosopher of Bishop BERKLEY." ALCIPHRON did, indeed, well deserve to be mentioned on this occasion; notwithstanding it has been treated with contempt by writers much inferior to BERKLEY in genius, learning, and taste †. Omitting those passages in the fourth dialogue,

* Dr. Hurd, in Moral and Political Dialogues, Preface, p. 14.

† But Sherlock thought highly of ALCIPHRON, and presented it to Queen Caroline with many encomiums; who used to be delighted with the conversation of Berkley. Lord Bathurst told me, that the members of the *Scriblerus-club*, being met at his house at dinner, they agreed to rally Berkley, who was also his guest, on his scheme at Bermudas. Berkley having listened to the many lively things they had to say, begged to be heard in his turn; and displayed his plan with such an astonishing and animating force of eloquence and enthusiasm, that they were struck dumb, and, after some pause, rose up all together with earnestness, exclaiming—Let us set out with him immediately.

where

5

where he has introduced his fanciful and whimſical opinions about *viſion*, an attentive reader will find that there is ſcarce a ſingle argument that can be urged in defence of Revelation, but what is here placed in the cleareſt light, and in the moſt beautiful diction: in this work there is a happy union of reaſoning and imagination. The two different characters of the two different ſorts of free-thinkers, the ſenſual and the refined, are ſtrongly contraſted with each other, and with the plainneſs and ſimplicity of *Euphranor*.

THESE Dialogues of Addiſon * are written with that *ſweetneſs* and *purity* of ſtyle, which conſtitute him one of the firſt of our proſe-writers. The Pleaſures of Imagination, the Eſſay on the Georgics, and his laſt papers in the Spectator and Guardian, are models of language. And ſome

* It is obſervable how much he improved after he wrote his *Travels*. In Swift's Preface to Sir W. Temple's works, and in his tranſlations from the French, &c. in that book, there are many inaccurate and almoſt ungrammatical expreſſions: theſe were the very firſt publications of Swift.

late

late writers, who ſeem to have miſtaken *ſtiffneſs* for *ſtrength*, and are grown popular by a pompous rotundity of phraſe, make one wiſh that the riſing generation may abandon this unnatural, falſe, inflated, and florid ſtyle, and form themſelves on the *chaſter* model of Addiſon. The chief imperfection of his treatiſe on medals, is, that the perſons introduced as ſpeakers, in direct contradiction to the practice of the ancients, are *fictitious*, not *real*: for CYNTHIO *, PHILANDER, PALÆMON, EUGENIO, and THEOCLES, cannot equally excite and engage the attention of the reader with SOCRATES and ALCIBIADES, ATTICUS and BRUTUS, COWLEY and SPRATT, MAYNARD and SOMERS. It is ſomewhat ſingular, that ſo many modern dialogue-writers ſhould have failed in this particular, when ſo many of the moſt celebrated wits of modern Italy had given them eminent examples of the contrary proceeding, and,

* How ill the forms and ceremonies and compliments of modern good-breeding would bear to be exactly repreſented, ſee *Characteriſtics*, vol. i. p. 209.

closely

closely following the steps of the ancients, constantly introduced living and real persons in their numerous compositions of this sort; in which they were so fond of delivering their sentiments both on moral and critical subjects; witness the *Il Cortegiano* of B. CASTIGLIONE, the *Asolani* of P. BEMBO, *Dialoghi* del S. SPERONE, the *Naugerius* of FRACASTORIUS, and *Lil.* GYRALDUS *de Poetis*, and many others. In all which pieces, the famous and living geniuses of Italy are introduced discussing the several different topics before them.

37. Huge theatres, that now unpeopled woods *,

is not so poetical as what ADDISON says of an amphitheatre,

> That on its public shews unpeopled Rome,
> And held, *uncrowded*, nations in its womb †.

BUT the beginning of the nineteenth line is eminently beautiful;

> AMBITION sigh'd ‡ ———

* Ver. 7. † Letter from Italy.

‡ Such short personifications have a great effect: *Silence was pleas'd*, says *Milton*; which personification is taken, though it happens not to be observed by any of his commentators, from the *Hero* and *Leander* of *Musæus*, v. 280.

38. And

38. And ſcarce are ſeen the *proſtrate* NILE or RHINE;
A ſmall EUPHRATES thro' the piece is roll'd,
And little eagles wave their wings in gold *.

THE two firſt-mentioned *rivers* having been *perſonified*, the *Euphrates* ſhould not have been ſpoken of as a *mere river*. The circumſtance in the laſt line is puerile and little.

39. To gain Peſcennius one employs his ſchemes,
One graſps a Cecrops in ecſtatic dreams †.

How his eyes languiſh! how his thoughts adore
That painted coat which *Joſeph never* wore?
He ſhews, on *holidays*, a ſacred pin,
That toucht the ruff, that toucht Queen Beſs's chin ‡.

A GREAT deal of wit has been waſted on *Antiquarians*; whoſe ſtudies are not only pleaſing to the imagination, but attended with many advantages to ſociety, eſpecially ſince they have been improved, as they lately have been, in elucidating the moſt important part of all hiſtory, the *Hiſtory of Manners*.

40. Oh when ſhall Britain, conſcious of her claim,
Stand emulous of Greek and Roman fame?

* Ver. 28. † Ver. 39. ‡ Young, Satire iv.

In

In living medals see her wars enroll'd,
And vanquish'd realms supply recording gold *.

ADDISON, in the ninety-sixth paper of the Guardian, has given us a proposal, here alluded to, which he drew up and delivered to the Lord Treasurer: The paper ends thus: "It is proposed, 1. That the English farthings and halfpence be re-coined upon the union of the two nations. 2. That they bear devices and inscriptions alluding to all the most remarkable parts of her Majesty's reign. 3. That there be a society established for the finding out of proper subjects, inscriptions, and devices. 4. That no subject, inscription, or device, be stamped without the approbation of this society, nor, if it be thought proper, without the authority of privy-council. By this means, medals, that are at present only a dead treasure, or mere curiosities, will be of use in the ordinary commerce of life, and, at the same time, perpetuate the glories of her Majesty's reign,

* Ver. 53.

reward the labours of her greateſt ſubjects, keep alive in the people a gratitude for public ſervices, and excite the emulation of poſterity. To theſe generous purpoſes nothing can ſo much contribute as medals of this kind, which are of undoubted authority, of neceſſary uſe and obſervation, not periſhable by time, nor confined to any certain place; properties not to be found in books, ſtatues, pictures, buildings, or any other monuments of illuſtrious actions."

41. Then ſhall thy CRAGGS (and let me call him mine)
On the caſt ore, another POLLIO ſhine *.

TICKELL †, in his preface to the works of Addiſon, concludes a copy of highly elegant, poliſhed and pathetic verſes, addreſſed to the Earl of Warwick, with the following fine lines:

These works divine, which, on his death-bed laid,
To thee, O *Craggs*, th' expiring ſage convey'd,
Great, but ill-omen'd monument of fame,
Nor he ſurviv'd to give, nor thou to claim.

* Ver. 62.

† In the few things that Tickell wrote, there appear to be a peculiar terſeneſs and neatneſs.

Swift

Swift after him thy ſocial ſpirit flies,
And cloſe to his, how ſoon! thy coffin lies.
Bleſt pair! whoſe union future bards ſhall tell,
In future tongues; each other's boaſt *, farewell!
Farewell! whom join'd in fame, in friendſhip try'd,
No chance could ſever, nor the grave divide.

42. Stateſman, yet friend to truth! of ſoul ſincere,
In action faithful, and in honour clear;
Who broke no promiſe, ſerv'd no private end,
Who gain'd no title, and who loſt no friend;
Ennobled by himſelf, by all approv'd,
And prais'd, unenvy'd, by the muſe he lov'd †.

THESE nervous and finiſhed lines were afterwards inſcribed as an epitaph on this worthy man's monument in Weſtminſter Abbey, with the alteration of two words in the laſt verſe; which there ſtands thus:

Prais'd, wept, and honour'd by the muſe he lov'd.

* Addiſon's works (ſays Atterbury, Letter x. v. 8.) came to my hands yeſterday, Oct. 15, 1721. I cannot but think it a very odd ſet of incidents, that the book ſhould be dedicated by a dead man to a dead man (Mr. Craggs) and even that the new patron (Lord Warwick) to whom Tickell choſe to inſcribe his verſes, ſhould be dead alſo before they were publiſhed. Had I been in the Editor's place, I ſhould have been a little apprehenſive for myſelf, under a thought that every one who had any hand in that work, was to die before the publication of it.

† Ver. 67.

It was Craggs, who in the moſt friendly and alluring manner offered our author a penſion of three hundred pounds per annum; which if he had accepted, we ſhould have been deprived of his beſt ſatires. Poets have a high ſpirit of liberty and independence. They neither ſeek or expect rewards. Mecænases do *not* create geniuſes. Neither Spencer or Milton, or Dante or Tasso, or Corneille *, were patronized by the governments under which they lived. And Horace and Virgil and Boileau were *formed*, before they had an opportunity of flattering Augustus and Lewis XIV.

Though Pope enliſted under the banner of Bolingbroke, in what was called the country party, and in violent oppoſition to the meaſures of Walpole, yet his clear and good ſenſe enabled him to ſee the fol-

* Il n' aimoit point le Cour, (ſays Fontenelle, ſpeaking of his uncle *Corneille*) il y apportoit un viſage preſqu' inconnu, un grand nom qui ne s' attiroit que des louanges, & un merite qui n' etoit point le merite de ce pays-là. Tom. iii. p. 126.

lies

lies and virulence of all parties; and it was his favourite maxim, that, however factious men thought proper to diſtinguiſh themſelves by *names*, yet when they got into power they all acted much in the ſame manner; ſaying,

> I know how like *Whig* miniſters to *Tory*.

And among his manuſcripts were four very ſenſible, though not very poetical, lines, which contain the moſt ſolid apology that can be made for a miniſter of this country:

> Our miniſters like *gladiators* live;
> 'Tis half their buſineſs blows to *ward*, or *give*;
> The good their *virtue* would effect, or *ſenſe*,
> Dies, between *exigents* and *ſelf-defence*.

Yet he appears ſometimes to have forgotten this candid reflection.

S E C T. XI.

Of the Epistle *to* Dr. Arbuthnot.

1. SHUT, ſhut the door, good John! fatigu'd, I ſaid,
Tie up the knocker, ſay I'm ſick, I'm dead!
The dog-ſtar rages! nay, 'tis paſt a doubt,
All Bedlam or Parnaſſus is let out:
Fire in each eye, and papers in each hand,
They rave, recite, and madden round the land *.

This abrupt exordium is animated and dramatic. Our poet, wearied with the impertinence and ſlander of a multitude of mean ſcribblers that attacked him, ſuddenly breaks out with this ſpirited complaint of the ill uſage he had ſuſtained. This piece was publiſhed † in the year 1734, in the form of an epiſtle to Dr. Arbuthnot; it is now given as a *Dialogue*,

* Ver. 1.

† With this motto, ſince omitted: Neque ſermonibus *Vulgi* dederis te, nec in premiis humanis ſpem poſueris rerum tuarum: ſuis te oportet illecebris *ipſa Virtus* trahat ad verum decus. Quid de te alii loquantur, ipſi videant, ſed loquentur tamen. Tully.

in

3

in which a very ſmall ſhare indeed is allotted to his friend. *Arbuthnot* was a man of conſummate probity *, integrity, and ſweetneſs of temper: he had infinitely more learning than POPE or SWIFT, and as much wit and humour as either of them. He was an excellent mathematician and phyſician, of which his letter on the uſefulneſs of mathematical learning, and his treatiſe on air and aliment, are ſufficient proofs. His tables of ancient coins, weights, and meaſures †, are the work of a man intimately acquainted with ancient hiſtory and literature, and are enlivened with many curious and intereſting particulars of the manners and ways of living of the ancients. *The Hiſtory of John Bull*, the *beſt parts* of the *Memoirs of Scriblerus*, the *Art of Political Lying*, the *Freeholders*

* Swift ſaid, "he was a man that could do every thing but walk." His chearfulneſs was remarkable: "As for your humble ſervant, *with a great ſtone in his kidneys*, and a family of men and women to provide for, he is as chearful as ever in public affairs." Letters, vol. xx. p. 2c6.

† Oh, ſays Swift, if the world had but a dozen of Arbuthnots in it, I would burn my *Travels!* Letters, vol. ix. p. 56.

Catechism, It cannot rain but it pours, &c. abound in strokes of the most exquisite humour. It is known that he gave numberless hints to Swift, and Pope, and Gay, of some of the most striking parts of their works. He was so neglectful of his writings, that his children tore his manuscripts and made paper-kites of them. Few letters in the English language are so interesting, and contain such marks of Christian resignation * and calmness of mind, as one that he wrote to Swift a little before his death, and is inserted in the 3d vol. of Letters, page 157. He frequently, and ably, and warmly, in many conversations, defended the cause of revelation against the

* "I make it my last request (says Arbuthnot in his last letter to POPE) that you will continue that noble disdain and abhorrence of vice, which you seem naturally endued with; but still with a due regard to your own safety; and study more to *reform* than *chastise*, though the one cannot be effected without the other." Letters, vol. viii. p. 290. The words are remarkable, and cannot fail of raising many reflections in the mind of the reader. POPE, in his answer, says, "To *reform*, and not to *chastise*, is impossible; and the best precepts, as well as the best laws, would prove of small use, if there were no examples to enforce them." This is not a sufficient and solid defence of *personal* satire.

attacks

attacks of BOLINGBROKE and CHESTERFIELD.

THE ſtrokes of ſatire, in many parts of this epiſtle, have ſuch an extraordinary energy and poignancy, that our author's want of temper has been much cenſured; and I know not whether it will be a ſufficient juſtification to ſay, that theſe malevolent ſcribblers, however impotent and inſignificant, attacked his *perſon*, *morals*, and *family*. If Boileau ridicules and rallies vile writers, with more ſeeming pleaſantry and good-humour, yet we ought to recollect, that *Boileau* was the aggreſſor, and had received no previous abuſe, when he fell upon *Cotin*, *de Pure*, *Quinault*, *St. Amand*, *Colletet*, *Chapelain*, and *Theophyle*. It was on this account that the *Duke de Montauſier*, a man of rigid virtue, ſo much condemned Boileau, that it was with great difficulty he was brought to read his works, and be reconciled to him. The authors that POPE proſcribed were in truth ſo mean and contemptible, that Swift ſaid, " Give

me

me a ſhilling, and I will inſure you that poſterity ſhall never know you had a ſingle enemy, excepting thoſe whoſe memory you have preſerved."

Laiſſez mourir un fat dans ſon obſcurité.
Un auteur ne peut-il pourir en ſeureté?
Le Jonas inconnu ſeche dans la pouſſiere.
Le David imprimé n'a point veu la lumiere.
Le Moïſe commence à moiſir par les bords.
Quel mal cela fait-il? Ceux qui ſont morts ſont morts.
Le tombeau contre vous ne peut-il les défendre,
Et qu'on fait tant d'auteurs pour remuer leur cendre?
Que vous ont fait Perrin, Bardin, Pradon, Hainaut,
Colletet, Pelletier, Titreville, Quinaut *.
Dont les noms en cent lieux, placez comme en leurs niches,
Vont de vos vers malins remplir les hemiſtiches.

BOILEAU, Satire ix. v. 89.

This is exquiſitely pleaſant; and expreſſed with that purity and force, both of thought and diction, that happy Horatian mixture of jeſt and earneſt, that contribute to place *Deſpreaux* at the head of modern *claſſics* †.

* Quinaut did not deſerve to be ſo ſeverely ſatirized. See his *Atys*, *Armide*, & *Alceſte*.

† His generoſity was equal to his genius. PATRU was reduced to great extremities, and compelled to ſell his very valuable library. He not only gave PATRU a larger ſum for his books than he could get of any body elſe, but added to the conditions of the ſale, that he ſhould continue to uſe his library as long as he lived.

I think

I think it muſt be confeſſed, that he has caught the manner of Horace more ſucceſsfully than POPE. It is obſervable that Boileau, when he firſt began to write, copied JUVENAL; whoſe *violent, downright, declamatory* ſpecies of ſatire, is far more eaſy to be imitated, than the oblique, indirect, delicate touches of Horace. The judgment of L. GYRALDUS concerning Juvenal ſeems to be judicious and well-founded. "If you think my opinion worth regarding, I would ſay, that the ſatires of Juvenal ought never to be read, till our taſte is fixed and confirmed, and we are thoroughly tinctured with a knowledge of the Latin language; and I mention this my opinion more freely, becauſe I perceive many maſters uſe a contrary method." Dial. iv.

2. Is there a Parſon, much be-mus'd in beer,
A maudlin Poeteſs, a rhyming Peer,
A Clerk, pre-doom'd his father's ſoul to croſs,
Who pens a ſtanza when he ſhould *engroſs*?
Is there, who lock'd from ink and paper, ſcrawls
With deſp'rate charcoal round his darken'd walls?

All fly to *Twitnam*, and in humble ſtrain
Apply to me to keep them mad and vain!
Arthur, whoſe giddy ſon neglects the laws,
Imputes to me and my damn'd works the cauſe *.

BEFORE this epiſtle was publiſhed, Dr. Young addreſſed two epiſtles to our author, in the year 1730, concerning the authors of the age; in which are many paſſages that bear a great reſemblance to many of POPE's; though POPE has heightened, improved, and condenſed the hints and ſentiments of Young.

Shall we not cenſure all the motley train,
Whether with ale irriguous, or champain?
Whether they tread the vale of Proſe, or climb,
And whet their appetites on cliffs of Rhyme;
The college Sloven, or embroider'd Spark,
The purple Prelate, or the Pariſh-clerk,
The quiet Quidnunc, or demanding Prig,
The plaintiff Tory, or defendant Whig;
Rich, poor, male, female, young, old, gay, or ſad,
Whether extremely witty, or quite mad;
Profoundly dull, or ſhallowly polite,
Men that read well, or men that only write:
Whether peers, porters, taylors, tune their reeds,
And meaſuring words to meaſuring ſhapes ſucceeds;

* Ver. 15.

For

For bankrupts write, when ruin'd ſhops are ſhut,
As maggots crawl from out a periſh'd nut.
His hammer this, and that his trowel quits,
And, wanting ſenſe for tradeſmen, ſerve for wits.
Thus his material, paper, takes it's birth,
From tatter'd rags of all the ſtuff on earth *.

3. Seiz'd and ty'd down to judge, how wretched I † !

Odiſti & fugis, ut Druſonem debitor æris;
Qui, niſi cum triſtes miſero venere Calendæ,
Mercedem aut nummo unde unde extricat, amaras
Porrecto jugulo hiſtorias, captivus ut, audit.

Few paſſages in Horace are more full of humour, than this ludicrous puniſhment of the poor creditor.

4. Nine years! cries he, who high in Drury-Lane,
Lull'd by ſoft zephyrs thro' the broken pane,
Rhymes ere he wakes ‡ ————

Qui facit in parvâ ſublimia carmina cellâ §.

Lo! what from *cellars* riſe, what ruſh from high,
Where Speculation rooſted near the ſky:
Letters, eſſays, ſock, buſkin, ſatire, ſong,
And all the *garret* thunders on the throng ‖ !

* Epiſtle on the authors of the age, page 5, 1730.
† Ver. 33.
‡ Ver. 41.
§ Juv. Sat. vii.
‖ Young, Epiſtle i. p. 4.

5. Bleſs

5. Bleſs me! a packet—'tis a ſtranger ſues,
A virgin tragedy, an orphan muſe.
If I diſlike it, furies, death, and rage!
If I approve, commend it to the ſtage.
Then, thank my ſtars, my whole commiſſion ends,
The play'rs and I are luckily no friends *.

THIS alludes to a tragedy acted at the Threatre-Royal in Lincoln'-Inn-Fields, and publiſhed in the year 1729, called, *The Virgin Queen*, written by Mr. Richard Barford; who dared to adopt the fine machinery of the Sylphs, in an heroicomical poem, called *The Aſſembly*, in five cantos, publiſhed 1726, and not well received.

6. 'Tis ſung, when Midas' ears began to ſpring,
(Midas, a ſacred perſon, and a king)
His very miniſter, who ſpy'd them firſt,
Some ſay his queen, was forc'd to ſpeak, or burſt.
And is not mine, my friend, a ſorer caſe,
When ev'ry coxcomb *perks* them in my face †?

THE abruptneſs with which this ſtory from Perſius is introduced, occaſions an obſcurity in the paſſage; for there is no connexion with the foregoing paragraph.

* Ver. 55.

† Ver. 69.

Boileau

Boileau ſays, Satire ix. v. 221, I have nothing to do with *Chapelain*'s * honor, or probity, or candor, or civility, or complaiſance: but if you hold him up as a model of good writing, and as the king of authors,

> Ma bile alors s' echauffe, & je brûle d'ecrire;
> Et s'il ne m'eſt permis de le dire au papier;
> J'irai creuſer la terre, & comme ce *barbier*,
> Faire dire aux roſeaux par un nouvel organe,
> " Midas, le Roi Midas a des oreilles d'Aſne."

THERE is more humour in making the prying and watchful eyes of the miniſter, inſtead of the barber, firſt diſcover the aſs's ears;

* Notwithſtanding his *La Pucelle* was ſo dull and tireſome an epic poem, yet was *Chapelain* a man of learning, and a good critic, and treated too harſhly by *Boileau*. His avarice was extreme.

The candid Abbé *d' Olivet*, in the 2d. tom. of his Hiſtory of the French Academy, p. 145, has zealouſly defended the abilities and character of *Chapelain*. It was at the deſire of *Malherbe* and *Vaugelas*, that *Chapelain* wrote the famous Preface to the *Adone* of *Marino*. And it was he who corrected the very firſt poetical compoſition of *Racine*, his Ode to the Queen, who introduced *Racine* to *Colbert*, and procured him a penſion. It is remarkable, that *Chapelain* ſhould be the perſon who firſt pointed out to Cardinal *Richlieu*, and the poets whom he employed, the neceſſity of obſerving the three unities in a drama.

ears; and the word *perks* has particular force and emphaſis. Sir *Robert Walpole* and *Queen Caroline* were here pointed at.

7. Who ſhames a ſcribbler? break one cobweb thro',
He ſpins the ſlight, ſelf-pleaſing thread anew:
Deſtroy his fib or ſophiſtry, in vain!
The creature's at his dirty work again;
Thron'd in the center of his thin deſigns,
Proud of a vaſt extent of flimſy lines *.

The *metaphor* † is moſt happily carried on through a variety of correſponding particulars, that exactly hit the natures of the two *inſects* in queſtion. It is not purſued

* Ver. 89.

† Berkley, in his Alciphron, Dialogue vi. p. 107, has beautifully employed an image of this ſort, on a more ſerious ſubject. "To tax or ſtrike at this divine doctrine, on account of things foreign and adventitious, the ſpeculations and diſputes of curious men, is, in my mind, an abſurdity of the ſame kind, as it would be to cut down a fine tree, yielding fruit and ſhade, becauſe its leaves afforded nouriſhment to caterpillars, or becauſe ſpiders may now and then weave cobwebs among the branches." Berkley had a brilliant imagination. See his charming deſcription of the iſland *Inarime,* in Letters to P. vol. vii. p. 330. I have been told, that Blackwell received his juſt idea of *Homer*, and of the *reaſons* and *cauſes* of *Homer*'s ſuperior excellence, from Berkley, with whom he had been connected, and had travelled with him.

too

too far, nor jaded out, ſo as to become *quaint* and *affected*, as is the caſe of many, perhaps, in *Congreve's* too witty *Comedies*, particularly in the Way of the World, and in *Young*'s Satires. For inſtance:

Critics on verſe, as *ſquibs* on triumphs, wait,
Proclaim the glory, and augment the ſtate;
Hot, envious, noiſy, proud, the ſcribbling fry *,
Burn, hiſs, and bounce, waſte paper, ſtink and die †.

THE epithets *envious*, and *proud*, have nothing to do with *ſquibs*. The laſt line is brilliant and ingenious, but perhaps too much ſo.

8. There are who to my perſon pay their court:
I cough like *Horace*, and tho' *lean*, am *ſhort*;
Ammon's great ſon one ſhoulder had too high,
Such *Ovid*'s noſe, and, Sir, you have an eye ‡.

THE ſmalleſt *perſonal* particularities are intereſting in eminent men. We liſten with pleaſure to *Montaigne*, when he familiarly tells us, " My face is not puff'd,

* See alſo a paſſage in his two Epiſtles, where the tranſmigrations of Proteus are adapted to the various ſhapes aſſumed by modern ſcribblers.

† Univerſal Paſſion, Sat. iii.

‡ Ver. 115.

but full, and my complexion between jovial and melancholy, moderately ſanguine and hot. In dancing, tennis, or wreſtling, I could never arrive at any excellence; in ſwimming, fencing, vaulting, and leaping, to none at all. My hands are ſo clumſy, that I cannot read what I write myſelf. I cannot handſomely fold up a letter, nor could I ever make a pen, nor carve at table, nor carry a hawk." This is delivered with ſuch an air, ſays old *Paſquier*, that it pleaſes me as much as if it had been ſpoken of ſome other perſon.

WHAT paſſages in Horace * are more agreeable than—

Me *pinguem* & nitidum bene curatâ cute viſes—
Luſum it Mæcænas, *dormitum* ego Virgiliuſque—
Namque pila *lippis* inimicum & ludere *crudis*—
Me primis urbis *belli* placuiſſe *domique*;
Corporis *exigui*, *præcanum*, *ſolibus aptum*,
Iraſci *celerem*, tamen ut *placabilis* eſſem.

* "My converſation (ſays Dryden very entertainingly of himſelf) is ſlow and dull, my humour ſaturnine and reſerved. In ſhort, I am none of thoſe who endeavour to break jeſts in company, or make repartees."
Preface to his Indian Emperor.

Above all, the pleaſing detail he gives of his way of life, the deſcriptions of his mule, his dinner, his ſupper, his furniture, his amuſements, his walks, his time of bathing and ſleeping, &c. from the 105th line, to the end, of the 6th ſatire of the firſt book.

WHAT Addiſon ſays in jeſt, and with his uſual humour, is true in fact:—"I have obſerved that a reader ſeldom peruſes a book with pleaſure, 'till he knows whether the writer of it be a black or fair man, of a mild or cholerick diſpoſition, married or a batchelor." I will add, at the hazard of its being reckoned a trifling and minute remark, that many of our Engliſh poets have been in their perſons remarkably handſome; ſuch were SPENCER, MILTON, COWLEY, BUTLER, WALLER, WYCHERLEY, ROWE, ADDISON, CONGREVE, GARTH, GAY.—VIRGIL and VIDA are ſaid, by LIL. GYRALDUS, to have had a plain ruſtic look; and OVID and CARDINAL BEMBO, to be ſlender and active; as alſo was TI-

BULLUS.—The portraits of DANTE, PETRARCH, and BOCCACIO, are thus given, in the curious and entertaining hiſtory of their lives by JANNOT. MANETTUS, a celebrated writer of the fifteenth century, but not publiſhed till 1746, at Florence. DANTE, he ſays, was of a becoming and middle ſtature, had a long face, very large eyes, an aquiline noſe, broad cheeks, an under-lip that projected a little, a dark complexion, a beard and hair long, black, and curling. In the form of PETRARCH, there was a happy mixture of majeſty and grace. He had ſo much agility and dexterity, that no one could gain the maſtery over him. He enjoyed a firm ſtate of health to his old age. Of BOCCACIO he ſays, he was of a full and large habit of body, of a tall ſtature, a round face, an aſpect chearful and pleaſant, ſo facetious and well-bred, that a certain elegance and urbanity appeared in every word he uttered. P. 81.

9. Why did I write? what ſin, to me unknown,
Dipt me in ink, my parents or my own?

As yet a child, nor yet a fool to fame,
I lisp'd in numbers, for the numbers came.
I left no calling for this idle trade,
No duty broke, no father disobey'd *.

Boileau says, in his fifth epistle, verse 110, that his father left him a decent patrimony, and made him study the law:

Mais bien-tost amourex d'un plus noble métier,
Fils, frere, oncle, cousin, beau-frere de Greffier,
Pouvant charger mon bras d'une utile liasse,
J'allay loin du Palais errer sur de Parnasse.
La famille en pâlit, & vit en frémissant,
Dans la Poudre du Greffe un poete naissant.
On vit avec horreur une muse effrenée
Dormir chez un Greffier la grasse matinée †.

10. But why then publish? *Granville* the polite,
And knowing *Walsh*, would tell me I could write;
Well-natur'd *Garth* ‡ inflam'd with early praise,
And *Congreve* lov'd, and *Swift* endur'd my lays:

* Ver. 125.

† He was a great sleeper; got up late, and always was accustomed to sleep after dinner: as also was Pope.

‡ Every word and epithet here used is characteristical, and peculiarly appropriated to the temper and manner of each of the persons here mentioned; the elegance of *Lansdown*, the open free benevolence of *Garth*, the warmth of *Congreve*, the difficulty of pleasing *Swift*, the very gesture that *Atterbury* used when he was pleased, and the animated air and spirit of *Bolingbroke*.

The courtly *Talbot*, *Somers*, *Sheffield* read,
Ev'n mitred *Rochester* would nod the head;
And *St. John*'s ſelf (great Dryden's friends before)
With open arms received one poet more *.

To the *three* firſt names, that encouraged his earlieſt writings, he has added other friends, whoſe acquaintance with him did not commence till he was a poet of eſtabliſhed reputation. From the many commendations which *Walſh*, and *Garth*, and *Granville* beſtowed on *his Paſtorals*, it may fairly be concluded how much the public taſte has been improved, and with how many good compoſitions our language has been enriched, ſince that time. When *Gray* † publiſhed his exquiſite ode on Eton College, his firſt publication, little notice was taken of it; but I ſuppoſe no

* Ver. 135.

† Sweet BARD, who ſhun'ſt the noiſe of folly,
Moſt muſical, moſt melancholy!
Thee oft, the lonely woods among,
I woo to hear thy even-ſong;
And think thy thrilling ſtrains have power
To raiſe MUSÆUS from his bower,
Or bid the tender SPENCER come
From his lov'd haunt, ſweet Fancy's tomb!

critic

critic can be found, that will not place it far above POPE's Paſtorals.

11. From theſe the world will judge of men and books,
Not from the *Burnets*, *Oldmixons*, and *Cooks* *.

SUCH authors as the two laſt, are a kind of literary harpies; whatever ſubject they touch, they debaſe and defile;

——Magnis quatiunt clangoribus alas,
Diripiuntque dapes, *contactûque* omnia *fœdant*
Immundo; tum *vox* tetrum *dira* inter *odorem* †.

As to *Burnet*, his character is thus drawn by the very ſenſible and judicious tranſlator of Polybius, Mr. Hampton, in a pamphlet that deſerves to be more known, entitled, *Reflections on Ancient and Modern Hiſtory*: printed in quarto, at Oxford, 1746. " His perſonal reſentment put him upon writing hiſtory. He relates the actions of a perſecutor and benefactor: and it is eaſy to believe that a man in ſuch circumſtances muſt violate the laws of truth. The remembrance of his injuries is always pre-

* Ver. 145. † Virg. Æn. iii. v. 225.

ſent, and gives venom to his pen. Let us add to this, that intemperate and malicious curioſity, which penetrates into the moſt private receſſes of vice. The greateſt of his triumphs is to draw the veil of ſecret infamy, and expoſe to view tranſactions that were before concealed from the world; though they ſerve not in the leaſt, either to embelliſh the ſtyle, or connect the ſeries, of his hiſtory; and will never obtain more credit, than perhaps to ſuſpend the judgment of the reader, ſince they are ſupported only by one ſingle, ſuſpected teſtimony." P. 28 *.

12. Yet then did *Gildon* draw his venal quill;
I wiſh'd the man a dinner, and ſat ſtill:
Yet then did *Dennis* rave in furious fret;
I never anſwer'd, I was not in debt:
If want provok'd, or madneſs made them print,
I wag'd no war with *Bedlam* or the *Mint* †.

THE ‡ unexpected turn in the *ſecond* line

* Theſe animadverſions obviouſly relate to the Hiſtory of his own Times, and not to his Hiſtory of the Reformation, and his other important works.

† Ver. 151.

‡ Ingenii plurimum eſt in eo, & acerbitas mira, & urbanitas, & vis ſumma; ſed plus ſtomacho quam conſilio dedit. Præterea ut amari ſales, ita frequenter amaritudo ipſa ridicula eſt. M. F. Quintil. lib. x. c. 1.

of

of each of these three *couplets*, contains as cutting and bitter strokes of satire, as perhaps can be written.

It is with difficulty we can forgive our author for upbraiding these wretched scribblers for their poverty and distresses, if we do not keep in our minds the grossly abusive pamphlets they published, without previous provocation from him; and even, allowing this circumstance, we ought to separate *rancour* from *reproof*.

13. Yet ne'er one sprig of laurel grac'd these ribalds,
From *slashing Bentley* ———— *.

Swift imbibed from Sir W. Temple, and Pope from Swift, an inveterate and unreasonable aversion and contempt for Bentley; whose admirable *Boyle*'s *Lectures*, *Remarks* on Collins, Emendations of Menander and Callimachus, and Tully's *Tuscul. Disp.* whose edition of Horace, and above all, *Dissertation* on the Epistles of Phalaris, (in which he

* Ver. 163.

gained

gained the most complete victory over a whole army of wits) all of them exhibit the most striking marks of accurate and extensive erudition, and a vigorous and acute understanding. He degraded himself much by his edition of the *Paradise Lost*, and by his strange and absurd hypothesis of the faults which Milton's amanuensis introduced into that poem. But I have been informed that there was still an additional cause for POPE's resentment; that ATTERBURY, being in company with BENTLEY and POPE, insisted upon knowing the Doctor's opinion of the English Homer; and that, being earnestly pressed to declare his sentiments freely, he said, "The verses are good verses, but the work is not Homer, it is *Spondanus*." It may however be observed, in favour of POPE *, that Dr. CLARKE, whose critical exactness is

* And yet POPE, in a letter which Dr. Rutherforth shewed me at Cambridge, in the year 1771, written to a Mr. Bridges, at Fulham, mentions his consulting Chapman and Hobbes, and talks of "their authority, joined to the knowledge of my own imperfectness in the language, over-ruled me." These are the very words, which I transcribed at that time.

well

well known, has not been able to point out above three or four miſtakes in the ſenſe through the whole Iliad. The real faults of that tranſlation are of a different kind. They are ſuch, as remind us of Nero's gilding a brazen ſtatue of Alexander the Great, caſt by Lyſippus.

14. ———— down to *piddling* Tibalds.

YET this very dull and laborious man was the firſt publiſher of *Shakeſpear*, that hit upon the true and rational method of correcting and illuſtrating his author, that is, by reading ſuch books (whatever traſh POPE * might call them) as SHAKESPEAR read, and by attending to the genius, learning, and notions of his times †. By purſuing and perfecting which method, the public has lately been preſented with a moſt valuable and complete edition of all

* POPE was irritated at the many blunders in his Shakeſpear, that Theobald pointed out.

† In this manner alſo has SPENCER been illuſtrated. See Obſervations on the *Faery Queen*, by T. Warton, A.M. London, 1762, 8vo. 2d. edit. and the Canterbury Tales of Chaucer, with incomparable remarks by Mr. *Tyrwhit*.

his

his works, by the united labours of ſuch excellent critics as JOHNSON, STEEVENS, TYRWHIT, and MALONE.

15. Each wight, who reads not, and but ſcans and ſpells,
Each word-catcher, that lives on ſyllables *.

IT is very eaſy, but very ungrateful, to laugh at collectors of various readings, and adjuſters of texts, thoſe poor pioneers of literature, who drag forward

A waggon-load of meanings for one word,
While *A's* *depos'd*, and *B* with pomp *reſtor'd* †.

* Ver. 165.

† Many are the ridiculous ſtories told of the violent conteſts and quarrels of grammarians and commentators. PHILELPHUS, who married the daughter of EMANUEL CHRYSOLORAS, laid a wager of one hundred crowns with TIMOTHEUS, a Greek grammarian, about the termination of a *tenſe*; which ſum he ſtaked againſt the long flowing beard of the grammarian; and gaining his wager, abſolutely cut off the beard of TIMOTHEUS.

This CHRYSOLORAS ought not to be reckoned, as he commonly is, among the Greeks whom the taking of Conſtantinople forced into Italy; ſince he died at the Council of Conſtance, in 1415, thirty-eight years before the Turks took that city; which was on the twenty-ninth of May, in 1453; and moreover, Leonard of Arezzo, in p. 253 of his Hiſt. Rerum Ital. plainly ſays, that Chryſoloras was in Italy from the year 1398.

To the indefatigable researches of many a Dutch commentator and German editor, are we indebted for that ease and facility with which we now are enabled to read. "I am persuaded," says BAYLE, "that the ridiculous obstinacy of the first critics, who lavished so much of their time upon the question, whether we ought to say Virgilius or Vergilius, has been ultimately of great use; they thereby inspired men with an extreme veneration for antiquity; they disposed them to a sedulous enquiry into the conduct and character of the ancient Grecians and Romans, and that gave occasion to their improving by those great examples." Dict. tom. v. p. 795. I have always been struck with the following words of a commentator *, who was also a great philosopher, I mean Dr. CLARKE,

* MALLET, to gratify Pope, by abusing Bentley, published, about this time, a very feeble and flimsy poem, *on Verbal Criticism*, stuffed with illiberal cant about pedantry, and collators of manuscripts. Real scholars will always speak with due regard of such names as the *Scaligers*, *Salmasius's*, *Heinsius's*, *Burmans*, *Gronovius's*, *Reiskius's*, *Marklands*, *Gesners*, and *Heynes*.

who

who thus finiſhes the preface to his incomparable edition of Homer *:

"Levia quidem hæc, & parvi forte, ſi per ſe ſpectentur momenti. Sed ex elementis conſtant, ex principiis oriuntur, omnia: Et ex judicii conſuetudine in rebus *minutis* adhibitâ, pendet ſæpiſſimè in *maximis* vera atque accurata ſcientia."

16. Pretty! in amber to obſerve the forms
Of hairs, or ſtraws, or dirt, or grubs, or worms †!

Very elegant imagery, happily applied! *Addiſon* has made a beautiful uſe of a ſimilar image to a contrary purpoſe, and to illuſtrate excellence. "Shakeſpear," ſays he, Spectator 398, "was born with all the ſeeds of poetry, and may be compared to the ſtone in *Pyrrhus*'s ring, which, as *Pliny* tells us, had the figure of Apollo and the nine Muſes in the veins of it, produced by the ſpontaneous hand of nature, without any help of art."

* Whenever Dr. Clarke, who was of a tranquil and ſedate temper, ſpoke of Homer, he did it, as his friend Dr. Sykes informed me, with a vehement and enthuſiaſtic admiration, very unuſual to him on other ſubjects.

† Ver. 169.

17. Did

17. Did ſome more ſober critic come abroad;
If wrong, I ſmil'd; if right, I kiſs'd the rod *.

SUCH he eſteemed to be Mr. SPENCE's judicious Eſſay on his tranſlation of the Odyſſey; a work of the trueſt taſte, and ſoundeſt criticiſm, and which POPE was ſo far from taking amiſs, that it was the origin of a laſting friendſhip betwixt them. I have ſeen, by the kindneſs of the preſent Biſhop of London, a copy of this work, with marginal obſervations written in POPE's own hand †, and generally acknowledging the juſtneſs of SPENCE's obſervations, and in a few inſtances pleading, humorouſly enough, that ſome favourite lines might be ſpared. I am indebted to this learned and amiable man, on whoſe friendſhip I ſet the greateſt value, for moſt of the anecdotes relating to POPE, mentioned in this work, which he gave me, when I was making him a viſit at *Byfleet*, in the year 1754.

* Ver. 171.

† Which do you look upon (ſays Spence one day to POPE) as the beſt age of our Poetry? "Why the laſt, I think; but now the old ones are all gone, and the young ſeem to have no emulation among them."

18. The

18. The bard whom pilfer'd pastorals renown,
Who turns a Persian tale for half a crown *.

And in a line before,

Still to one Bishop PHILIPS seems a wit.

PHILIPS, certainly not a very animated or first-rate writer, yet appears not to deserve quite so much contempt, if we look at his first and fifth pastoral, his epistle from Copenhagen, his ode on the death of Earl Cowper, his translations † of the two first olympic odes of Pindar, the two odes of Sappho, and above all, his pleasing tragedy ‡ of the Distrest Mother §.

* Ver. 180.

† The secret grounds of Philips's malignity to Pope, are said to be the ridicule and laughter he met with from all the Hanover Club, of which he was secretary, for mistaking the incomparable ironical paper in the Guardian, N° 40, which was written by Pope, for a serious criticism on pastoral poetry. The learned *Heyne* also mistook this irony, as appears by p. 202. v. 1. of his Virgil.

‡ Racine, in his remarks on his father's Andromaque, has censured this play of Philips, p. 207. t. i.

§ I have heard Mr. Garrick say, that Addison wrote the celebrated epilogue to this tragedy, published in the name of Budgell: that this was a fact he received from some of the Tonsons. And Addison is said also to have largely corrected and improved Budgell's translation of Theophrastus.

How

How far Addison, as hath been insinuated, was concerned in altering and improving Philips's works, cannot now be ascertained. He was accused of reporting that Mr. POPE was an enemy to the government, and that he had a hand in the famous party paper called The Examiner.

19. And own'd that nine such poets made a *Tate* *.

YOUNG says, with equal pleasantry, of the same *Nahum Tate*,

He's now a *scribbler*, who was once a *man* †.

20. Peace to all such! but were there one whose fires
True genius kindles, and fair fame inspires:
Blest with each talent and each art to please,
And born to write, converse, and live with ease:
Should such a man, too fond to rule alone,
Bear, like the Turk ‡, no brother near the throne,
View

* Ver. 190. † Sat. i.

‡ This is from Bacon de Augmentis Scient. lib. iii. p. 180. Etsi enim Aristoteles, more Ottomannorum, regnare se haud tutè posse putaret, nisi fratres suos omnes contrucidasset.

Which thought, and also that of *Cato*'s little senate, are used in a letter to Mr. Craggs, dated July 15, 1715. Our author frequently has versified passages from his own letters.

View him with ſcornful, yet with jealous eyes,
And hate for arts that caus'd himſelf to riſe;
Damn with faint praiſe, aſſent with civil leer,
And, without ſneering, teach the reſt to ſneer:
Willing to wound, and yet afraid to ſtrike,
Juſt hint a fault, and heſitate diſlike;
Alike reſerv'd to blame, or to commend,
A tim'rous foe, and a ſuſpicious friend;
Dreading ev'n fools, by flatterers beſieg'd,
And ſo obliging that he ne'er oblig'd;
Like *Cato*, give his little ſenate laws,
And ſit attentive to his own applauſe;
While wits and Templars ev'ry ſentence raiſe,
And wonder with a fooliſh face of praiſe—
Who but muſt laugh, if ſuch a man there be?
Who would not weep, if *Atticus* were he *!

THIS is that famous character of ADDISON †, which has been ſo much com-

" It is uſual with the ſmaller party to make up in intereſt what they want in number; and this is the caſe with the little ſenate of Cato. We have, it ſeems, a Great Turk in poetry, who can never bear a brother on the throne; and has his mutes too, a ſet of nodders, winkers, and whiſperers, whoſe buſineſs it is to ſtrangle all other offspring of wit in their birth." Vol. vii. p. 300.

* Ver. 192.

† Old Jacob Tonſon hated Addiſon. You will ſee him, ſays he, one day a Biſhop. He intended to have given a tranſlation of all the Pſalms, of which deſign his verſion of the 23d is a beautiful ſpecimen. Addiſon uſed to ſpeak contemptuouſly of his own account of the Engliſh poets, addreſſed to his old friend *Sacheverell*. It is remarkable, that Addiſon declared he had never read *Spencer*, when he gave *his* character in that account.

6 mended

mended for it's wit and poignancy, and ſo much cenſured for it's bitterneſs and malignity. The provocations that induced our author to write it, which he did ſo early as 1721, though it was not inſerted in this epiſtle till 1733, have been touched upon in the firſt volume of this eſſay, at page 159. Since that time, a writer, of the firſt eminence, who, to a conſummate knowledge of the laws, hiſtory, and antiquities of his country, joined the moſt exquiſite taſte in polite literature, the late much-lamented Sir William Blackſtone, drew up, with his uſual preciſion and penetration, a paper that minutely inveſtigated all the facts that have been urged againſt Addiſon's conduct to Pope. The chain of his reaſoning would be injured, by endeavouring to abridge this paper; I muſt therefore refer the reader to the ſecond volume of the Biographia Britannica, publiſhed by Dr. Kippis, page 56, and ſhall only inſert the concluſion of it; which is as follows: "Upon the whole, however Mr. Pope may be excuſable for penning ſuch a character of his friend in the firſt tranſports of poetical indignation, it reflects no great honour on his feelings, to have kept it in petto for ſix years, till after the death of Mr. Addiſon, and then to permit its publication (whether by recital or copy makes no material difference;) and at length, at the diſtance of 18 years, hand it down to poſterity ingrafted into one of his capital productions. Nothing ſurely could juſtify ſo long and ſo deep a reſentment, unleſs the ſtory be true of the commerce between Addiſon and Gildon; which will require to be very fully proved, before it can be believed of a gentleman who was ſo amiable in his moral character, and who (in his own caſe) had two years before expreſsly diſapproved of a perſonal abuſe upon Mr. Dennis. The perſon, indeed, from whom Mr. Pope is ſaid to have received this anecdote, about the time of his writing the character (viz. about July 1715) was no other than the Earl of Warwick, ſon-in-law to Mr. Addiſon himſelf; and the ſomething about Wycherley,

(in

(in which the ſtory ſuppoſes that Addiſon hired Gildon to abuſe Pope and his family) is explained by a note on the Dunciad, vol. i. p. 296, to mean a pamphlet containing Mr. Wycherley's life. Now it happens, that in July 1715, the Earl of Warwick (who died at the age of twenty-three, in Auguſt 1721) was only a boy of ſeventeen, and not likely to be entruſted with ſuch a ſecret, by a ſtateſman between forty and fifty, with whom it does not appear he was any-way connected or acquainted. For Mr. Addiſon was not married to his mother the Counteſs of Warwick till the following year, 1716; nor could Gildon have been employed in July 1715 to write Mr. Wycherley's life, who lived till the December following. As therefore ſo many inconſiſtencies are evident in the ſtory itſelf, which never found its way into print till near ſixty years after it is ſaid to have happened, it will be no breach of charity to ſuppoſe that the whole of it was founded on ſome miſapprehenſion in either Mr. Pope or the Earl; and unleſs better proof can be given, we ſhall readily acquit Mr. Addiſon of this moſt odious part of the charge."

I BEG leave to add, that as to the other accuſation, Dr. Young, Lord Bathurſt, Mr. Harte, and Lord Lyttelton, each of them aſſured me, that Addiſon himſelf certainly tranſlated the firſt book of Homer. Yet I have very lately heard, that ſome proofs to the contrary have been juſt diſcovered, which every man of candour will be glad to ſee publiſhed.

21. Proud as Apollo on his forked hill,
Sate full-blown *Bufo*, puff'd by ev'ry quill;
Fed with ſoft Dedication all day long,
Horace and he went hand in hand in ſong.
His library (where buſts of poets dead *,
And a true Pindar ſtood without a head)
Receiv'd

* The poverty of Butler is often mentioned among the diſtreſſes of poets, as a reproach to his age, and particularly to Charles II. who was ſo fond of Hudibras. But Dr. Pearce, the late Biſhop of Rocheſter, related, that Mr. Lowndes, then belonging to the Treaſury, and in the reigns of King William and Queen Anne Secretary to it, aſſured him, that, by order of King Charles II. he had paid to Butler a yearly penſion of 100l. to the time of his deceaſe.—After having been in many important offices, and an

Receiv'd of wits an undiftinguifh'd race,
Who firft his judgment afk'd, and then a place;
Much they extoll'd his pictures, much his feat,
And flatter'd ev'ry day, and fome days eat;
Till, grown more frugal in his riper days,
He paid fome bards with port, and fome with praife *.

DR. YOUNG's parafites and flatterers are painted with equal humour, and a generous contempt of fervility;

Who'd be a crutch to prop a rotten peer;
Or living pendant dangling at his ear;
For ever whifp'ring fecrets, which were blown,
For months before, by trumpets thro' the town?
Who'd be a glafs, with flattering grimace,
Still to reflect the temper of his face;
Or happy pin to ftick upon his fleeve,
When my lord's gracious, and vouchfafes it leave;
Or cufhion, when his Heavinefs fhall pleafe
To loll, or thump it for his better eafe;
Or a vile butt, for noon or night befpoke,
When the peer rafhly fwears he'll club his joke?
Who'd fhake with laughter, tho' he cou'd not find
His Lordfhip's jeft, or, if his nofe broke wind,
For bleffings to the Gods profoundly bow—
That can cry chimney-fweep, or drive a plough?

an Ambaffador at *Paris*, *Prior* had, at one time of his life, nothing left but the income of his fellowfhip of St. John's College, Cambridge. Bufo is faid to mean Lord Halifax.

* Ver. 231.

22. *Dryden* alone * (what wonder?) came not nigh;
Dryden alone efcap'd his judging eye;
But ftill, the great have kindnefs in referve,
He help'd to bury whom he help'd to ftarve †.

Our poet, with true gratitude, has feized every opportunity of fhewing his reverence for his great mafter, *Dryden*: whom Swift as conftantly depreciated and maligned. "I do affirm (fays he, feverely, but with exquifite irony indeed, in the

* Alluding to the fubfcription that was made for his funeral. Garth fpoke an oration over him. His neceffities obliged him to produce (befides many other poetical pieces) twenty-feven plays in twenty-five years. He got 25l. for the copy, and 70l. for his benefits generally. Dramatic poetry was certainly not his talent. His plays, a very few paffages excepted, are infufferably unnatural. It is remarkable, that he did not fcruple to confefs, that he could not relifh the pathos and fimplicity of Euripides. When he publifhed his fables, Tonfon agreed to give him two hundred and fixty-eight pounds for *ten thoufand verfes*. And, to complete the full number of lines ftipulated for, he gave the bookfeller the epiftle to his coufin, and the celebrated mufic ode.—" Old Jacob Tonfon ufed to fay, that Dryden was a little jealous of rivals. He would compliment *Crown* when a play of his failed, but was very cold to him if he met with fuccefs. He fometimes ufed to fay that *Crown* had fome genius; but then he added always, that his father and Crown's mother were very well acquainted." Mr. Pope to Mr. Spence.

† Ver. 245.

Dedication

Dedication of the Tale of *a Tub* to Prince Pofterity) upon the word of a fincere man, that there is now actually in being a certain poet, called *John Dryden*, whofe tranflation of Virgil was lately printed in a large folio, well-bound, and, if diligent fearch were made, for aught I know is yet to be feen." And he attacks him again in the Battle of Books. SHAFTESBURY is alfo very fond of petulantly carping at Dryden. "To fee the incorrigiblenefs of our poets, in their pedantic manner (fays he, vol. iii. p. 276) their vanity, defiance of criticifm; their rhodomontade, and poetical bravado; we need only turn to our famous poet-laureat, the very Mr. BAYS himfelf, in one of his lateft and moft valued pieces, *Don Sebaftian* *, writ many years after the ingenious author of the *Rehearfal* had drawn his picture." Shaftefbury's refent-

* The dramatic works of *Lope de Vega* make twenty-fix volumes, befides four hundred fcriptural dramatic pieces, his *Autos Sacramentales*. His biographer affirms, that he often finifhed a play in twenty-four hours, nay fome of his comedies in lefs than five. He wrote during his life 21,316,000 verfes.

ment

ment * was excited by the admirable poem of *Absalom* and *Achitophel*; and particularly by four lines in it, that related to Lord Ashley, his father;

And all to leave, what with his toil he won,
To that unfeather'd, two-legg'd thing a son;
Got while his soul did huddled notions try,
And born a shapeless lump, like anarchy.

But Dryden's works will remain, when the *Characteristics* will be forgotten.

23. Blest be the Great for those they take away,
And those they left me; for they left me GAY;
Left me to see neglected genius bloom,
Neglected die, and tell it on his tomb.
Of all thy blameless life the sole return
My verse, and Queensb'ry weeping o'er thy urn † !

* I remember to have heard my father say, that Mr. Elijah Fenton, who was his intimate friend, and had been his master, informed him, that Dryden, upon seeing some of Swift's earliest verses, said to him, "Young man, you will never be a poet." And that this was the cause of Swift's rooted aversion to Dryden, mentioned above. *Baucis* and *Philemon* was so much and so often altered, at the instigation of Addison, who mentioned this circumstance to my father, at Magdalen College, that not above eight lines remain as they originally stood. The violence of party disputes never interrupted the sincere friendship that subsisted between Swift and Addison, though of such opposite tempers as well as principles.

† Ver. 255.

THE

The ſweetneſs and ſimplicity of Gay's temper and manners, much endeared him to all his acquaintance, and made them always ſpeak of him with particular fondneſs and attachment. He wrote with neatneſs, and terſeneſs, æquali quâdam mediocritate, but certainly without any elevation; frequently without any ſpirit. Trivia * appears to be the beſt of his poems, in which are many ſtrokes of genuine humour and pictures of London-life, which are now become curious, becauſe our manners as well as our dreſſes, have been ſo much altered and changed within a few years. His fables, the moſt popular of all his works, have the fault of many modern fable-writers †, the aſcribing to the different animals

* The fable of Cloacina is indelicate. I ſhould think this was one of the hints given him by Swift, who himſelf was indebted, for many ſtrokes in his Gulliver, to Biſhop *Godwin*'s *Man in the Moon*, or Voyage of Domingo Gonzales, 1638.

† The long and languid introductions to the fables in the ſecond volume (which is indeed much inferior to the firſt) read like party pamphlets verſified. *Dione* has not reſcued us from the imputation of having no paſtoral-comedy, that can be compared, in the ſmalleſt degree, to the

animals and objects introduced, ſpeeches and actions inconſiſtent with their ſeveral natures. An elephant can have nothing to do in a bookſeller's ſhop. They are greatly inferior to the fables of *La Fontaine*, which is perhaps the moſt unrivalled work in the whole French language. The Beggar's Opera has ſurely been extolled beyond it's merits; I could never perceive that fine vein of concealed ſatire ſuppoſed to run through it; and though I ſhould not join with a bench of Weſtminſter Juſtices in forbidding it to be repreſented on the ſtage, yet I think pickpockets, ſtrumpets, and highwaymen, may be hardened in their vices by this piece; and that *Pope* and *Swift* talked too highly of it's moral good effects. One undeſigned and accidental miſchief attended it's ſucceſs: it was the parent of that moſt monſtrous of

the Aminta or Paſtor Fido. The paſtorals were written to ridicule thoſe of Philips, and conſequently very acceptable to Pope. *Polly*, the ſecond part of the Beggar's Opera, though it brought him a good deal of money, above 1200 pounds, being publiſhed by ſubſcription, is not equal to the firſt.

all

all dramatic abſurdities, the *Comic Opera.* The friendſhip of two ſuch excellent perſonages as the Duke and Dutcheſs of Queenſberry, did, in truth, compenſate poor Gay's want of penſion * and preferment. They behaved to him conſtantly with that delicacy, and ſenſe of ſeeming equality, as never to ſuffer him for a moment to feel his ſtate of dependence. Let every man of letters, who wiſhes for patronage, read D'Alembert's *Eſſay on living with the Great*, before he enters the houſe of a patron. And let him always remember the fate of Racine, who having drawn up, at Madame Maintenon's † ſecret requeſt, a memorial that ſtrongly painted the diſtreſſes of the French nation, the

* I was informed by Mr. Spence, that Addiſon, in his laſt illneſs, ſent to deſire to ſpeak with Mr. Gay, and told him he had much injured him; probably with reſpect to his gaining ſome appointment from the court: but, ſaid he, if I recover, I will endeavour to recompenſe you.

† The moſt exact account of the occaſion on which Racine wrote his excellent *Eſther* and *Athaliah*, at the requeſt of Madame Maintenon, for the uſe of the young ladies at St. Cyr, is to be found in, *Les Souvenirs de Mad. De Caylus*, p. 183. There alſo are ſome very intereſting and authentic particulars of the life of *Mad. Maintenon.*

weight

weight of their taxes, and the expences of the court, ſhe could not reſiſt the importunity of Lewis XIV. but ſhewed him her friend's paper: againſt whom the king immediately conceived a violent indignation, becauſe a poet ſhould dare to buſy himſelf with politics. Racine had the weakneſs to take this anger of the king ſo much to heart, that it brought on a low fever, which haſtened his death. The Dutcheſs of Queenſberry would not have ſo betrayed her poetical friend Gay.

24. Curs'd be the verſe, how well ſoe'er it flow,
That tends to make one worthy man my foe,
Give virtue ſcandal, innocence a fear,
Or from the ſoft-ey'd virgin ſteal a tear * !

M. DESPREAUX s'applaudiſſoit fort à l'age de ſoixante & onze ans, de n'avoir rien mis dans ſes vers qui choquât les bonnes mœurs. C'eſt une conſolation, diſoit il, pour les vieux poetes, qui doivent bientôt rendre compte à Dieu de leurs actions. L. 2. Tom. v. 4. P. 18.

* Ver. 283.

HAPPY

HAPPY indeed was the poet, of whom his worthy and amiable * friend could ſo truly ſay, that in all his works was not to be diſcovered

> One line, that dying, he could wiſh to blot!

WOULD to God, ſaid AVERROES (regretting the libertiniſm of ſome verſes which he had made in his youth) I had been born old!

> FONTAINE and CHAUCER, dying, wiſht unwrote
> The ſprightlieſt effort of their wanton thought:
> SIDNEY and WALLER, brighteſt ſons of fame,
> Condemn'd the charm of ages to the flame †.

25. Let Sporus tremble—What! that thing of ſilk,
Sporus, that mere white curd of aſs's milk?
Satire or ſenſe, alas! can Sporus feel?
Who breaks a butterfly upon a wheel?—
Yet let me flap this bug with gilded wings,
This painted child of dirt, that ſtinks and ſtings;
Whoſe buzz the witty and the fair annoys,
Yet wit ne'er taſtes, and beauty ne'er enjoys;
So well-bred ſpaniels civilly delight
In mumbling of the game they cannot bite.

* Lord Lyttelton, in the Prologue to Thomſon's Coriolanus.

† Young's Epiſtle to Authors.

Eternal

Eternal ſmiles his emptineſs betray,
As ſhallow ſtreams run dimpling all the way.
Whether in *florid impotence* he ſpeaks,
And as the prompter breathes the puppet ſqueaks;
Or at the ear of Eve, familiar toad *,
Half froth, half venom, ſpits himſelf abroad.
In puns, or politics, or tales, or lyes,
Or ſpite, or ſmut, or rhymes, or blaſphemies.—
Amphibious thing! that acting either part,
The trifling head, or the corrupted heart,
Fop at the toilet, flatt'rer at the board,
Now trips a lady, and now ſtruts a lord.
Eve's tempter thus, the rabbins have expreſt,
A cherub's face, a reptile all the reſt,
Beauty that ſhocks you, pride that none will truſt,
Wit that can creep, and pride that licks the duſt †.

LANGUAGE cannot afford more glowing or more forcible terms to expreſs the utmoſt bitterneſs of contempt. We think we are here reading MILTON againſt SAL-

* It is but juſtice (ſaid Pope in the firſt advertiſement, ſince omitted) to own that the hint of Eve and the Serpent was taken from the verſes to the Imitator of Horace—

When God created thee, one would believe
He ſaid the ſame as to the ſnake of Eve;
To human race antipathy declare,
'Twixt them and thee be everlaſting war.
But oh! the ſequel of the ſentence dread,
And whilſt you bruiſe their heel, beware your head.

† Ver. 305.

MASIUS,

MASIUS *. The raillery is carried to the very verge of *railing*, some will say *ribaldry*. He has armed his muse with a scalping-knife. The portrait is certainly *over-charged:* for Lord H. for whom it was designed, whatever his morals might be, had yet considerable abilities, though marred indeed by affectation. Some of his speeches in parliament were much beyond *florid impotence*. They were, it is true, in favour of Sir *R. Walpole* †, and this was sufficiently offensive to *Pope*. The fact that particularly incited his indignation, was Lord H.'s *Epistle* to a *Doctor* of *Divinity*, (Dr. Sherwin) *from a Nobleman at Hampton Court*, 1733; as well as his having been concerned with Lady M.W.M.

* That strong expression in the discourse pro Populo Anglicano of "*Nerone* ipso *Neronior*," applied to Charles I. is taken from what Peter, King of Arragon, wrote to Charles Duke of Anjou, who had caused to be beheaded the son of the Emperor Conrad.

† Lord H. fought a duel with Mr. Pulteney upon a political quarrel.—See also a pamphlet, entitled, The *Court Secret*, occasioned by Lord Scarborough's death, for a severe character of *Ibrahim*, intended for this Lord. Printed 8vo. 1741.

in * *Verſes to the Imitator of Horace,* 1732. This lady's beauty, wit, genius, and travels, of which ſhe gave an account in a ſeries of elegant and entertaining letters, very characteriſtical of the manners of the Turks, and of which many are addreſſed to Pope; are well known, and juſtly celebrated. With both theſe noble perſonages had Pope lived in a ſtate of intimacy. And juſtice obligeth us to confeſs, that he himſelf was the aggreſſor in the quarrel with them; as he firſt aſſaulted and affronted Lord H. by theſe two lines in his imitation of the 1ſt Sat. of Horace's ſecond book,

> The lines are weak, another's pleas'd to ſay,
> Lord Fanny *ſpins* a thouſand ſuch a day.

* After her quarrel with Mr. Pope, which Lord Peterborough in vain endeavoured to reconcile, ſhe wrote thus from Florence, to the Counteſs of ——— "The word malignity, and a paſſage in your letter, call to my mind the wicked waſp of Twickenham, his lyes affect me now no more; they will be all as much deſpiſed as the ſtory of the ſeraglio and the handkerchief, of which I am perſuaded he was the only inventor. That man has a malignant and ungenerous heart; and he is baſe enough to aſſume the maſk of a moraliſt, in order to decry human nature, and to give a decent vent to his hatred of man and womankind."

And Lady M. W. M. by the eighty-third *line* of the ſame piece, too *groſs* * to be here repeated.

It is a ſingular circumſtance, that our author's indignation was ſo vehement and inexhauſtible, that it furniſhed him with another invective, of equal power, in proſe, which is to be found at the end of the eighth volume, containing his letters. The reader that turns to it, page 253 (for it is too long to be here inſerted, and too full of matter to be abridged) will find, that it abounds in ſo many new modes of irony, in ſo many unexpected ſtrokes of ſarcaſm, in ſo many ſudden and repeated blows, that he does not allow the poor devoted peer a moment's breathing-time:

Nunc dextrâ ingeminans ictus, nunc ille ſiniſtrâ;
Nec mora, nec requies; quam multâ grandine nimbi

* So alſo are lines 87, 88, 89, 90 of the third epiſtle concerning Fulvia and old Narſes. But let us remember, that,

As the ſoft plume gives ſwiftneſs to the dart,
Good-breeding ſends the ſatire to the heart. Young.

Culminibus crepitant; ſic denſis ictibus heros
Creber utrâque manû pulſat, verſatque——— *.

It is indeed the maſter-piece of *invective*, and perhaps excels the character of *Sporus* itſelf, capital as that is, above quoted. Who however would wiſh to be the author of ſuch a cutting invective? But can this be the nobleman (we are apt to aſk) whom *Middleton*, in his dedication to the Hiſtory of the Life of Tully, has ſo ſeriouſly and earneſtly praiſed, for his ſtrong good ſenſe, his conſummate politeneſs, his real patriotiſm, his rigid temperance, his thorough knowledge and defence of the laws of his country, his accurate ſkill in hiſtory, his unexampled and unremitted diligence in literary purſuits, who added credit to this very hiſtory, as Scipio and Lælius did to that of Polybius, by reviſing and correcting it; and brightening it †, as he expreſſes it,

* Æn. v. ver. 456.

† The life of Tully procured Dr. Middleton a great reputation, and a great ſum of money. It is a pleaſing and uſeful work, eſpecially to younger readers, as it gives a comprehenſive view of a moſt intereſting period in the Roman hiſtory, and of the characters principally concerned in thoſe

it, by the ſtrokes of his pencil? The man that had written this ſplendid encomium on Lord H. could not, we may imagine,

thoſe important events. It may be worth obſerving, that he is much indebted, without acknowledging it, to a curious book little known, entitled, *G. Bellendini*, Scoti, de *Tribus Luminibus Romanorum*, Libri 16. *Pariſiis. Apud Taſſanum du Bray*. 1634. *Folio*; dedicated to King Charles. It comprehends a hiſtory of Rome, from the foundation of the city to the time of Auguſtus, drawn up in the very words of *Cicero*, without any alteration of any expreſſion. In this book *Middleton* found every part of Cicero's own hiſtory, in his own words, and his works arranged in chronological order, without farther trouble. The impreſſion of this work being ſhipped for England, was loſt in the veſſel, which was caſt away, and only a few copies remained, that had been left in France. I venture to ſay, that the ſtyle of Middleton, which is commonly eſteemed very *pure*, is blemiſhed with many *vulgar* and *cant* terms. Such as Pompey *had a month*'s mind, &c. He has not been ſucceſsful in the tranſlations of thoſe many epiſtles of Tully which he has inſerted; which, however curious, yet break the thread of the narration. *Mongault* and *Melmoth* have far exceeded him in their excellent tranſlations of theſe pieces, which are, after all, ſome of the moſt precious remains of antiquity. What a treaſure would it have been, if the letters of Tully to Julius Cæſar had remained! As alſo his Journal and Ephemerides; and the Commentaries of Sylla, Lucullus, and Pollio. It is uſual to lament the loſs of the Decads of Livy; but ſurely we might as much wiſh to recover the loſt books of Diodorus Siculus, and Polybius, and the account of Annibal mentioned by Cornelius Nepos. I will juſt add, that great part of *Middleton*'s Letter from Rome is taken from a little unknown French book, entitled, *Les Conformitez des Ceremonies Modernes avec les Anciennes. A Leydæ, chez I. Sambix*, 1667.

be very well affected to the bard who had painted Lord Fanny in so ridiculous a light. We find him writing thus to Dr. Warburton, Jan. 7, 1740: "You have evinced the *orthodoxy* of Mr. Pope's principles; but, like the old Commentators on his Homer, will be thought perhaps, in some places, to have found a meaning for him, that he himself never dreamt of. However, if you did not *find* him a *philosopher*, you will *make* him one; for he will be wise enough to take the benefit of your reading, and make his future essays more *clear* and *consistent*."

26. That not in Fancy's maze he wander'd long,
But stoop'd to *Truth*, and moraliz'd his song *.

HERE is our author's own declaration, delivered in the most precise and positive terms, that he early left the *more poetical* provinces of his art, to become a moral, didactic, and satiric poet.

27. Of gentle blood † (part shed in honour's cause,
While yet in Britain honour had applause)

Each

* Ver. 340.

† When Mr. Pope published the notes on the Epistle to Dr. Arbuthnot, giving an account of his family, Mr. Pottinger,

Each parent ſprung; what fortune pray their own,
And better got than Beſtia's from the throne.
Born to no pride, inheriting no ſtrife,
Nor marrying diſcord in a noble wife;
Stranger to civil and religious rage,
The good man walk'd innoxious thro' his age.
No courts he ſaw, no ſuits would ever try,
Nor dar'd an oath, nor hazarded a lye.
Unlearn'd, he knew no ſchoolman's ſubtile art,
No language, but the language of the heart.
By nature honeſt, by experience wiſe,
Healthy by temp'rance, and by exerciſe;
His life, tho' long, to ſickneſs paſt unknown,
His death was inſtant, and without a groan *.

tinger, a relation of his, obſerved, that his couſin Pope had made himſelf out a fine pedigree, but he wondered where he got it; that he never had heard any thing himſelf of their being deſcended from the Earls of Down; and, what is more, he had an old maiden aunt, equally related, a great genealogiſt, who was always talking of her family, but never mentioned this circumſtance; on which ſhe certainly would not have been ſilent, had ſhe known any thing of it. Mr. Pope's grandfather was a clergyman of the church of England, in Hampſhire. He placed his ſon, Mr. Pope's father, with a merchant at Liſbon, where he became a convert to Popery. (Thus far Dr. *Bolton*, late Dean of *Carliſle*, a friend of Pope; from *Mr. Pottinger.*) The burying-place and monuments of the family of the Popes, Earls of Down, is at Wroxton, Oxfordſhire. The Earl of Guildford ſays, that he has ſeen and examined the pedigrees and deſcents of that family, and is ſure that there were then none of the name of Pope left, who could be deſcended from that family.—*(From John Loveday, of Caverſham, Eſquire.)*

* Ver. 388.

Boileau *, who has been ſo frequently quoted, becauſe he was the model of our author, ſpeaks thus of his father and family, in an epiſtle that was juſtly one of his favourite works, addreſſed (in imitation of Horace's *Vertumnum Janumque*) *to his verſes*.

Que ſi quelqu'un, mes vers, alors vous importune,
Pour ſcavoir mes parens, ma vie & ma fortune,
Contès-lui, qu' alliè d'aſsès hauts Magiſtrats,
Fils d'un Pere Greffier, né d'ayeux Avocats;
Dès le berceau perdant une fort jeune mere,
Reduit ſeize ans après à pleurer mon vieux Pere,
J'allai d'un pas hardi, par moi-meſme guidé,
Et de mon ſeul Genie en marchant ſecondé,
Studieux amateur, & de Perſe & d'Horace,
Aſsès près de Regnier m'aſſeoir ſur le Parnaſſe;

* He had no aſperity in his temper. Mad. de Sevigné uſed to ſay, he is cruel only in verſe. Being punctual in performing all acts of religion, he was one day in the country, and went to confeſſion to a prieſt who did not know him. What is your occupation? ſaid the good man — To make verſes, replied Boileau.—So much the worſe, ſaid the Prieſt—And what ſort of verſes?—Satires.—Still worſe and worſe, ſaid the confeſſor.—And againſt whom?—Againſt thoſe, ſaid Boileau, who make bad verſes; againſt ſuch miſchievous works as operas and romances.—Ah! my friend, ſays the Confeſſor, there is no harm in this, and I have nothing more to ſay to you.

Memoires de J. Racine, p. 196.

Que

Que par un coup de ſort au grand jour amenè
Et de bords du Permeſſe à la Cour entraiſné,
Je ſçeûs, prenant l'eſſor par de routes nouvelles
Eſlever aſsès haut mes poetiques âiles;
Que ce Roy * dont le nom fait trembler tant de Rois
Voulut bien que ma main crayonnait ſes exploits:
Que plus d'un grand m'aima juſques à la tendreſſe;
Que ma veüe a Colbert inſpiroit, l'allegreſſe;
Qu' aujourd'hui meſme encor de deux ſens affoibli
Retiré de la cour & non mis en oubli;
Plus d'un Heros epris des fruits de mon eſtude,
Vient quelquefois ches moi gouter la ſolitude †.

ALL theſe particularities of his father, family, and fortunes, become intereſting.

* He was appointed Hiſtoriographer to the King, with Racine, in October 1677. They both, together with Vander-Meulen, the painter, accompanied Lewis XIV. in his oſtentatious expedition to Flanders. After the death of Racine, he went once to Verſailles, to inform the King of the loſs of his colleague; and when he took his leave, Louis obligingly ſaid to him, ſhewing him his watch, which he happened to hold in his hand, "Remember that I have always one hour in the week to give you, whenever you will come to me."

It is to be regretted that Boileau never finiſhed, what he told his friends he had ſketched out, the life of Diogenes the Cynic, a comic romance, in which much literature, ſatire, and knowledge of life and manners, would have appeared. Let me take this occaſion of adding, that it is alſo to be regretted, that Monteſquieu never finiſhed a political romance he intended to give, called *Arſaces*.

† Epiſtre x. ver. 93.

There

There is in this paſſage the true manner of Horace, his eaſy vigour, and *firma facilitas*. It is on occaſion of this epiſtle that *Boileau* wrote his celebrated letter to *Monſ. de Maucroix*, from which I ſhall, without any ſcruple, give a large extract, as it is ſo replete with good ſenſe and ſolid criticiſm, and contains ſo many judicious obſervations on the more remote and interior beauties of ſtyle. Tom. iii. p. 185. Par M. de Saint Marc. 1747.

RACAN excelle ſur tout, à mon avis, à dire les petites choſes, & c'eſt en quoi il reſſemble mieux aux anciennes, que j'admire ſur tout par cet endroit. Plus les choſes ſont ſeches & mal aiſées à dire en vers, plus elle frapent quand elles ſont dites noblement, & avec cette elégance qui fait proprement la poéſie. Je me ſouviens que M. de la Fontaine m'a dit plus d'une fois, que les deux vers de mes ouvrages qu'il eſtimoit davantage c'eſtoit ceux oû je loue le Roi d'avoir établi la manufacture des points de France, à la place des points

de

de Venise. Les voici. C'est dans la premiere Epistre à sa Majesté.

Et nos voisins frustrez de ces tributs serviles,
Que payoit à leur art le luxe de nos villes.

VIRGILE & Horace sont divins en cela, aussi bien qu' Homere. C'est tout le contraire de nos Poëtes, qui ne disent que des choses vagues, que d'autres ont déja dites avant eux, & dont les expressions sont trouvées. Quand ils sortent de là, ils ne sçauroient plus s'exprimer, & ils tombent dans une secheresse qui est encore pire que leurs larcins. Pour moy, je ne sçay pas si j'y ay réussi : mais quand je fais des vers, je songe toûjours à dire ce qui ne s'est point encore dit en nostre langue. C'est ce que j'ay principalement affecté dans une nouvelle epistre, que j'ay faite à propos de toutes les Critiques, qu'on a imprimées contre ma derniere satire. J'y conte tout ce que j'ay fait depuis que je suis au monde, j'y rapporte mes defauts, mon âge, mes inclinations, mes mœurs. J'y dis de quel Pere & de quelle Mere je suis né. J'y

marque

marque les degrés de ma fortune; comment j'ay éfté à la cour, comment j'en fuis forti; les incommodités qui me font furvenuës; les ouvrages que j'ay faits. Ce font bien de petites chofes dites en affés peu de mots, puifque la piece n'a pas plus de cent trente vers. Elle n'a pas encore veu le jour, & je ne l'ay pas mefme encore écrite. Mais il me paroift que tous ceux à qui je l'ay recitée, en font auffi frappez que d'aucun autre de mes ouvrages. Croiriez-vous, Monfieur, qu'un des endroits où ils fe recrient le plus, c'eft un endroit qui ne dit autre chofe, finon qu' aujourd'huy que j'ai cinquante-fept ans, je ne dois plus pretendre à l'approbation publique. Cela eft dit en quatre vers que je veux bien vous écrire ici, afin que vous me mandiez fi vous les approuvez.

Mais aujourd'hui qu' enfin la Vieilleffe venue,
Sous mes faux cheveux blonds déja toute chenue,
A jetté fur ma tefte avec fes doigts pefans,
Onze luftres complets furchargez de deux ans.

Il me femble que la Perruque eft affés heureufement frondée dans ces quatres vers.

28. O friend!

28. O friend! may each domeſtic bliſs be thine!
Be no unpleaſing melancholy mine!
Me, let the tender office long engage,
To rock the cradle of repoſing age*;
With lenient arts extend a mother's breath,
Make languor ſmile, and ſmooth the bed of death;
Explore the thought, explain the aſking eye,
And keep awhile one parent from the ſky†!

These exquiſite lines give us a very intereſting picture of the exemplary filial piety of our author‡. There is a penſive and pathetic ſweetneſs in the very flow of them. The eye that has been wearied and oppreſt by the harſh and auſtere colouring of ſome of the preceding paſſages, turns away with pleaſure from theſe aſperities, and repoſes with complacency on the ſoft tints of domeſtic tenderneſs. We are naturally gratified to ſee great men deſcending

* See a letter to Mr. Richardſon, deſiring him to come to Twickenham, and take a ſketch of his mother, juſt after ſhe was dead, June 20, 1733. "It would afford, ſays he, the fineſt image of a ſaint expired, that ever painting drew." Vol. viii. p. 233.

† Ver. 406.

‡ For which alſo another truly great poet was remarkable. See Memoirs of Mr. *Gray*'s Life, paſſim; and ſo alſo was *Arioſto*.

 from

from their heights, into the familiar offices of common life; and the ſenſation is the more pleaſing to us, becauſe *admiration* is turned into *affection*. In the very entertaining memoirs of the life of Racine (publiſhed by his ſon) we find no paſſage* more amuſing and intereſting, than where that great poet ſends an excuſe to Mon[r]. the Duke, who had earneſtly invited him to dine at the Hotel de Conde, becauſe he had promiſed to partake of a great fiſh that his children had got for him, and he could not think of diſappointing them.

MELANCTHON appeared in an amiable light, when he was ſeen holding a book in one hand, and attentively reading, and with

* Memoires ſur la Vie de Jean Racine, p. 182, printed 1747: by the author of the didactic poems on *Religion* and *Grace*, of *Reflections on Poetry*, of *Two Epiſtles* on *Man*, and ſome excellent *Sacred Odes*, particularly one from Iſaiah, c. xiv. He endeavours, but I fear in vain, to vindicate his father from the report of having had any connexion with the celebrated actreſs Chammelè, whom Racine taught to ſpeak and declaim, and for whom it was thought he had a ſtrong paſſion; of which he afterwards repented, and became a remarkably good huſband.

the

the other rocking the cradle of his infant child. And we read with more ſatisfaction,

——— ου παιδος ορεξατο φαιδιμος Εκτωρ,
Αψ δ' ὁ παῖς προς κολπον ευζωνοιο τιθηνης
Εκλινθη ιαχων — *

than we do,

Τρις μεν ορεξατ' ιων· το δε τετρατον ικετο τεκμωρ
Αιγας ——— †.

* Iliad vi. v. 467. † Iliad xiii. v. 20.

SECT.

SECT. XII.

Of the Satires and Epiſtles of Horace *imitated, of the Satires of* Donne *verſified, and of the Epilogue to the Satires.*

"WHEN I had a fever one winter in town (ſaid POPE to Mr. SPENCE) that confined me to my room for five or ſix days, Lord BOLINGBROKE came to ſee me, happened to take up a Horace that lay on the table, and in turning it over, dipt on the firſt ſatire of the ſecond book. He obſerved, how well that would ſuit my caſe, if I were to imitate it in Engliſh. After he was gone, I read it over, tranſlated it in a morning or two, and ſent it to preſs in a week or fortnight after. And this was the occaſion of my imitating ſome other of the Satires and Epiſtles. To how caſual a beginning (adds SPENCE) are we obliged, for the

moſt

most delightful things in our language! When I was saying to him, that he had already imitated near a third part of Horace's satires and epistles, and how much it was to be wished that he would go on with them; he could not believe that he had gone near so far; but upon computing it, it appeared to be above a third. He seemed on this not disinclined to carry it farther; but his last illness was then growing upon him, and robbed us of him, and of all hopes of that kind, in a few months *."

No parts of our author's works have been more admired than these imitations. The aptness of the allusions, and the happiness of many of the parallels, give a pleasure that is always no small one to the mind of a reader, the pleasure of *comparison*. He that has the least acquaintance with these pieces of Horace, which resemble the *Old Comedy*, immediately perceives, indeed, that our author has assumed a higher tone,

* Transcribed from Spence's Anecdotes, 1754.

and frequently has deserted * the free colloquial air, the insinuating Socratic manner of his original. And that he clearly resembles in his style, as he did in his natural temper, the severe and serious Juvenal, more than the smiling and sportive Horace. Let us select some passages, in which he may be thought to have equalled, excelled, or fallen short of, the original; the latter of which cannot be deemed a disgrace to our poet, or to any other writer, if we consider the extreme difficulty of transfusing into another language the subtle beauties of Horace's dignified *familiarity*, and the uncommon union of so much *facility* and *force*.

I. ———————————————— Trebati
Quid faciam? prescribe. T. Quiescas. H. Ne faciam, inquis,
Omnino versus? T. Aio. H. Peream male, si non

* After all that has been said of Horace, by so many critics, ancient and modern, perhaps no words can describe him so exactly and justly, as the following of Tully, spoken on another subject. Lib. i. de Oratore. Accedit lepos quidam, facetiæque, & eruditio libero digna, celeritasque & brevitas respondendi & lacessendi subtili venustate & urbanitate conjuncta.

Optimum

I

Optimum erat: verum nequeo dormire. T. Ter uncti
Transnanto Tiberim, somno quibus est opus alto;
Irriguumve mero sub noctem corpus habento *:

Tim'rous by nature, of the rich in awe,
I come to counsel learned in the law:
You'll give me, like a friend, both sage and free
Advice; and as you use, without a fee.
F. I'd write no more. P. Not write? but then I think,
And for my soul I cannot sleep a wink.
I nod in company, I wake at night,
Fools rush into my head, and so I write.
F. You could not do a worse thing for your life:
Why, if the night seem tedious, take a wife.
Or rather truly, if your point be rest,
Lettuce and cowslip-wine, probatum est.
But talk with Celsus, Celsus will advise,
Hartshorn, or something that shall close your eyes †.

Horace, with much seeming seriousness, applies for advice to the celebrated Roman lawyer, *C. Trebatius Testa*, an intimate friend of *Julius Cæsar*, and of *Tully*, as appears from many of his epistles to *Atticus*. The gravity and self-importance of whose character is admirably supported throughout this little drama. His answers are short, authoritative, and decisive. *Qui-*

* Sat. 1. lib. 1. v. 4.

† Ver. 8.

 escas.

escas. Aio. And, as he was known to be a great *drinker* and *swimmer*, his two absurd pieces of advice have infinite pleasantry. All these circumstances of humour are dropt in the copy. The Lettuce and Cowslip-wine are insipid and unmeaning prescriptions, and have nothing to do with Mr. *Fortescue*'s character. The third, fourth, and ninth lines of this *imitation* are flat and languid. We must also observe (from the old Commentator *) that the verbs *transnanto*, and *habento*, are, in the very style of the Roman law, "Vide ut directis jurisconsultorum verbis utitur ad Trebatium jurisconsultum.

2. Aut si tantus amor scribendi te rapit, aude
Cæsaris invicti res dicere, multa laborum
Præmia laturus———— †.

Or, if you needs must write, write Cæsar's praise,
You'll gain at least a *knighthood*, or *the bays* ‡.

* There are many excellent remarks in *Acro* and *Porphyrio*; from whom, as well as from *Cruquius*, *Dacier* has borrowed much, without owning it. *Dacier*'s translation of Horace is not equal to his *Aristotle*'s Poetics. In the former, he is perpetually striving to discover new meanings in his author, which Boileau called, The Revelations of Dacier.

† Ver. 10. ‡ Ver. 21.

 THIS

THIS is ſuperior to the original, becauſe *præmia laturus* is general and flat, in compariſon of the particular rewards here ſpecified.

3. —— neque enim quivis horrentia pilis *
Agmina, nec fractâ pereuntes cuſpide Gallos,
Aut labentis equo deſcribat vulnera Parthi †.

What! like Sir Richard, rumbling, rough, and fierce,
With ARMS, and GEORGE, and BRUNSWICK crowd the verſe,
Rend with tremendous ſound your ears aſunder,
With gun, drum, trumpet, blunderbuſs, and thunder.

POPE has turned the compliment to Auguſtus into a ſevere ſarcaſm. All the wits ‡

* Of theſe verſes ſays *Porphyrio*, Eleganter in hâc ipſâ excuſatione, poſſe ſe ſcribere oſtendit.

† Ver. 13.

‡ *Swift* never could forgive *Blackmore* the following ſtrictures on a Tale of a Tub, in his eſſays, London, 1717. "Had this writing been publiſhed in a Pagan or Popiſh nation, who are juſtly impatient of all indignity offered to the eſtabliſhed religion of their country, no doubt but the author would have received the puniſhment he deſerved. But the fate of this *impious buffoon* is very different; for in a Proteſtant kingdom, zealous of their civil and religious immunities, he has not only eſcaped affronts, and the effects of public reſentment, but he has been careſſed and patronized by perſons of great figure, and of all denominations."

feem to have leagued againft Sir Richard Blackmore. In a letter now lying before me, from ELIJAH FENTON to my father, dated, Jan. 24, 1707, he fays, "I am glad to hear Mr. Phillips will publifh his POMONA: Who prints it? I fhould be mightily obliged to you, if you could get me a copy of *his* verfes *againft* Blackmore." As the letter contains one or two literary particulars, I will tranfcribe the reft. "As to what you write about making a collection, I can only advife you to buy what poems you can, that *Tonfon* has printed, except the *Ode to the Sun*; unlefs y[illegible]il take it in, becaufe I writ it; [illegible] I am the freer to own, that *Mat. Prior* may not fuffer in his reputation, by having [illegible] afcribed to him. My humble fervice to Mr. *Sacheverell*, and tell him I will never imitate *Milton* more, till the author of *Blenheim* is forgotten." In vain was Blackmore extolled by *Molyneux* and *Locke*: but *Locke*, to his other fuperior talents, did not add a good tafte. He affected to defpife poetry, and he depreciated the an-

cients;

cients *; which circumſtance, as I am informed from undoubted authority, was the ſource of perpetual diſcontent and diſpute betwixt him and his pupil Lord *Shafteſbury*; who, in many parts of the Characteriſtics, has ridiculed Locke's philoſophy, and endeavoured to repreſent him as a diſciple of *Hobbes* †; from which

* Another, and a better philoſopher, thought very differently on this ſubject; and has given ſo high an encomium on the utility of the ancient claſſics, that the paſſage deſerves a particular notice. Annon ideo fit, ut ſcriptorum priſcorum præſtantiſſimi libri & ſermones, (quibus ad virtutem homines efficaciſſimè invitati ſunt, tam auguſtam ejus majeſtatem omnium oculis repreſentando, quam opiniones populares, in virtutis ignominiam, tanquam habidû paraſitorum indutas, deriſui propinando) tam parum proſint, ad vitæ honeſtatem, & mores pravos corrigendos, qui a perlegi & revolvi non conſueverunt, a viris ætate & judicio maturis, ſed Pueris tantum & Tyronibus relinquuntur. BACON de Augmentis. Scient. Lib. 7. c. 3

† No author in that age, ſays Hume, was more celebrated both abroad and at home than Hobbes: In our times, he is much neglected: a lively inſtance, how precarious all reputations founded on reaſoning and philoſophy! A pleaſant comedy, which paints the manners of the age, and expoſes a faithful picture of nature, is a durable work, and is tranſmitted to the lateſt poſterity. But a ſyſtem, whether phyſical or metaphyſical, owes commonly its ſucceſs to its novelty; and is no ſooner canvaſſed with impartiality than its weakneſs is diſcovered.

Hiſt. Vol. vi. p. 127.

writer, however, it is certain that *Locke* borrowed frequently and largely.

4. ———— nisi dextro tempore, Flacci
Verba per attentam non ibunt Cæsaris aurem.
Cui male si palpere recalcitrat undique tutus *.

Alas! few verses touch their nicer ear,
They scarce can bear their *Laureate* twice a year.
And justly Cæsar scorns the poet's lays;
It is to *History* he trusts for praise †.

SUPERIOR to the original, on account of the mention of the Laureate; and the sudden unexpected turn in the last line, which is uncommonly *sly* and *severe*.

5. Quid faciam? saltat Milonius, &c. ‡

Each mortal has his pleasure §.

THESE words, indeed, open the sense of Horace; but the *quid faciam* is better, as it leaves it to the reader to discover what is one of Horace's greatest beauties, his secret and delicate *transitions* and *connections*, to which they who do not carefully attend, lose half the pleasure of reading him.

* Ver. 18. † Ver. 33. ‡ Ver. 24. § Ver. 45.

5. —— none

5. ——————— none deny
——————— *Darty* his ham-pye *.

Lyttelton, in his Dialogues of the Dead, has introduced *Darteneuf*, in a pleasant discourse betwixt him and *Apicius*, bitterly lamenting his ill fortune, in having lived before *turtle-feasts* † were known in England. "Alas!" says he, "how imperfect is human felicity! I lived in an age when the pleasure of eating was thought to be carried to its highest perfection in England and France. And yet a turtle-feast is a novelty to me! Would it be impossible, do you think, to obtain leave from Pluto, of going back for one day, just to taste of that food? I would promise to kill myself by the quantity I would eat before the next morning."

6. Castor gaudet equis; ovo prognatus eodem,
Pugnis——————‡.

F. loves the senate, Hockley-hole his brother,
Like in all else, as one egg to another §.

* Ver. 45.

† He might have said the same of the *Chinese Bird's Nest*, a piece of Oriental luxury lately imported.

‡ Ver. 26. § Ver. 49.

This

This parallel is not happy and exact; to shew the variety of human passions and pursuits, Castor and Pollux were unlike, even though they came from one and the same egg. This is far more extraordinary and marvellous than that two common brothers should have different inclinations.

7. ——Me pedibus delectat claudere verba,
Lucilî ritu———*.

I love to pour out all myself, as plain
As downright *Shippen*, or as old *Montaigne* †.

"My chief pleasure is to write satires like Lucilius," says Horace. "My chief pleasure, says Pope, is,—What? *to speak my mind freely and openly*." There should have been an instance of some *employment*, and not a virtuous *habit*; there follows in the original, a line which *Bentley* has explained very acutely, and in a manner different from the other commentators—

———— neque si malè gesserat, usquam
Decurrens alio, neque si bene— ‡.

* Ver. 28. † Ver. 51. ‡ Ver. 31.

He

He affirms, that the true reading ſhould be malè *ceſſerat*, and that it does not mean, whether his *affairs* went ill or not, but whether he *wrote* ſucceſsfully or not. "Nuſquam alio præterquam ad libros decurrens, ſeu bene ei ceſſerat in *ſcribendo*, ſeu malè. Scilicet quovis ille die ſcribere amabat, ſive aptus tum ad ſtudium, ſeu, ut ſæpe uſû venit, ineptior: ſeu muſis faventibus ſive averſis."

The paſſage that immediately follows, in the original, at verſe the thirty-fifth,—Nam Venuſinus arat—down to verſe the thirty-ninth, to the words, incuteret violenta, which are frequently printed in a parentheſis, and have been ſuppoſed to be an awkward interpolation, were undoubtedly intended by Horace to repreſent the looſe, incoherent, and verboſe manner * of

* ——— amat ſcripſiſſe ducentos
Ante cibum verſus, totidem cænatus——
Hor. ſat. x. lib. 1. v. 61.

Ad. Baillet, in his *Jugemens*, among his numerous blunders and falſe judgments, is ſo abſurd, as to take literally the expreſſion of Lucilius—Stans pede in uno.

Lucilius

Lucilius (incompoſito pede) who loaded his ſatires with many uſeleſs and impertinent thoughts.

8. ———————— O Pater & Rex,
Jupiter, ut pereat poſitum rubigine telum *.

Save but our *army!* and let Jove incruſt
Swords, pikes, and guns, with everlaſting ruſt †!

He could not ſuffer ſo favourable an opportunity to paſs, without joining with his friends, the patriots of that time, in the cry againſt a ſtanding army. The ſentiment in the original is taken, as the old ſcholiaſt obſerves, from *Callimachus*;

Ζευ πατερ, ὡς χαλυβων παν απολοιτο ‡ γενος.

* Ver. 42. † Ver. 73.

‡ He imitates two other epigrams of Callimachus, in verſe 8. of the 2d Sat. lib. 1.

Præclaram ingratâ ſtringat malus ingluvie rem—

and alſo, as Heinſius obſerves, in the 105th verſe of the ſame ſatire————

Leporem venator ut altâ
In nive ſectatur————

In the ſixth ſatire of the ſecond book, he has *Sophocles* in his eye;

Luſerat in campo fortunæ filius————
Εγω δ' εμαυτον παιδα της τυχης νεμων.

Œdip. Tyrann. 1090.

NUMBERLESS

Numberless are the paſſages in Horace, which he has ſkilfully adopted and interwoven from the Greek writers; with whom he was minutely and intimately acquainted; perhaps more ſo than any other Roman poet, having ſtudied at Athens longer than any of them.

Quidquid ſub terrâ eſt in apricum proferet ætas
Defodiet condetque nitentia—— *,

is from the Ajax of Sophocles, verſe 659.

Απανθ' ὁ μακρος κἀναριθμητος χρονος
Φυει τ' αδηλα, και φανεντα κρυπτεται.

Pernicies & *Tempeſtas*, Barathrumque macelli—— †.

Grotius, in that very entertaining book, his *Excerpta ex Tragœdiis & Comœdiis Græcis*, has preſerved, page 583, a fragment of *Alexis*, to which this paſſage of Horace alludes:

Δειπνει δ' αφωνος Τηλεφος, νευων μονον
Προς τους επερωτωντας τι, ωστε πολλακις
Αυτον κεκληκως τοις Σαμοθραξιν ευχεται
Ληξαι πνεοντα και γαληνισαι ποτε.
Χειμων ὁμειρακισκος εστι τοις φιλοις,

* Ep. vi. v. 24. † Ver. 31. Ep. 15.

Per

Per mare pauperiem fugiens, per saxa, per ignes *,

is from *Theognis*;

Ην δη χρη φευγοντα και ες μεγακητεα ποντον
Ριπτειν, καὶ πετρων, Κυρνε κατ' ηλιβατων.

Sunt verba & voces quibus hunc lenire dolorem
Possis, & magnam morbi deponere partem †,

is from the Hippolitus of Euripides;

Εισιν δ' επωδαι και λογοι θελκτηριοι.

—— Si quid novisti rectius istis
Candidus imperti, si non, his utere mecum ‡,

is taken, as *Cruquius* remarks, from *Isocrates* to *Nicocles*;

Χρῶ τοις ειρημενοις, η ζητει βελτιω τυτων.

Spes jubet esse ratas, in prælia trudit inermem §,

from an elegant fragment of *Diphilus*; in which Bacchus is addressed:

Ω πασι, τοισι φρονῦσι προσφιλεστατε,
Διονυσε, και σοφωτατ' ως ηδυς τις ει,
'Οταν ταπεινον μεγα φρονειν ποιεις μονος,
Τον τας οφρυς αιροντα συμπειθεις γελᾶν,
Τον τ' ασθενη τολμαν τι, τον δειλον θρασειν.

* Ep. i. lib. 1. 46.
† Ep. i. lib. 1. ver. 35.
‡ Ep. vi. 67.
§ Ver. 17. Ep. 5.

The

The bold and beautiful metaphor in the fourth ode of the fourth book.

Per Siculas *equitavit* undas,

is from the *Phœnissæ* of *Euripides*, verse 222, (the Oxford edition in 4to. by Dr. Musgrave, 1778)

——— ——— Ζεφυρȣ πνοιαις
Ἱππευσαντος εν ȣρανω ——

The beginning of the first ode of the first book, which points out the different inclinations and pursuits of men, alludes to a passage in *Pindar*, preserved by *Sextus Empiricus*, in the first *Pyrrh. Hypothes.*

Αελλοποδων μεν τιν' ευφραινȣσιν ἱππων τιμαι και στεφανοι,
Τȣς δ' εν πολυχρυσοις θαλαμοις βιωτα·
Τερπεται δε τις επ οιδμα ἀλιον ναϊ θοα σων διαστειβων.

And line the 25th of the second * ode of the third book, is taken from a fragment of *Simonides* †, cited by *Aristides*. 2. *Platonica*.

* See P. Petiti. Misc. Obs. lib. iii. cap. 25.

† The words, Mors & fugacem persequitur virum, in Ode 2. book iii. are even translated from *Simonides*;

Ὁ δ' αυ θανατοι εκιχε και τον φυγομαχον.

Est

Eſt & fideli tuta Silentio
Merces ———

——σιωπης ακινδυνον γερας.

Bentley, with his uſual acuteneſs, conjectured, that an obſcure paſſage in Horace would be illuſtrated, if ever the Greek epigram of Philodemus, to which he alluded, ſhould be diſcovered.

Gallis *, hanc, *Philodemus* ait——L. i. ſat. 2, 121.

Reiſkius has ſince printed the very epigram, and the laſt words of it confirm Bentley's conjecture.

——την δ' αρα Γαλλος εχοι.

9. Nec quiſquam noceat cupido mihi pacis! at ille
Qui me commôrit (melius non tangere clamo)
Flebit, & inſignis totâ cantabitur urbe †.

Peace is my dear delight—*not Fleury*'s *more*:
But touch me, and *no miniſter ſo ſore*.
Whoe'er offends, at ſome unlucky time,
Slides into verſe, and hitches into rhyme ‡.

* See Anthol. Græc. Lib. tres Oxonii, 1766, p. 93. Philodemus lived at Rome in the time of Tully, and is mentioned by him as a friend of *Piſo*.

† Ver. 44. ‡ Ver. 75.

SUPERIOR

Superior to the original, on account of the lively and unexpected satire at the end of each of the two first lines; a high improvement of *Cupido mihi pacis*.

10. Cervius iratus leges minitatur & urnam;
Canidia Albutî, quibus est inimica, venenum;
Grande malum Turius, si quid se judice certas—*

Slander or poison dread from Delia's rage,
Hard words, or hanging, if your judge be Page †.

It is difficult to say which passage is the more spirited. But what follows in Pope,

It's proper power to hurt each creature feels,

is inferior to

——— utque
Imperet hoc natura potens, sic collige mecum.
Dente lupus, cornu taurus petit; unde nisi intus
Monstratum?— ‡

But then again these two lines,

So drink with Walters, or with Chartres eat,
They'll never poison you, they'll only cheat §,

* Ver. 46. † Ver. 81.
‡ Ver. 51. § Ver. 89.

is expreſſed with an archneſs and a dryneſs beyond the original, that follows:

——— Scævæ vivacem crede nepoti
Matrem; nil faciet ſceleris pia dextera (mirum;
Ut neque calce lupus quemquam, nec dente petit bos)
Sed mala tollet anum vitiato melle cicuta *.

11. Ne longum faciam: ſeu me tranquilla ſenectus
Expectat, ſeu mors atris circumvolat alis;
Dives, inops; Romæ, ſeu fors ita juſſerit exul;
Quiſquis erit vitæ ſcribam color †.

Then, learned Sir! (to cut the matter ſhort)
Whate'er my fate, or well or ill at court:
Whether old age, with faint but chearful ray,
Attends to gild the ev'ning of my day,
Or death's black wing already be diſplay'd,
To wrap me in the univerſal ſhade;
Whether the darken'd rooms to muſe invite,
Or whiten'd wall provoke the ſkewer to write;
In durance, exile, Bedlam, or the mint,
Like Lee or Budgell, I will rhyme and print ‡.

The brevity and force of the original is evaporated in this long and feeble paraphraſe. The *third*, and *three* ſucceeding lines, are languid and verboſe, and ſome of the worſt he has written.

* Ver. 53. † Ver. 54. ‡ Ver. 91.

12.——Quid

12. —— Quid cum eſt Lucilius auſus
Primus in hunc operis componere carmina morem,
Detrahere & pellem, nitidus quâ quiſque per ora
Cederet, introrſum turpis—— *.

What? arm'd for virtue when I point the pen,
Brand the bold front of ſhameleſs guilty men,
Daſh the proud gameſter from his gilded car,
Bare the mean heart that lurks beneath a ſtar;
Can there be wanting, to defend her cauſe,
Lights of the church or guardians of the laws †?

That ſtrain ‡ I heard was of a higher mood—,

than the original pretends to aſſume. Our author's *Horace* differs as much from his original as does his *Homer*; yet *both* will be always read with great pleaſure and applauſe.

13. Could penſion'd *Boileau* laſh, in honeſt ſtrain,
Flatt'rers and *Bigots* ev'n in *Louis'* reign §?

Boileau acted with much caution and circumſpection, when he firſt publiſhed his *Lutrin*, here alluded to; and endeavoured to cover and conceal his ſubject, by a preface intended to miſlead his reader from

* Ver. 64.
† Ver. 105.
‡ Milton's Lycidas, 87.
§ Ver. 111.

 the

the real ſcene of action; which preface is mentioned in the firſt volume of this eſſay, page 214; but it ought to be obſerved, that he afterwards, in the year 1683, threw aſide this diſguiſe; openly avowing the occaſion that gave riſe to the poem, the ſcene of which was not *Bourges* or *Pourges*, as before he had ſaid, but *Paris* itſelf; the quarrel he celebrated being betwixt the Treaſurer * and the Chanter of the *Holy Chapel*, in that city. The canons were ſo far from being offended, that they ſhewed their good ſenſe and good temper by joining in the laugh. Upon which *Boileau* compliments them, and adds, that many of that ſociety were perſons of ſo much wit and learning, that he would as ſoon conſult them upon his works, as the members of the French Academy †.

14. Quin ubi ſe a vulgo & ſcenâ in ſecreta remorânt
Virtus Scipiadæ & mitis ſapientia Læli,

* His name was *Barrin*; that of the Treaſurer was *Claude Auvri*, Biſhop of *Coutance*; in Normandy. The quarrel began in July, 1667. See Letters of *Broſſette* to *Boileau*. A Lyon. 1770. Page 242, v. 1.

† Oeuvres de M. Boileau, Deſpreaux, par M. de Saint Marc. Tom. ii. 177, Paris, 1747.

Nugari

Nugari cum illo, & discincti ludere, donec
Decoqueretur olus, soliti——*

There, my retreat the best companions grace,
Chiefs out of war, and statesmen out of place;
There St. John mingles with my friendly bowl
The feast of reason, and the flow of soul:
And he, whose lightning pierc'd th' Iberian lines,
Now forms my quincunx, and now ranks my vines,
Or tames the genius of the stubborn plain,
Almost as quickly as he conquer'd Spain †.

I KNOW not whether these lines, spirited and splendid as they are, give us more pleasure than the natural picture of the great *Scipio* and *Lælius* ‡, unbending themselves from their high occupations, and descending to common and even trifling sports: for the old commentator says, that they lived in such intimacy with *Lucilius*, "ut quodam tempore *Lælio* circum lectos triclinii fugienti Lucilius superveniens, eum obtortâ mappâ quasi percussurus sequeretur." For this is the fact to which Horace seems to allude, rather than to what

* Ver. 71. † Ver. 125.

‡ Whose character is finely touched by that sweet expression, *mitis sapientia*.

Tully mentions in the ſecond book *De Oratore*, of their amuſing themſelves in picking up ſhells and pebbles on the ſea-ſhore. *Bolingbroke* is here repreſented as pouring out himſelf to his friend, in the moſt *free* and *unreſerved* converſations on topics the moſt intereſting and important. But *Pope* was deceived; for it is aſſerted that the philoſopher never diſcovered his *real principles* to our poet; who is ſaid, ſtrange as this appears, not even to have been acquainted with the *tenets* and *contents* of thoſe very eſſays which were addreſt to himſelf, at the beginning of Bolingbroke's Philoſophical Works. And it is added, that Pope was ſurpriſed, in his laſt illneſs, when a common acquaintance informed him, that his Lordſhip, in a late converſation, had deny'd the *moral* attributes of God. There is a remarkable paſſage in a letter from Bolingbroke to Swift, dated June 1734:—" I am glad you approve of his *Moral Eſſays*. They will do more good than the ſermons and writings of ſome, who had a mind to *find great fault* with them.

them. And if the doctrines TAUGHT, HINTED AT, and IMPLIED in them, and the TRAINS of CONSEQUENCES DEDUCIBLE from these doctrines, were to be disputed in prose, I think he would have no reason to apprehend, either the free-thinkers on one hand, or the narrow dogmatists on the other. Some few things may be expressed a little *hardly*; but none are I believe unintelligible." With respect to the doctrines of the Essay on Man, I shall here insert an anecdote copied exactly from the papers of Mr. *Spence*, in the words of Pope himself. "In the moral poem, I had written an address to our Saviour, imitated from *Lucretius*'s compliment to *Epicurus*; but omitted it, by the advice of *Dean Berkley*. One of our priests, who are *more narrow* than yours, made a less sensible objection to the epistle on happiness. He was very angry that there was nothing said in it of our eternal happiness hereafter; though my subject was expressly to treat only of the state of man here."

There are not, perhaps, four more finiſhed lines in our author's works, than thoſe above mentioned, relating to Lord Peterborough: particularly the very ſtriking turn of compliment in the laſt line, which ſo beautifully and vigorouſly figures the rapidity of his conqueſt of Valencia.

15. ——————— tamen me
Cum magnis vixiſſe invita fatebitur uſque
Invidia————— *

Envy muſt own, I live among the Great,
No pimp of pleaſure, and no ſpy of ſtate †.

Pope triumphs and felicitates himſelf upon having lived with the Great, without deſcending into one of thoſe characters which he thinks it unavoidable to eſcape, in ſuch a ſituation. From the generoſity and openneſs of Horace's character, I think he might be pronounced equally free (at leaſt from the *laſt*) of theſe imputations. There muſt have been ſomething uncommonly captivating in the temper and manners of Horace, that could have made Au-

* Ver. 75. † Ver. 133.

guſtus

6

gustus so fond of him, though he had been so avowed an enemy, and served under Brutus. I have seen some manuscript *Letters of Shaftesbury*, in which he has ranged in three different classes the *Ethical* writings of Horace, according to the different periods of his life in which he supposes them to have been written. The first, during the time he professed the Stoic philosophy, and was a friend of Brutus. The second, after he became dissolute and debauched, at the court of Augustus. The third, when he repented of this abandoned Epicurean life, wished to retire from the city and court, and become a private man and a philosopher.

16. ———— et fragili quærens illidere dentem,
Offendet solido—— *

POPE has omitted this elegant allusion. Horace seems to have been particularly fond of those exquisite morsels of wit and genius, the old *Æsopic* † fables. He fre-

* Ver. 77.

† See the learned Dissertation, DE BABRIO, lately published by Mr. Tyrwhit; in which are several of the greatest elegance.

quently

quently alludes to them, but always with a *brevity*, very different from our modern writers of fable; even the natural *La Fontaine* has added a quaint and witty thought to this very fable. The *File* ſays to the Viper, Fab. 98,

> Tu te romprois toutes les dents.
> Je ne crains que *celles* du *Temps*.

17. Si mala condiderit in quem quis carmina, jus eſt
Judiciumque. *H.* Eſto ſi quis mala, ſed bona ſi quis
Judice condiderit laudatus Cæſare—— *

To laugh at the ſolemnity of Trebatius, Horace puts him off with a play upon words: But our important lawyer takes no notice of the jeſt, and finiſhes with a gravity ſuited to his character.

> Solventur riſû tabulæ, Tu miſſus abibis.

This dialogue I heard lately ſpoken † with ſo much ſpirit and propriety, that if our author could have been preſent, he perhaps might have been inclined to alter an opinion, of which he ſeems very fond,

* Ver. 83.

† At Eton School.

in the fourth book of the Dunciad, "that WORDS only are learnt at our GREAT SCHOOLS."

18. Non meus hic *ſermo*; ſed quæ præcepit *Oſellus*
Ruſticus, abnormis ſapiens, craſſâque Minervâ *.

Hear *Bethel*'s ſermon, one not vers'd in ſchools,
But ſtrong in ſenſe, and wiſe without the rules †.

THIS diſcourſe in praiſe of Temperance loſes much of it's grace and propriety, by being put into the mouth of a perſon of a much higher rank in life than the honeſt countryman *Oſellus*; whoſe patrimony had been ſeized by Auguſtus, and given to one of his ſoldiers named *Umbrenus*; and whom, perhaps, Horace recommended to the emperor, by making him the chief ſpeaker in this very ſatire. We may imagine that a diſcourſe on temperance from Horace, raiſed a laugh among the courtiers of Auguſtus; and we ſee, he could not venture to deliver it in his own perſon. This imitation of *Pope* is not equal to moſt of his others.

* Sat. ii. lib. 2. v. 2.

† Ver. 10.

19. ——Leporem

19. ———— Leporem sectatus, equove
Lassus ab indomito, vel, (si Romana fatigat
Militia assuetum græcari) seu pila velox,
Molliter austerum studio fallente laborem;
Seu te discus agit, pete cedentem aera disco;
Cum labor extuderit fastidia, siccus, inanis,
Sperne cibum vilem; nisi * Hymettia mella Falerno
Ne biberis diluta. Foris est promus & atrum
Defendens pisces hiemat mare; cum sale panis
Latrantem stomachum bene leniet. Unde putas aut
Quî partum? non in caro nidore voluptas
Summa, sed in teipso est. Tu pulmentaria quære
Sudando. Pinguem vitiis albumque neque ostra
Nec scarus, aut poterit peregrina juvate lagois †.

Go hunt, work, exercise! he thus began,
Then scorn a homely dinner if you can.
Your wine lock'd up, your butler stroll'd abroad,
Or fish deny'd (the river yet unthaw'd)
If then plain bread and milk will do the feat,
The pleasure lies in you, and not the meat ‡.

THIS paragraph is much inferior to the original; in which the mention of many particular *exercises* gives it a pleasing va-

* We are informed by Mr. Stuart, in his Athens, that the honey of Hymettus, even to this time, continues to be in vogue, and that the seraglio of the Grand Seignor is served with a quantity of it yearly.

† Ver. 9. ‡ Ver. 11.

riety.

riety. The ſixth and ſeventh lines in Horace are nervous and ſtrong. The third in Pope languid and wordy, which renders *foris eſt promus*. *Defendens*, & *latrantem*, & *caro*, & *pinguem*, & *album*, are all of them very expreſſive epithets. And the alluſion to *Socrates*'s conſtant exerciſe, *tu pulmentaria*, &c. ought not to have been omitted. Pope's two laſt lines in this paſſage are very exceptionable.

20. Vix tamen eripiam, poſito *pavone*, velis quin
Hoc potius quam *gallinâ* tergere palatum *.

Preach as I pleaſe, I doubt our curious men
Will chuſe a pheaſaut ſtill before a hen †.

He might have inſerted the original word *peacocks*, as many of our Engliſh epicures are fond of them. Q. Hortenſius had the honour of being the firſt Roman that introduced this bird to the table as a great dainty, in a magnificent feaſt which he made on his being created Augur. The price of a peacock, ſays Arbuthnot, page 129, was 50 denarii, that is, 1*l*. 12*s*. 3*d*.

* Ver. 23. † Ver. 17.

A flock

A flock of a hundred was sold at a much dearer rate, for 322*l.* 18*s.* 4*d.* of our money. M. Aufidius Lurco, according to Varro, used to make every year of his peacocks 484*l.* 7*s.* 6*d.*

21. Unde datum sentis *Lupus* hic Tiberinus, an alto
Captus hiet? pontesne inter jactatus, an amnis
Ostia sub Tusci? laudas insane trilibrem
Mullum; in singula quem minuas pulmenta necesse
est *.

Of carps and mullets why prefer the great,
Tho' cut in pieces ere my Lord can eat;
Yet for small turbots such esteem profess?
Because God made these large, the other less †.

VERY inferior to the original; and principally so, because that pleasant stroke is omitted, of the eater's knowing in what part of the river the *Lupus* ‡ was taken,

* Ver. 31.

† Ver. 21.

‡ Pliny, in his Natural History, b. ix. c. 34. mentions an extraordinary circumstance that gave value to their fish. Tot piscium saporibus, quibus pretia capientium periculo fiunt. The fish were esteemed, and supposed to have a higher flavour, in proportion to the dangers that had been undergone in the catching them. We are not yet arrived to the height to which Roman luxury was carried, however we may flatter ourselves on our improvements in eating.

and

and whether or no betwixt the two bridges, which was deemed an eſſential circumſtance. The reader will be well entertained on this ſubject, if he will look into the ſeventeenth chapter of the third book of Macrobius, particularly into a curious ſpeech of *C. Titius* * there recited. But Horace ſeems to have had in his eye a paſſage of Lucilius, quoted by Macrobius: Sed & Lucilius acer & violentus poeta, oſtendit ſcire ſe hunc piſcem egregii ſaporis, qui inter duos pontes captus eſſet. Lucilii verſus hi ſunt;

Fingere præterea afferri quod quiſque volebat;
Illum ſumina ducebant atque Altilium Lanx,
Hunc pontes Tiberinos duo inter captus catillo.

With reſpect to the *mullus* (which is ſuppoſed to be what the French and we call *ſurmoullet*) Juvenal † ſpeaks of one bought

* Cujus verba ideo póno, quia non ſolum de lupo inter duos pontes capto erunt teſtimonio, ſed etiam *mores*, quibus plerique *tunc vivebant*, facile publicabunt. Deſcribens enim homines prodigos in forum ad judicandum ebrios commeantes: quæque ſoleant inter ſe ſermocinari, ſic ait; "Ludunt aleâ, &c." p. 335. Pariſiis, 1585.

† *Arbuthnot* of Ancient Coins, p. 130. The expences of *Vitellius*'s table for one year amounted to 7,265,625 pounds

bought for 48*l.* 8*s.* 9*d.* According to *Macrobius,* there was paid for another 56*l.* 10*s.* 1*d.* For a third, according to *Pliny,* 64*l.* 11*s.* 8*d.* Our age is as yet unacquainted with the niceneſs of the ancients in weighing their fiſhes *at table,* and beholding them *expire.* The death of a *mullus,* with the variety and change of colours in it's laſt moments, was reckoned one of the moſt entertaining ſpectacles in the world, by the men of taſte at Rome.

21. Preſentes Auſtri, coquite horum obſonia——— *

pounds ſterling. In Macrobius, lib. ii. c. 9. is a bill of fare, and an account of the company who ſupped with *Lentulus,* when he was made prieſt of *Mars.* And in *Suetonius,* (Life of *Vitellius,* cap. 13.) is the deſcription of a coſtly ſupper which his brother gave him, in which there were two thouſand of the choiceſt birds; one diſh, for its amplitude and capacity, was called *Minerva's* buckler, which conſiſted chiefly of the livers of *Scari,* the brains of pheaſants and peacocks, the tongues of phænicopteræ, and lampreys bellies, brought from the moſt diſtant coaſts in *Triremes.* Claudius Æſopus, the tragedian, had one diſh that coſt him 600 ſeſtertia, (4,843l. 10s.) in which, to enhance the price of it, he had put ſinging-birds. VESTRIS, the modern *Bathyllus,* is not *yet* rich enough to give ſuch a diſh to his admirers. I know not what *Æſopus's* ſalary was for acting; Roſcius had thirty-two pounds five ſhillings a day.

* Ver. 41.

Oh!

Oh! blaſt it ſouth winds! till a ſtench exhale,
Rank as the ripeneſs of a rabbit's tail *.

A VERY filthy and offenſive image, for the happy and decent word *coquite*; it muſt be owned our author, as well as Swift, was but too fond of ſuch diſguſtful images.

22. Tutus erat Rhombus, tutoque Ciconia nido,
Donec vos autor docuit Prætorius——†.

The Robin-red-breaſt till of late had reſt,
And children ſacred held a Martin's neſt.
'Till Beccafico's ſold ſo dev'liſh dear,
To one that was, or would have been, a peer ‡.

HE has happily ſubſtituted for the *ſtork* two ſorts of birds that among us are held as it were ſacred. *Aſellus Sempronius Rufus* was the perſon § who firſt taught the Romans to eat *ſtorks*, for which he was ſaid to have loſt the prætorſhip. On which ſubject the following verſes were written, and have been preſerved by the old commentator *Porphyrio*.

* Ver. 27. † Ver. 49. ‡ Ver. 37.

§ See the Horace of *Badius Aſcenſius*, printed at Paris in folio, 1519, f. 213.

Ciconiarum Rufus iste Conditor,
Hic est duobus elegantior Plancis;
Suffragiorum puncta non tulit septem:
Ciconiarum populus ultus est mortem.

23. Porrectum magno magnum spectare catino
Vellem, ait, Harpyiis Gula digna rapacibus *.

Oldfield, with more than Harpy throat endu'd,
Cries, send me, Gods! a whole hog barbecu'd † !

He has happily introduced this large unwieldy instance of gluttony, supposed to be peculiar to the West Indies. But *Athenæus* ‡ speaks of a cook that could dress a whole hog with various puddings in his belly. I unfortunately know not with what wine it was basted. The slow movement of the lines in the original, loaded with spondees, aptly represent the weight and vastness of the dish. *Gula* is used personally: as it is also by *Juvenal*, Sat. xiv. v. 10.

* Ver. 40. † Ver. 25.

‡ An author that deserves to be more read and regarded, as abounding with entertaining anecdotes, and various accounts of the manners and ways of living of the ancients, and in quotations of elegant fragments of writers now lost. The same may be said of *Stobæus*, a work full of curious extracts upon important and pleasing subjects.

24. Si

3

24. Si quis nunc mergos suaves *edixerit* assos,
Parebit pravi docilis Romana juventus *.

Let me extol a cat, on oysters fed,
I'll have a party at the Bedford-Head;
Or ev'n to crack live craw-fish recommend,
† I'd never doubt at Court to have a friend ‡.

To dine upon a cat fattened with oysters, and to crack live craw-fish, is infinitely more pleasant and ridiculous than to eat *mergos assos*. But then the words *extol*, and *recommend*, fall far below *edixerit*; give out a *decree*: So Virgil, Georgic the third, line 295, does not advise but raises his subject by saying,

Incipiens stabulis *edico* in mollibus herbam
Carpere oves——

25. Ille repotia natales aliosque dierum
Festos albatus celebret—— §

But on some lucky day (as when they found
A lost Bank-bill, or heard their son was drown'd ||.

Much heightened and improved by two

* Ver. 51.

† This fourth line is feeble and unmeaning.

‡ Ver. 41. § Ver. 60. || Ver. 55.

ſuch ſuppoſed occaſions of the unnatural feſtivity and joy of a true miſer.

26. Dulcia ſe in bilem vertent, ſtomachoque *tumultum*
Lenta feret pituita——— *.

When bile, and phlegm, and wind, and acid jar,
And all the man is one inteſtine war †.

Τα γαρ ανομοια στασιαζει, ſays *Hippocrates:* the very metaphor here employed by *Horace*. Two writers of ſcience, in Greek, have uſed a ſtyle eminently pure, preciſe, and elegant, *Hippocrates* and *Euclid*.

27. ——————vides, ut pallidus omnis
Cæna deſurgat dubiâ——‡.

How pale each worſhipful and rev'rend gueſt
Riſe from a clergy or a city feaſt §.

Our author has been ſtrangely guilty here of falſe Engliſh and falſe grammar, by uſing *riſe* for *riſes*. The expreſſion in the original is from *Terence*; in the ſecond act of the *Phormio*.

* Ver. 75. † Ver. 71. ‡ Ver. 77. § Ver. 76.

Ph. Cæna

PH. Cæna *dubia* apponitur:

GETA. Quid iſtud verbi eſt? PH. Ubi tu dubites quid ſumas potiſſimum.

From which paſſage it is worth obſerving, that Terence was the firſt writer that uſed this expreſſion.

28. —————— Hos utinam inter
Heroas natum tellus me prima tuliſſet *.

Why had I not in theſe good times my birth,
Ere coxcomb-pyes, or coxcombs, were on earth †.

THE laſt line, and the conceit of coxcomb-*pyes* and *coxcombs*, ſink it below the original; which, by the way, ſays *Cruquius*, ſeems to allude to that of *Heſiod*, *Oper*. & *Dieb*.

Μηκετ' επειτ' ωφειλον εγω πεμπτοισι μετειναι
Ανδρασιν——————

29. Das aliquid Famæ, quæ carmine gratior aurem
Occupet humanam—— ‡

Unworthy he, the voice of Fame to hear,
That ſweeteſt muſic to an honeſt ear §.

* Ver. 93. † Ver. 97. ‡ Ver. 94. § Ver. 99.

Two very beautiful lines, that excel the original; though in truth the word *occupat* has much force. Horace again alludes to his favourite Grecians. Antiſthenes philoſophus, ſays the old commentator, cum vidiſſet adoleſcentem Acroamatibus multum delectari, O te, ait, infelicem, qui ſummum Acroama, hoc eſt, Laudem tuam non audiviſti.

30. Cur * eget indignus quiſquam te divite † ?

> How *dar'ſt* thou let one worthy man be poor ‡ ?

Very ſpirited, and ſuperior to the original; for *dar'ſt* is far beyond the mere *eget*.

31. Non aliquid patriæ tanto emetiris acervo § ?

> Or to thy country let that heap be lent,
> As M———o's was—but not at five per cent ||.

He could not forbear this ſtroke againſt a nobleman, whom he had been for many years accuſtomed to hear abuſed by his

* "Ev'n modeſt want may bleſs your hand unſeen,
"Tho' huſh'd in patient wretchedneſs at home."
Which ſecond line (of Dr. Armſtrong) is exquiſitely tender.

† Ver. 103. ‡ Ver. 118. § Ver. 105. || Ver. 121.

moſt

moſt intimate friends. A certain paraſite, who thought to pleaſe Lord Bolingbroke by ridiculing the avarice of the Duke of M. was ſtopt ſhort by Lord Bolingbroke; who ſaid, He was ſo very great a man, that I forget he had that vice.

32. Non ego, narrantem, temere edi luce profeſta
Quidquam, &c. ——— *

THIS ſpeech of Ofellus continues in the original to the end of this ſatire. Pope has taken all that follows out of the mouth of *Bethell*, and ſpeaks entirely in his own perſon. 'Tis impoſſible not to tranſcribe the pleaſing picture of his way of life, and the account he gives of his own table, in lines that expreſs common and familiar objects with dignity and elegance. See therefore his bill of fare, of which you will long to partake, and wiſh you could have dined at *Twickenham*.

32. 'Tis true, no turbots dignify my boards,
But gudgeons, flounders, what my Thames affords:
To Hounſlow-Heath I point, and Banſted-Down,
Thence comes your mutton, and theſe chicks my own.

* Ver. 116.

From yon old walnut-tree a ſhow'r ſhall fall,
And grapes, long ling'ring on my only wall,
And figs from ſtandard and eſpalier join;
The dev'l is in you if you cannot dine.
Then chearful healths (your miſtreſs ſhall have place)
And, what's more rare, a poet ſhall ſay * grace †.

33. Nam propriæ Telluris herum natura neque illum
Nec me nec quemquam ſtatuit——— ‡

What's *property?* dear Swift! you ſee it alter,
From you to me, from me to Peter Walter §.

Swift was always reading lectures of œconomy, upon which he valued himſelf, to his poetical friends. A ſhilling, ſays he, is a ſerious thing. His favourite maxim was, "Have money in your head, but not in your heart." Our author would have been pleaſed, if he could have known that his pleaſant villa would, after his time, have been the property of a perſon of diſtinguiſhed learning, taſte, and virtue ‖.

* Which Swift always did, with remarkable decency and devotion.

† Ver. 141. ‡ Ver. 130. § Ver. 167.

‖ The Right Honourable Welbore Ellis.

34. —— quocirca

3

34. ———— quocirca vivite fortes,
Fortiaque adverſis opponite pectora rebus *.

Let lands and houſes have what lords they will,
Let us be fix'd, and our own maſters ſtill †.

The majeſtic plainneſs of the original is weakened and impaired, by the addition of an antitheſis, and a turn of wit, in the laſt line.

35. Primâ dicte mihi, ſummâ dicende Camænâ,
Spectatum ſatis, & donatum jam rude quæris,
Mæcenas ‡; iterum antiquo me includere ludo.
Non eadem eſt ætas, non mens; Veianius armis
Herculis

* Ver. 135. † Ver. 179.

‡ It has been ſuſpected that his affection to his friend was ſo ſtrong, as to make him reſolve not to outlive him; and that he actually put into execution his promiſe of *ibimus, ibimus*, Od. xvii. l. 3. Both died in the end of the year 746; U. C. *Horace* only three weeks after *Mæcenas*, November 27. Nothing can be ſo different as the plain and manly ſtyle of the former, in compariſon with what Quintilian calls the *calamiſtros* of the latter, for which *Suetonius*, and *Macrobius*, c. 86, ſays Auguſtus frequently ridiculed him, though Auguſtus himſelf was guilty of the ſame fault. As when he ſaid, *Vapidè* ſe habere, for *malè*. The learned *C. G. Heyne*, in his excellent edition of Virgil, after obſerving, that the well-known verſes uſually aſcribed to Auguſtus, on Virgil's ordering his Æneid to be burnt, are the work of ſome bungling grammarian, and not of that Emperor, adds, " Videas tamen *Voltairium*, horridos hos & ineptos verſus non modo Auguſto tribuere, verum etiam

Herculis ad poſtem fixis, latet abditus agro,
Ne populum extremâ toties exoret arenâ *.

St. John, whoſe love indulg'd my labours paſt,
Matures my preſent, and ſhall bound my laſt.
Why will you break the ſabbath of my days?
Now ſick alike of envy and of praiſe.
Public too long, ah let me hide my age!
See modeſt Cibber now has left the ſtage:
Our gen'rals now, retir'd to their eſtates,
Hang their old trophies o'er the garden gates †.

There is more pleaſantry and humour in Horace's comparing himſelf to an old gladiator, worn out in the ſervice of the public, from which he had often begged his life, and has now at laſt been diſmiſſed with the uſual ceremonies, than for Pope to compare himſelf to an old actor or retired general. Pope was in his forty-ninth year, and Horace probably in his forty-ſeventh, when he wrote this epiſtle. Bentley

etiam magnopere probare; ils ſont beaux & ſemblent partir du cœur. Eſſai ſur la Poeſie Epique, c. 3. Ita vides, ad verum pulchrarum ſententiarum ſenſum & judicium, ſermonis intelligentiam aliquam eſſe neceſſariam."

P. V. Maronis Opera, tom. i. p. 131. Lipſiæ, 1767.

* Ep. i. lib. i. v. 1.

† Ver. 1. ep. i.

ley has arranged the writings * of Horace in the following order. He composed the first book of his Satires, between the twenty-sixth and twenty-eighth years of his age; the second book, from the years thirty-one to thirty-three; next, the Epodes, in his thirty-fourth and fifth year; next, the first book of his Odes, in three years, from his thirty-sixth to his thirty-eighth year; the second book in his fortieth and forty-first year; the third book, in the two next years; then, the first book of the Epistles, in his forty-sixth and seventh year; next to that, the fourth book of his Odes, in his forty-ninth to his fifty-first year. Lastly, the Art of Poetry, and second book of the Epistles, to which an exact date cannot be assigned.

36. Est mihi purgatam crebro qui personet aurem,
Solve senescentem mature sanus equum, ne
Peccet ad extremum ridendus & ilia ducat †.

* *J. Masson*, author of the Latin Life of Horace, does not agree to this arrangement of Horace's works; but does not seem to be able to substitute a more probable chronological order. See Hist. Crit. Repub. Lit. tom. v. p. 51.

† Ver. 7.

A voice

A voice there is that whiſpers in my ear *,
('Tis Reaſon's voice, which ſometimes one can hear)
Friend Pope, be prudent, let your muſe take breath,
And never gallop Pegaſus to death,
Leſt ſtiff and ſtately, void of fire and force,
You limp like Blackmore, on a Lord Mayor's horſe †.

HORACE plainly alludes to the good genius of Socrates, which conſtantly warned him againſt approaching evils and inconveniences. POPE has happily turned it to Wiſdom's voice, and as happily has added, "which *ſometimes* one can hear." The *purged* ear is a term of philoſophy. The idea of the jaded Pegaſus, and the Lord Mayor's horſe, are high improvements on the original. A Roman reader was pleaſed

* He has excelled Boileau's imitation of theſe verſes, Ep. x. ver. 44. And Boileau himſelf is excelled by an old poet, whom indeed he has frequently imitated, that is, *Le Freſnaie Vauquelin*, who was the father of N. V. des Yvetaux, the preceptor of Louis XIII. whoſe poems were publiſhed towards the end of his life, 1612. He ſays that he profited much by the ſatires of *Arioſto*. Boileau has borrowed much from him. He alſo wrote an Art of Poetry. One of his beſt pieces is an imitation of Horace's *Trebatius*, being a dialogue between himſelf and the Chancellor of France.

† Ver. 11.

with

with the allusion to two well-known verses of Ennius *.

37. Virtutis veræ custos, rigidusque satelles †.

> Free as young LYTTELTON her cause pursue,
> Still true to virtue, and as warm as true ‡.

A JUST, and not over-charged encomium, on an excellent man, who always served his friends with warmth (witness his kindness to Thomson) and his country with activity and zeal. His Poems, and Dialogues of the Dead, are written with elegance and ease; his Observations on the conversion of St. Paul, with clearness and

* Sicut fortis equus spatio qui forte supremo
Vicit Olympia, nunc senio confectu quiescit.

Ennius, poeta antiquus (says Jos. Scaliger, with his usual bluntness) in Scaligerana, magnifico ingenio. Utinam hunc haberemus integrum, & amissemus, Lucanum, Statium, Silium Italicum, & *tous ces garçons-la.* The learned *M. Monoye,* to whom we are indebted for so many additions to the *Menagiana,* reads with great acuteness, *Gascons-la,* by which term he thinks Scaliger points out the inflated, bombastic style of Lucan and Statius. How elegantly, and even poetically, does Quintilian give his judgment of Ennius; Hunc sicut sacros vetustate lucos adoremus, in quibus grandia & antiqua robora, jam non tantam habent speciem, quantam religionem. Lib. x. c. 1.

† Ver. 17. ‡ Ver. 29.

closeness

closeness of reasoning; and his History of Henry II. with accuracy, and knowledge of those early times, and of the English constitution; and which was compiled from a laborious search into authentic documents, and the records lodged in the Tower and at the Rolls. A little before he died, he told me, that he had determined to throw out of the collection of all his works, which was then soon to be published, his first juvenile performance, the *Persian* * *Letters*, written, 1735, in imitation

* Montesquieu himself also says, that in this agreeable work there were some *juvenilia*, that he would wish to correct; " for though a Turk ought necessarily to see, think, and speak like a Turk, and not like a Christian, yet many persons do not attend to this circumstance, in reading my Persian Letters." See an entertaining collection of his Original Letters, p. 180. In this collection are some curious particulars relating to his great work, The Spirit of Laws. He tells his friend, the Count de Guasco, " Though many kings have not done me that honour, yet I know one who has read my work; and *M. de Maupertuis* has informed me, that this monarch is not always of my opinion. I have answered Maupertuis, and told him, I would lay a wager, I could easily put my finger on those passages which the King dislikes." In page 166, he thus speaks of *Voltaire*; " Quant à Voltaire, il a trop d'esprit pour m'entendre; tous les livres qu'il lit, il les fait, après quoi il approuve ou critique ce qu'il a fait. And afterwards,

imitation of thoſe of his friend *Monteſquieu*, whom he had known and admired in England; in which he ſaid there were

wards, ſpeaking of Voltaire's diſmiſſion from Berlin, "Voilà donc Voltaire qui paroit ne ſçavoir ou repoſer ſa tête; ut eadem tellus quæ modo victori defuerat, deeſſet ad ſepulturam. Le bon eſprit vaut beaucoup mieux que le bel eſprit." p. 198. It is much to be lamented, that the hiſtory of *Louis* the Eleventh, which Monteſquieu had written, was burnt by a miſtake of his ſecretary, p. 98. Mr. Stanley, for whom Monteſquieu had a ſincere eſteem and regard, told me, that Monteſquieu aſſured him, he had received more information from the commentaries of *Azo* on the Codex and Digeſt, a famous civilian of Bologna in the twelfth century, than from any other writer on the civil law. He is ſaid to have had 10,000 ſcholars. Trithemius mentions him, c. 487. See Ariſii Cremonam Litteratam. Tom. i. p. 89.

I beg to add, that Lyttelton was not blind to the faults and blemiſhes of his friend Monteſquieu. See notes on the Hiſtory of the Life of Henry II. p. 291, 4to, where he is cenſured for an exceſſive deſire of ſaying ſomething new upon every ſubject, and differing from the common opinions of mankind.

That accompliſhed lady the Dutcheſs *D'Aiguillon*, conſtantly attended Monteſquieu in his laſt illneſs, to the time of his death, 1755. One day, during her abſence of a few hours from his chamber, an Iriſh jeſuit, Father *Roth* (author of ſome ſevere criticiſms againſt the Paradiſe Loſt) got introduced to the dying philoſopher, and inſiſted on having the key of his bureau, that he might take away his papers. When the Dutcheſs ſuddenly returned, and reproached the jeſuit for this proceeding, he only anſwered, Madam, I muſt obey my ſuperiors. It was owing to the interpoſition of the celebrated phyſician, *Van Swieten*, that the Spirit of Laws was permitted to be ſold and read at Vienna.

principles and remarks that he wiſhed to retract and alter. I told him, that, notwithſtanding his caution, the bookſellers, as in fact they have done, would preſerve and inſert theſe letters. Another little piece, written alſo in his early youth, does him much honour; the *Obſervations on the Life of Tully*, in which, perhaps, a more diſpaſſionate and impartial character of Tully is exhibited, than in the panegyrical volumes of Middleton.

38. Nunc in Ariſtippi furtim præcepta relabor *.

> Sometimes with Ariſtippus, or St. Paul,
> Indulge my candor, and grow all to all †.

THERE is an impropriety and indecorum, in joining the name of the moſt profligate paraſite of the court of Dionyſius with that of an apoſtle. In a few lines before, the name of *Montaigne* is not ſufficiently contraſted by the name of *Locke*; the place required that two philoſophers, holding very different tenets, ſhould have been introduced. *Hobbes* might have been

* Ver. 19. † Ver. 31.

oppoſed

opposed to *Hutcheson*. I know not why he omitted a strong sentiment that follows immediately,

Et mihi res, non me rebus subjungere conor *.

Which line Corneille took for his motto.

39. Non tamen idcirco contemnas lippus inungi †.

I'll do what MEAD and Chefelden advise ‡.

MEAD, a judge of pure Latinity, having disputed with Pope on the impropriety of the expression, *Amor* publicus, on Shakespear's monument, ended the controversy by giving up his opinion, and saying to him,

Omnia vincit amor & nos cedamus amori.

I mention this circumstance, because it may be amusing to the lovers of anecdotes, just to add, that in a public inscription at Rheims in France, RACINE, who drew it up, used the words Amor publicus, in the very same sense. I believe both these great poets were wrong.

* Ver. 20. † Ver. 29. ‡ Ver. 51.

40. Invidus, *iracundus*, *iners*, *vinosus*, *amator* *.

Be furious, envious, flothful, mad, or drunk,
Slave to a wife, or vaffal to a punk †.

I CANNOT forbear thinking that Horace glanced at his ‡ own frailties and imperfections, as he frequently does, in the *four* laft epithets of this verfe, in the original. As to *envy*, he had not a grain of it in his nature.

41. Virtus eft vitium fugere §.

'Tis the firft virtue, vices to *abhor*,
And the firft wifdom, to be fool no *more* ||.

DR. KING informed me, that *thefe* were two of the rhymes to which Swift, who was fcrupuloufly exact in this refpect, ufed to object, as he did to fome others in

* Ver. 38. † Ver. 61.

‡ As he does at his paffion for building, in verfe 100, below,

Diruit, ædificat, mutat quadrata rotundis.

So alfo, Sat. iii. lib. ii. v. 308.

———— Accipe, primum
Ædificas; hoc eft longos imitaris, ab imo
Ad fummum totus moduli bipedalis——

§ Ver. 41. || Ver. 65.

Pope;

Pope; particularly to two in the Essay on Criticism, v. 237, where *delight* is made to rhyme to *wit*.

42. Per mare pauperiem fugiens, per saxa, per ignes *.

> Scar'd at the spectre of pale POVERTY † !

POPE has given life to the image, and added terror to the simple expression *pauperiem*.

43. At pueri ludentes, Rex eris, aiunt,
Si recte facies ——— ‡.

> Yet ev'ry child another song will sing,
> Virtue, brave boys! 'tis virtue makes a king §.

SOME commentators think Horace alluded to an old Greek play among children, called, Βασιλινδα. But Lambinus observes, that the sport alluded to is mentioned in the *Theætetus* of Plato; where Socrates says, he that fails in his pursuit will be reckoned an ass, as the children say of him who cannot catch the ball; and he that catches it is called their king.

* Ver. 46. † Ver. 70. ‡ Ver. 59. § Ver. 91.

44. Ut propius ſpectes lacrymoſa * poemata Pupi † !

For what? to have a box when eunuchs ſing,
And foremoſt in the circle eye a king ‡.

OUR author is ſo perpetually expreſſing an affected contempt for kings, that it becomes almoſt a nauſeous cant;

—the pride of kings—
—ſome monſter of a king—
—pity kings—the gift of kings—
—Gods of kings—much above a king—
—Settle wrote of kings—&c.—

HAWKINS BROWN laughed at him for this affectation, in the pleaſant Imitations of Engliſh poets, on Tobacco.

Come, let me taſte thee, *unexcis'd by kings!*

45. Olim quod vulpes ægroto cauta leoni
Reſpondit, referam: Quia me veſtigia terrent,
Omnia te adverſum ſpectantia, nulla retrorſum §.

Faith, I ſhall give the anſwer Reynard gave:
I cannot like, dread Sir! your royal cave;

* The epithet *lacrymoſa* is ironical.

† Ver. 67. ‡ Ver. 105. § Ver. 73.

Becauſe

5

Becauſe I ſee, by all the tracks about,
Full many a beaſt goes in, but none comes out *.

BOTH poets have told the fable with an elegant brevity. Why did Pope omit *ægroto?* *Dread Sir,* and *Royal cave,* are good additions. Plato was alſo fond of this fable. He has put it into the mouth of Socrates, in the firſt Alcibiades †.

46. Exci-

* Ver. 114.

Conciſeneſs was the quality, for which *Babrius*, if we may judge from the fragments, ſeems to have been ſo excellent. See Diſſertat. de Babrio, Fab. 97, 50, 242; and above all, the exquiſite fable of the Swallow and Nightingale, Fable 149, and the laſt in this curious and elegant diſſertation. In the *Fabularum Æſopicarum Delectus*, a book not ſufficiently known, and now out of print, publiſhed at Oxford, 1698, are *ſixty* fables exquiſitely written, verſibus ſenariis, by *Ant. Alſop*. The beſt life of Æſop is by M. *Mezeriac*, the learned editor of *Diophantus*: a book ſo ſcarce, that *Bentley* complained he could never get a ſight of it; and *Bayle* had never ſeen it, when he firſt publiſhed his Dictionary. It was reprinted in the Memoires de Litterature of M. de Sallengre, 1717, tom. i. p. 87. This was the author, whom Malherbe aſked, when he ſhewed him the edition of Diophantus; "if it would leſſen the price of bread?"

† Αλλ' ατεχνως, κατα τον Αισωπυ μυθον, ον η Αλωπηξ προς τον Λεοντα ειπε, και τυ εις Λακεδαιμονα νομισματος εισιοντος μεν τα ιχνη τα εκεισε τετραμμενα δηλα, εξιοντος δε, υδαμη αν τις ιδοι. Tom. ii. p. 122. Serrani. Ed. H. Steph. 1578. Pope has *connected* the paſſage that imme-

 diately

46. Excipiantque senes quos in vivaria mittant *.

Some with fat bucks on childless dotards fawn †.

THE legacy-hunters, the *Hæredipetæ*, were a more common character among the ancients than with us. The ridicule, therefore, is not now so striking. Lucian has five pleasant Dialogues on the subject, from page 343 to 363, in the 4to edition of Hemsterhusius. Horace himself appears to have failed more in exposing this folly, than in any other of his satires; and principally so, by mixing ancient with modern manners, and making Tiresias instruct Ulysses in petty frauds, and artifices too subtle for the old prophet and hero to dictate and to practise. Sat. 5. lib. 2.

47. Multis occulto crescit res fœnore ——— ‡.

diately follows in a forced and quaint manner, which Horace never thought of;

Well, if a king's a *lion*, at the least
The people are a many-headed beast. V. 120.

as if the word *bellua* had any relation to the *lion* before-mentioned.

* Ver. 79. † Ver. 130. ‡ Ver. 80.

is far excelled in force and ſpirit by,

> While with the ſilent growth of ten per cent,
> In *dirt* and *darkneſs*, hundreds *ſtink* content *.

48. Nullus in orbe ſinus Baiis prælucet amœnis,
Si dixit dives ; lacus & mare ſentit amorem
Feſtinantis heri —— †.

> Sir Job ‡ ſail'd forth, the evening bright and ſtill,
> "No place on earth, he cry'd, like Greenwich-hill!"
> Up ſtarts a palace; lo, th' obedient baſe
> Slopes at its foot, the woods its ſides embrace,
> The ſilver Thames reflects its marble face §.

SUPERIOR to the original: a pleaſing little landſcape is added to the ſatire. But *Greenwich-hill* is not an exact parallel for *Baiæ*; where the Romans of the beſt taſte and faſhion built their villas. POPE's is the villa of a citizen. The abſurd and aukward magnificence of opulent citizens has, of late, been frequently expoſed; but no where with more humour than in the *Connoiſſeur*, and in the characters of *Sterling* and *Mrs. Heidelberg*, in the Clandeſtine Marriage.

* Ver. 132. † Ver. 83.

‡ More lively than the general word, *dives*.

§ Ver. 138.

49. ——Cui si vitiosa * libido
Fecerit auspicium; cras ferramenta Teanum
Tolletis, fabri———— †

Now let some whimsy, or that dev'l within,
Which guides all those who know not what they mean,
But give the knight (or give his lady) spleen;
Away, away! take all your scaffolds down,
For snug's the word;—my dear, we'll live in town ‡.

HORACE says, he will carry his buildings from so proper and pleasant a situation as *Baiæ*, to *Teanum*; a situation unhealthy and disagreeable. POPE says, he will not build at all, he will again retire to town. He has, I think, destroyed the connexion by this alteration. Mutability of temper is indeed equally exhibited in both instances, but Horace keeps closer to his subject.

50. Quo teneam vultus mutantem Protea nodo?
Quid pauper? ride; mutat cœnacula, lectos,
Balnea, tonsores; conducto navigio æque,
Nauseat ac locuples quem ducit priva triremis §.

* Scaliger observes, that Horace is fond of adjectives that end in *osus*.

† Ver. 85. ‡ Ver. 143. § Ver. 90.

Did

Did ever Proteus, Merlin, any witch,
Transform themſelves ſo ſtrangely as the rich.
Well, but the poor—the poor have the ſame itch.
They change their weekly barber, weekly news,
Prefer a new japanner to their ſhoes;
Diſcharge their garrets, move their beds, and run,
(They know not whither) in a chaiſe and one;
They hire their ſculler, and, when once aboard,
Grow ſick, and damn the climate—like a lord *.

THIS imitation is in truth admirable. It is, perhaps, one of his fineſt paſſages. All the parallels are fortunate, and exactly hit the original: and the images drawn from modern life are minutely applicable to the purpoſe.

51. Si curtatus inæquali tonſore capillos,
Occurro; rides: ſi forte ſubucula pexæ
Trita ſubeſt tunicæ, vel ſi toga diſſidet inpar;
Rides ——— †.

You laugh, half beau, half ſloven if I ſtand,
My wig all powder, and all ſnuff my band;
You laugh, if coat and breeches ſtrangely vary,
White gloves, and linen worthy Lady Mary ‡!

I AM inclined to think that Horace laughs at himſelf (not at Virgil, as has

* Ver. 152. † Ver. 94. ‡ Ver. 161.

been

been ſuppoſed) for the ungraceful appearance he ſometimes made, and the incongruity of his dreſs. Perhaps our *little, round, fat, oily* man, was ſomewhat of a ſloven. Poor POPE was ſo weak and infirm, and his body required ſo many wrappers and coverings, that it was hardly poſſible for him to be neat. No poet, except *Malherbe*, ever wore ſo many * pair of ſtockings. *Thomſon* ſpeaks elegantly of his perſon, in that delightful poem, The Caſtle of Indolence, ſtanza the 33d.

He came, the bard, a little Druid-wight,
Of wither'd aſpect; but his eye was keen,
With ſweetneſs mix'd. In ruſſet brown bedight,
As is his ſiſter of the copſes green,
He crept along, unpromiſing of mien.
Groſs he who judges ſo.——

52. Nil admirari, prope res eſt una, Numici,
Solaque quæ poſſit facere & ſervare beatum †.

"Not to admire, is all the art I know,
"To make men happy, and to keep them ſo."

* *Ten* in number, according to his friend RACAN, in the account of his life.

† Epiſt. vi.

Plain

Plain truth, dear MURRAY *, needs no flowers of speech,
So take it in the very words of CREECH †:

Who, in truth, is a much better ‡ translator than he is usually supposed and allowed to be. He is a nervous and vigorous writer: and many parts, not only of his Lucretius, but of his Theocritus and Horace (though now decried) have not been excelled by other translators. One of his pieces may be pronounced excellent; his translation of the thirteenth satire of Juvenal; equal to any that Dryden has given us of that author.

* He knew the exact taste and learning of the person he addresses, and has laboured this imitation accordingly.

† Ver. 1.

‡ Mr. Christopher Pitt has imitated the 7th sat. of Hor. b. ii.; the 19th epistle, b. ii.; the 4th epistle, b. i.; the 19th epistle, b. i.; the 18th epistle, b. i. (see his poems, vol. xliii. of the English poets) with a freedom and a facility of versification truly Horatian. Perhaps it may deserve consideration, whether the best manner of imitating these satires and epistles, which approach so near to comedy, and to common conversation, would not be to adopt the *familiar* blank verse, which Mr. *Colman* has so successfully employed in his Terence; a sort of verse no more resembling that of Milton, than the Hexameters of Homer resemble those of Theocritus.

52. Hunc.

53. Hunc solem & stellas & decedentia certis
Tempora momentis, sunt qui formidine nullâ
Imbuti spectent ——— *.

This vault of air, this congregated ball,
Self-center'd sun and stars, that rise and fall:
There are, my friend, whose philosophic eyes
Look through, and trust the Ruler with his skies †.

THIS last line is quaint and obscure; the two first vigorously expressed. Horace thought of a noble passage ‡ in Lucretius, book v. line 1185.

In cœloque, Deum sedes, & templa locârunt,
Per cœlum volvi quia sol, & luna videntur:
Luna, dies, & nox, & noctis signa serena,
Noctivagæque faces cœli, flammæque volantes,
Nubila, ros, imbres, nox, venti, fulmina, grando,
Et rapida fremitus, & murmura magna minarum,

* Ver. 3. † Ver. 5.

‡ To those who know the number of *thoughts that breathe, and words that burn*, in this animated writer, it is surprising that Tully could speak of him in so cold and tasteless a manner; Lucretii poemata non sunt lita multis luminibus *Ingenii*, multæ tamen *Artis*. Ep. ad Fratrem, Lib. ii. Ep. 11. Lucretius seems to have thought of the fine passage in the Sisyphus of Euripides, quoted by Grotius, Excerpta, p. 402. Sextus Empirius ascribes the lines to Critias; but Plutarch, with better reason, to Euripides.

53. Ludicra

54. Ludicra quid, plausus, & amici dona Quiritis *.

Or popularity? or stars and strings?
The mob's applauses, or the gifts of kings †

CONSIDERING the present state of politics, the abilities of politicians in this country, and the number of those who think themselves completely qualified to guide the state, might I be pardoned for the pedantry of recommending to them the few following words of Socrates; who thus addresses Alcibiades: Γυμνασαι πρωτον, ω μακαριε, και μαθε ἁ δει μαθοντα ιεναι επι τα της πολεως, προτερον δε μη. Alcibiad. 2d. p. 133. Serr. Platon. T. 2.

55. ——Cum bene notum
Porticus Agrippæ, & via te conspexerit Appî;
Ire tamen restat, Numa quo devenit & Ancus ‡.

Grac'd as thou art with all the pow'r of words,
So known, so honour'd, at the House of Lords;
Conspicuous scene!—another yet is nigh,
(More silent far!) where kings and poets lie;

* Ver. 7. † Ver. 13.

‡ Ver. 25.

Where

Where MURRAY, long enough his country's pride *,
Shall be no more than TULLY, or than HYDE †.

MUCH beyond the original; particularly on account of the very happy and artful uſe POPE has made of the neighbourhood of the Houſe of Parliament to Weſtminſter Abbey; and of the well-turned and unexpected compliment he has paid to his illuſtrious friend. The character of Lord Chancellor CLARENDON ‡ ſeems to grow

* What would our author have ſaid and thought, had he lived long enough to ſee the houſe of this venerable magiſtrate, like that of Tully, plundered and burnt, by an infamous band of bigots, rebels, ruffians, and enthuſiaſts? What a ſubject for the ſevereſt and deepeſt tones of his indignant Muſe!

† Ver. 48.

‡ During his retirement in Jerſey, he writes thus to Dr. G. Sheldon, " That you may not think I am idle, I have read over Livy, and Tacitus, and almoſt Tully's works." They who cenſure his ſtyle as too diffuſe, and too much embarraſſed with parentheſes, may conſult the 3d volume of the learned Lord Monbaddo's Origin of Languages. When Clarendon was going from court, juſt after his profligate and ungrateful maſter had obliged him to reſign the Great Seal, the Dutcheſs of Portſmouth meanly inſulted him from a window in the palace. He looked up at her, and only ſaid, with a calm and contemptuous dignity; " Madam, if you live *you* will grow old."

every

every day brighter, the more it is ſcrutinized, and his integrity and abilities are more aſcertained and acknowledged, even from the publication of private papers, never intended to ſee the light.

56. —— vis rectè vivere? quis non?
Si virtus hoc una poteſt dare, fortis omiſſis
Hoc age deliciis—— *

Would ye be bleſt? deſpiſe low joys, low gains;
Diſdain whatever CORNBURY diſdains;
Be virtuous, and be happy for your pains †.

THIS again is ſuperior to the original; where quis non, is feeble and flat: and the mention of a particular ſhining character gives a force and ſpirit to the line. This amiable young nobleman wrote, from Paris, 1752, a very preſſing remonſtrance to Mr. Mallet, to diſſuade him, but in vain, from publiſhing a very offenſive ‡ digreſſion on the

* Ver. 29. † Ver. 60.

‡ It appears that Swift ſuſpected the irreligious principles of Bolingbroke, ſo early as the year 1724; for he makes for himſelf the following apology to the Dean:— " I muſt on this occaſion ſet you right, as to an opinion, which

the Old Teſtament, in Lord Bolingbroke's Letters on Hiſtory. "I muſt ſay to you, Sir, for the world's ſake, and for his ſake, that part of the work ought by no means to be communicated further. If this digreſſion be made public, it will be cenſured, it muſt be cenſured, it ought to be cenſured. It will be criticiſed too by able pens, whoſe erudition, as well as their reaſonings, will not eaſily be anſwered." He concludes by ſaying, "I therefore recommend to you to ſuppreſs that part of the work, as a good citizen of the world, for the world's peace,

which I ſhould be very ſorry to have you entertain concerning me. The term *eſprit fort*, in Engliſh free-thinker, is, according to my obſervation, uſually applied to them, whom I look upon to be the *peſts* of ſociety; becauſe their endeavours are directed to looſen the bands of it, and to take at leaſt one curb out of the mouth of that wild beaſt man, when it would be well if he was checked by half a ſcore others." One of theſe *peſts*, however, he choſe to become, by ſtrictly enjoining Mr. Mallet to publiſh the writings he left againſt religion. See Letters of Swift by Hawkeſworth, vol. ii. p. 200. In this collection is the very entertaining journal which Swift wrote daily to Mrs. Johnſon, containing a minute account, and many private anecdotes of the miniſtry of Queen Anne. Perhaps the inſide of a court (vitæ poſtſcenia) was never ſo clearly diſplayed. But yet Swift does not ſeem to have known all the intrigues then carried on.

as one intrusted and obliged by Lord Bolingbroke, not to raise new storms to his memory."

57. ——Virtutem verba putas, ut
Lucum ligna?——*.

But art thou one, whom new opinions sway,
One who believes as TINDAL leads the way;
Who *Virtue* and a *Church* alike disowns,
Thinks *that* but words, and *this* but brick and stones†?

HERE we have a direct and decisive censure of a celebrated infidel writer; at this time, therefore, which was 1737, POPE was strongly and openly on the side of religion, as he knew the great lawyer to be to whom he was writing. Horace, it is said, alludes to the words of a dying Hercules in a Greek tragedy; and Dion Cassius relates, in the 27th book of his history, that these were the words which Brutus used just before he stabbed himself, after his defeat at Philippi. But it is observable, that this fact rests solely on the

* Ver. 31. † Ver. 62.

credit of this fawning and fulſome court-hiſtorian; and that Plutarch, who treats largely of Brutus, is ſilent on the ſubject. If Brutus had adopted this paſſage, I cannot bring myſelf to believe, that Horace would ſo far have forgotten his old republican principles, as to have mentioned the words adopted by the dying patriot, with a mark of reproach and reprobation.

58. Scilicet uxorem cum dote, fidemque & amicos,
Et genus & formam * regina PECUNIA donat,
Ac bene nummatum decorat SUADELA, VENUSQUE†.

For mark th' advantage; juſt ſo many ſcore
Will gain a wife with half as many more;
Procure her beauty, make that beauty chaſte,
And then ſuch friends as cannot fail to laſt.
A man of wealth is dubb'd a man of worth,
Venus ſhall give him form, and Anſtis birth ‡.

* The Duke of M. dining with Prince Eugene, in a very large company, ſpoke in high terms of *his* Queen Anne; the Prince whiſpered to the oldeſt and moſt venerable general officer *now living*, *Regina Pecunia* "*that's his Queen*." And the Prince immediately added, "There is a great difference in making war *en maitre*, or *en advocat*.

† Ver. 38. ‡ Ver. 77.

NOT

NOT imitated with the vigour and energy of the original. The firſt line is weak and languid. Three *Divinities*, for ſuch he makes them, PECUNIA, SUADELA, and VENUS, conſpire in giving their accompliſhments to this favourite of fortune. Modern images could not be found to anſwer theſe proſopopœias.

59.——Chlamydes Lucullus, ut aiunt,
Si poſſet centum ſcenæ præbere rogatus *,
" Quî poſſum tot? ait: tamen & quæram & quot habebo,
" Mittam"—poſt paulo ſcribit ſibi millia quinque
Eſſe domi chlamydum; partem vel tolleret omnes †.

* Orationis ſubtilitas imitabilis illa quidem videtur eſſe exiſtimanti, ſed nihil experienti minus. *Cicero.* See what Demetrius Phalereus ſays, in a paſſage full of taſte and judgment, περι τȣ ισχνȣ χαρακτηρος, pag. 113. Oxon. 1676.

Theſe lines of Horace are a ſtrong example of this ſpecies of ſtyle,

——parcentis viribus atque
Extenuantis eas conſulto——

This treatiſe of Demetrius Phalereus is not ſo much read, but perhaps is more uſeful than even Dionyſius de Struct. Some have imagined that Dionyſius was the author of it. There are many internal proofs why it could not be written ſo early as *D. Phalereus*.

† Ver. 40.

His wealth brave Timon gloriouſly confounds;
Aſk'd for a groat, he gives a hundred pounds;
Or, if three ladies like a luckleſs play,
Takes the whole houſe upon the poet's day *.

By no means equal to the original: there is ſo much pleaſantry in alluding to the known ſtory of the Prætor coming to borrow dreſſes (paludamenta) for a chorus in a public ſpectacle that he intended to exhibit, who aſked him to lend him a hundred, ſays Plutarch; but Lucullus bade him take *two hundred*. Horace humourouſly has made it *five thouſand*. We know nothing of Timon, or the three ladies here mentioned. There is ſtill another beauty in Horace; he has ſuddenly, according to his manner, introduced Lucullus ſpeaking; "*qui poſſum, &c.*" He is for ever introducing theſe little interlocutions, which give his ſatires and epiſtles an air ſo lively and dramatic. This alſo is very frequently the practiſe of Bayle, and is one of the circumſtances that has contributed to make

* Ver. 85.

his

his Dictionary ſo very entertaining; and he need not have ſaid, as he did to BOILEAU, that the reading his work was like the journey of a caravan over the deſerts of Arabia, which often went twenty or thirty leagues together, without finding a ſingle fruit-tree or fountain.

60. Mercemur ſervum, qui dictet nomina, lævum
Qui fodiat latus, & cogat trans * pondera dextram
Porrigere: hic multum in *Fabiâ* valet, ille *Velinâ*;
Cui libet is faſces dabit; eripietque curule,
Cui volet, importunus ebur: Frater, Pater, adde;
Ut cuique eſt ætas ita quemque facetus adopta †.

Then hire a ſlave, or, if you will, a lord,
To do the honours, or to give the word;

* Various are the opinions about the meaning of *trans pondera*; ſome commentators think it means, acroſs the carriages and waggons loaded with beams and ſtones, &c. or the *weight* of the gown *pulled* up. But *Geſner*'s interpretation ſeems the moſt ſenſible; ultra æquilibrium corporis, cum periculo cadendi; the candidate bows ſo low that he almoſt overſets his body. Fodit latus lævum candidati nomenclator; alacris nimium & cupidus candidatus ita protendit dextram, ut æquilibrium pœne perdat. And Ovid uſes *pondera* in this ſenſe; Ponderibus librata ſuis. Met. i. 13.

† Ver. 50.

Tell at your levee, as the crowds approach,
To whom to nod, whom take into your coach,
Whom honour with your hand: to make remarks,
Who rules in Cornwall, or who rules in Berks;
" This may be troublesome, is near the chair:
" That makes three members; this can chuse a may'r."
Instructed thus, you bow, embrace, protest,
Adopt him son, or cousin, at the least,
Then turn about, and laugh at your own jest *.

An admirable picture of septennial folly and meanness during an *election canvass*, in which the arts of English solicitation are happily applied to Roman. Some strokes of this kind, though mixed with unequal trash, in the *Pasquin* of Fielding, may be mentioned as capital, and full of the truest humour. It is indeed a fine and fruitful subject for a satyrist. As Pope could not use a *nomenclator (servum)* he has happily added—a *Lord*. And if he has omitted a lively circumstance, *fodiat latus*, he has made ample compensation by, *take into your coach*. *Importunus* is skilfully turned

* Ver. 110.

by,

by, *this may be troublesome*; as is *facetus*, by, *laugh at your own jest* *.

61. ———remigium vitiosum Ithacensis Ulyssei
Cui potior patriâ fuit interdicta voluptas †,

is admirably applied to the frequent mischievous effects of *early* foreign travel.

From Latian Syrens, French Circæan feasts,
Return well travell'd, and transform'd to beasts;
Or for a titled punk, or foreign flame,
Renounce our country, and degrade our name ‡?

62. Si, Mimnermus uti censet, sine amore jocisque,
Nil est jucundum, vivas in amore jocisque §.

If SWIFT cry wisely, "*Vive la Bagatelle* ‖!"

THE Dean made his old age despicable, by mis-spending it in *trifling* and in *railing*; in scribbling paltry riddles and rebusses, and venting his spleen in peevish invectives. His banishment to Ireland, for such he thought it, and his disappointed ambition,

* Yet Horace, lib. 1. sect. 10. uses *facetus* in another sense, as interpreted by Quintilian, lib. 6. c. 3.

† Ver. 63. ‡ Ver. 123.

§ Ver. 65. ‖ Ver. 129.

embittered and exasperated his mind and temper. An excellent man, and excellent philosopher, whose loss I shall long and sincerely deplore, has lately made the following strictures upon one of his capital works.

" *Misanthropy* is so dangerous a thing, and goes so far in sapping the very foundation of *morality* and *religion*, that I esteem the last part of *Swift*'s *Gulliver* (that I mean relative to his Houyhnhnms and Yahoos) to be a worse book to peruse, than those which we forbid, as the most flagitious and obscene. One absurdity in this author (a wretched philosopher, though a great wit) is well worth remarking: in order to render the nature of *men odious*, and the nature of *beasts amiable*, he is compelled to give *human* characters to his *beasts*, and *beastly* characters to his *men*; so that we are to admire the *beasts*, not for being *beasts*, but *amiable men*; and to *detest* the *men*, not for being men, but detestable beasts.

WHOEVER has been reading this *unnatural* FILTH, let him turn for a moment to a *Spectator* of ADDISON, and observe the PHILANTHROPY of that classical writer; I may add, the superior purity of his *diction*, and his *wit* *."

63. Cum tot sustineas & tanta negotia *solus*,
Res Italas armis tuteris, moribus ornes,
Legibus emendes, in publica commoda peccem,
Si longo sermone morer tua tempora, Cæsar †!

While you, great patron of mankind, sustain
The balanc'd world, and open all the main;
Your country, chief, in arms abroad defend,
At home with morals, arts, and laws amend;
How shall the Muse from such a monarch steal
An hour, and not defraud the public weal ‡?

ALL those nauseous || and outrageous compliments, which Horace, in a strain of abject

* Philological Inquiries, in three parts, by JAMES HARRIS, Esq; London, 1781. Part iii. page 537.

† Ep. 1. Lib. ii. v. 1. If an interrogation point is placed after *Cæsar?* in the original, it would remove a difficulty complained of by the commentators.

‡ Ver. 1.

|| Horace, says POPE, in the advertisement to this piece, made his court to this great prince (or rather this cool and subtle

abject adulation, degraded himſelf by paying to Auguſtus, Pope has converted into bitter and pointed ſarcaſms, conveyed under the form of the moſt artful irony. Of this irony the following ſpecimens ſhall be placed together, in one view, added to the preceding lines, which are of the ſame caſt.

Wonder of kings! like whom, to mortal eyes,
None e'er has riſen, and none e'er ſhall riſe *.
How ſhall we fill a library with wit,
When Merlin's cave is half unfiniſh'd yet †?

ſubtle tyrant) by writing with a decent freedom towards him, with a juſt contempt of his low flatterers, and with a manly regard to his own character." Surely he forgot,

Jurandaſque tibi per *Numen* ponimus *aras*,
Nil oriturum alias, nil ortum tale fatentes, &c.

We ſometimes ſpeak incorrectly of what are called the writers of the *Auguſtan* age. Terence, Lucretius, Catullus, Tully, J. Cæſar, and Salluſt, wrote *before* the time of Auguſtus; and Livy, Virgil, Horace, Tibullus, and Propertius, were not made good writers by his patronage and encouragement. Virgil had the courage to repreſent his hero aſſiſting the Etruſcans in puniſhing their tyrannical king. Lib. 8. v. 495. One of the moſt unaccountable prejudices that ever obtained, ſeems to be that of celebrating Auguſtus for clemency.

* Ver. 29. † Ver. 354.

My

My liege! why writers little claim your thought,
I guefs; and with their leave will tell the fault *.
Yet think, great Sir! fo many virtues fhown,
Ah, think what poet beft may make them known!
Or chufe at leaft fome minifter of grace,
Fit to beftow the Laureat's weighty place †.
Oh could I mount on the Mæonian wing,
Your arms, your actions, your *repofe*, to fing!
What feas you travers'd, and what fields you fought,
Your country's peace, how oft, how dearly bought!
How barbarous rage fubfided at your word,
And nations wonder'd while they dropp'd the fword!
How when you nodded, o'er the land and deep,
Peace ftole her wing, and wrapt the world in fleep;
Till earth's extremes your mediation own,
And Afia's tyrants tremble at your throne.
But verfe, alas! your majefty difdains,
And I'm not us'd to panegyric ftrains:
Befides, a fate attends on all I write,
That when I aim at praife, they fay I bite ‡.

It may be obferved, in general, that the imitations of thefe *two* epiftles of the *fecond* book of Horace, are finifhed with fo much accuracy and care, and abound in fo many applications and allufions moft nicely and luckily adapted to the original

* Ver. 356. † Ver. 376.

‡ Ver. 394.

paf-

passages *, that a minute comparison would be useless. In a very few instances, however, he may be thought to fall short of his model. This appears in the account of the rise of poetry among the Romans, v. 139—because he could not possibly find a parallel for the sacrifices paid to *Tellus*, and *Silvanus*, and the *Genius*, nor to the licentiousness of the Fescennine verses, which were restrained by a law of the Twelve Tables.

POPE has also failed in ascribing that introduction of our polite literature to *France*, which Horace attributes to Greece among the *Romans*, (v. 156. orig.) It was to Italy, among the moderns, that we owed our true taste in poetry. *Spencer* and *Milton* imitated the Italians, and not the French. And if he had correctness in his view, let us remember, that in point of *regularity* and *correctness*, the French †

* Particularly in Ep. i. v. 65. 80. 92. 181. 215. 315. 340. 390. In Ep. ii. v. 90. 105. 158. 203. 230. 270.

† The very first French play, in which the rules were observed, was the *Sophonisba* of *Mairet*, 1633.

had

had no dramatic piece equal to the *Silent Woman* of *Ben Johnſon*, performed 1609. At which time *Corneille* was but three years old. The *rules* of the *drama* are as much violated in the * *Cid*, 1637, beautiful as it is, as in the *Macbeth*, *Lear*, and *Othello*, all written before *Corneille* was born; whoſe firſt comedy, *Melite*, which is now never acted, was repreſented 1625. The pieces of the very fertile *Hardy* (for he wrote ſix hundred) the immediate prede-

* Father *Tournemine* uſed to relate, that M. de *Chalons*, who had been ſecretary to *Mary de Medicis*, and had retired to Rouen, was the perſon who adviſed Corneille to ſtudy the Spaniſh language; and read to him ſome paſſages of Guillon de *Caſtro*, which ſtruck Corneille ſo much, that he determined to imitate his *Cid*. The artifices uſed by *Richlieu*, and the engines he ſet to work to cruſh this fine play, are well known. Not one of the Cardinal's tools was ſo vehement as the Abbé *d' Aubignac*; who attacked Corneille on account of his family, his perſon, his geſture, his voice, and even the conduct of his domeſtic affairs. When the *Cid* firſt appeared (ſays Fontenelle) the Cardinal was as much alarmed as if he had ſeen the Spaniards at the gates of Paris. In the year 1635, *Richlieu*, in the midſt of the important political concerns that occupied his mighty genius, wrote the greateſt part of a play, called, *La comedie des Tuilleries*, in which Corneille propoſed ſome alterations to be made in the third act: which honeſt freedom the Cardinal never forgave.

ceſſor of *Corneille*, are full of improbabilities, indecorums, and abſurdities, and by no means comparable to *Melite*. As to the *correctneſs* of the French ſtage, of which we hear ſo much, the rules of the three unities are indeed rigorouſly and ſcrupulouſly obſerved *; but the beſt of their tragedies, even *ſome* of thoſe of the ſweet and exact *Racine*, have defects of another kind, and are what may be juſtly called, *deſcriptive* and *declamatory* dramas; and contain the ſentiments and feelings of the *author* or the *ſpectator*, rather than of the *perſon* introduced as ſpeaking. "After the reſtoration, ſays POPE in the margin, Waller, with the Earl of Dorſet, Mr. Godolphin, and others, tranſlated the Pompey of Corneille; and the more correct French poets began to be in reputation." But the model was unfortunately and injudiciouſly choſen; for the Pompey of Corneille is one of his moſt declamatory † tragedies.

* As they are certainly in *Samſon Agoniſtes*.

† See the Eſſay on Shakeſpeare by Mrs. Montague, in which ſhe has done honour to her ſex and nation; and which

gedies. And the rhyme tranſlation they gave of it, is performed pitifully enough. Even Voltaire confeſſes, that Corneille is always making his heroes ſay of themſelves, that they are great men. It is in this paſſage that POPE ſays of two great maſters of verſification;

Waller was ſmooth; but *Dryden* taught to join
The varying verſe, the full-reſounding line,
The long majeſtic march, and energy divine *.

WHAT! did Milton contribute nothing to the harmony and extent of our language?

which was ſent to Voltaire with this motto prefixed to it; by a perſon who admired it as a piece of exquiſite criticiſm:

—— PALLAS Te hoc Vulnere, PALLAS
Immolat———— VIRG.

The Iphigenie of Racine, it muſt be owned, is an incomparable piece; it is chiefly ſo, from Racine's attentive ſtudy of the pathetic Euripides. Corneille had not read the Greek tragedies. He was able to read Ariſtotle's Poetics only in Heinſius's tranſlation. It is remarkable, that there is not a ſingle line in Otway or Rowe from the Greek tragedies. And Dryden in his Œdipus has imitated Seneca and Corneille, not Sophocles.

Taſſo, in one of his letters to a friend, deſires him to procure for him a copy of Sophocles and Euripides; but adds, that he begs it may be in Latin, and not in Greek.

Smith, though a ſcholar, has ſcarcely imitated Euripides at all, in his Phædra.

* Ver. 267.

guage? nothing to our national taſte, by his noble imitations of Homer, Virgil, and the Greek tragedies? Surely his *verſes vary*, and *reſound* as much, and diſplay as much *majeſty* and *energy*, as any that can be found in *Dryden*. And we will venture to ſay, that he that ſtudies *Milton* attentively, will gain a truer taſte for genuine poetry, than he that forms himſelf on French writers, and their followers *. His name ſurely was not to be omitted on this occaſion.

The other paſſages in which Pope appears not to be equal to his original, are, in the three little ſtories which Horace has introduced into his ſecond epiſtle, with ſo much nature and humour; namely, the ſtory of the ſlave-ſeller, at verſe 2; that of the ſoldier of Lucullus, at verſe 26; and the ſtory of the madman at Argos,

* It is difficult, methinks, to read the following words of *Voltaire*, without feeling a little indignation. "It ſeems as if the ſame cauſe that deprives the Engliſh of a genius for Painting and Muſic, denies them alſo a genius for Tragedy." Letter to Maffei. T. 8. p. 225.

verſe

verſe 128. The laſt, particularly, loſes much of its grace and propriety, by transferring the ſcene from the theatre to the parliament-houſe, from poetry to politics.

64. Two noblemen of taſte and learning, the Duke of Shrewſbury and the Earl of Oxford, deſired POPE to melt down and caſt anew the weighty bullion of Dr. Donne's ſatires; who had degraded and deformed a vaſt fund of ſterling wit and ſtrong ſenſe, by the moſt harſh and uncouth diction. POPE ſucceeded in giving harmony to a writer, more rough and rugged than even any of his age, and who profited ſo little by the example *Spencer* had ſet, of a moſt muſical and mellifluous verſification; far beyond the verſification of *Fairfax*, who is ſo frequently mentioned as the greateſt improver of the harmony of our language. The ſatires of *Hall*, written in very ſmooth and pleaſing numbers, preceded thoſe of *Donne* many years; for his *Virgidemiarum* were publiſhed, in ſix books, in the year 1597; in which he calls him-

ſelf the very firſt Engliſh ſatiriſt. This, however, was not true in fact; for Sir Thomas Wyatt, of Allington Caſtle in Kent, the friend and favourite of *Henry VIII.* and, as was ſuggeſted, of *Ann Boleyn*, was our firſt writer of ſatire worth notice. But it was not in his numbers only that Donne was reprehenſible. He abounds in falſe thoughts, in far-ſought ſentiments, in forced unnatural conceits. He was the corrupter of *Cowley*. *Dryden* was the firſt who called him a *metaphyſical* poet. He had a conſiderable ſhare of * learning; and, though he entered late into orders, yet was eſteemed a good divine. *James I.* was ſo earneſt to prefer him in the church,

* He was one of our poets who wrote elegantly in Latin; as did *Ben Johnſon*, (who tranſlated into that language great part of Bacon de Augmentis Scient.) *Cowley*, *Milton*, *Addiſon*, and *Gray*. In Donne's introduction to his witty catalogue of curious books, written plainly in imitation of *Rabelais*, (whom alſo *Swift* imitated, in a catalogue of odd treatiſes, prefixed to the Tale of a Tub) there is a paſſage ſo minutely applicable to the preſent times, that I am tempted to tranſcribe it. Ævum ſortiti ſumus, quo planè indoctis nihil turpius, plenè doctis nihil rarius. Tam omnes in literis aliquid ſciunt, tam nemo omnia. Mediâ igitur plerumque itur viâ, & ad evitandám ignorantiæ turpitudinem, & legendi faſtidium.

that

that he even refufed the Earl of Somerfet, his favourite, the requeft he earneftly made, of giving Donne an office in the council. In the entertaining account of that converfation which *Ben Johnfon* is faid to have held with Mr. Drummond of Hawthornden in Scotland, in the year 1619, containing his judgments of the Englifh poets, he fpeaks thus of Donne, who was his intimate friend, and had frequently addreft him in various poems. "Donne was originally a poet; his grandfather on the mother's fide was Heywood the epigrammatift; that Donne, for not being underftood, would perifh. He efteemed him the firft poet in the world for fome things; his verfes of the loft Ochadine he had by heart, and that paffage of the calm, that duft and feathers did not ftir, all was fo quiet. He affirmed, that Donne wrote all his beft pieces before he was twenty-five years of age. The conceit of Donne's transformation, or metempfychofis, was, that he fought the foul of that apple which Eve pulled, and hereafter made it the ſoul of a bitch, then of a ſhe-wolf, and ſo of a woman; his general purpoſe was to have brought it into all the bodies of the heretics, from the ſoul of Cain, and at laſt left it in the body of Calvin. He only wrote one ſheet of this, and ſince he was made doctor repented earneſtly, and reſolved to deſtroy all his poems. He told Donne, that his Anniverſary was prophane, and full of blaſphemies; that if it had been written on the Virgin Mary, it had been tolerable: to which Donne anſwered, that he deſcribed the idea of a woman, and not as ſhe was *."

65. THE two Dialogues, entitled One thouſand ſeven hundred and thirty-eight, which are the laſt pieces that belong to this ſection, were more frequently tranſcribed, and received more alterations and

* And *B. Johnſon* again in his *Diſcoveries*:—" As it is fit to read the *beſt* authors to youth *firſt*, ſo let them be of the *openeſt* and the *cleareſt*. As *Livy* before *Salluſt*, and *Sydney* before *Donne*." But *Milton*, in one of his Latin letters, prefers *Salluſt* to all the Roman hiſtorians.

corrections,

corrections, than almost any of the foregoing poems. By long habit of writing, and almost constantly in one sort of measure, he had now arrived at a happy and elegant familiarity of style, without flatness. The satire in these pieces is of the strongest kind; sometimes, direct and declamatory, at others, ironical and oblique. It must be owned to be carried to excess. Our country is represented as totally ruined, and overwhelmed with dissipation, depravity, and corruption. Yet this very country, so emasculated and debased by every species of folly and wickedness, in about twenty years afterwards, carried its triumphs over all its enemies, through all the quarters * of the world, and astonished the most distant nations with a display of uncommon efforts, abilities, and virtues. So vain and groundless are the prognostications of poets, as well as politicians. It is to be lamented, that no genius could be

* We cannot ascribe these successes, as M. de Voltaire does, to the effects of *Brown's Estimate*. See Additions à l'Hist. Generale, p. 409.

found to write an *One Thousand Seven Hundred and Sixty-one*, as a counterpart to these two satires. Several passages deserve particular notice and applause. The design of the Friend, introduced in these dialogues, is to dissuade our poet from *personal* invectives. He desires him to copy the sly, insinuating style of Horace; and dexterously turns the very advice he is giving into the bitterest satire.

Horace would say, Sir Billy *serv'd the Crown*,
Blunt could *do business*, H—ggins *knew the town*:
In Sappho touch the *failings* of the sex,
In rev'rend bishops note some *small neglects*;
And own the Spaniard did a *waggish* thing,
Who cropt our ears and sent them to the king *.

THE character of Sir Robert Walpole was dictated by candour and gratitude; distinguishing the minister from the man.

Seen him I have, but in his happier hour
Of social pleasure, ill-exchang'd for pow'r;
Seen him, uncumber'd with the venal tribe,
Smile without art, and win without a bribe †.

* Ver. 13. † Ver. 28.

THIS

THIS character, together with that drawn of the ſame miniſter by Hume, in his fourth eſſay, will perhaps contribute to give a diſpaſſionate poſterity a more amiable idea of him than we uſually allow him, and counterwork the ſpirited and eloquent *Diſſertation* on Parties. Nothing can be more animated and lively, than where our author, ſeeming to follow the cautious admonitions of his friend, replies,

> Come, harmleſs characters, that no one hit,
> Come, Henley's oratory, Oſborn's wit,
> The honey dropping from Favonio's tongue,
> The flow'rs of Bubo, and the flow of Young!
> The gracious dew of pulpit eloquence,
> And all the well-whipt cream of courtly ſenſe * !

To which muſt be added a ſtroke that cuts to the quick; eſpecially the laſt line; which alludes to a very remarkable and particular anecdote, of the Queen's behaviour to her ſon.

> Or teach the melancholy muſe to mourn,
> Hang the ſad verſe on Carolina's urn;
> And hail her paſſage to the realms of reſt,
> All *parts* perform'd, and *all* her children bleſt †.

* Ver. 65. † Ver. 79.

I RECOLLECT no paſſage in Horace, Juvenal, or Boileau, more ſtrongly pointed, or more well-turned, than where our poet inſiſts that the *dignity* of *vice* muſt not be loſt.

Ye gods! ſhall * Cibber's ſon, without rebuke,
Swear like a lord, or Rich out-whore a duke?
A fav'rite's porter with his maſter vie,
Be brib'd as often, and as often lie?
Shall Ward draw contracts with a ſtateſman's ſkill,
Or Japhet pocket, like his Grace, a will?
Is it for Bond, or Peter, (paltry things!)
To pay their debts, or keep their faith like kings?
This, this, my friend, I cannot, muſt not bear,
Vice thus abus'd demands a nation's care †.

THE noble deſcription of the triumph of VICE, one of the moſt pictureſque in all his works, muſt not be here omitted.

Lo! at the wheels of her triumphal car,
Old England's Genius, rough with many a ſcar,
Dragg'd in the duſt; his arms hang idly round,
His flag inverted trails along the ground!
Our youth, all liv'ry'd o'er with foreign gold,
Before her dance; behind her, crawl the old!

* The names of *Cibber*, *Chartres*, *Ward*, *Walters*, *Japhet*, and ſome others, are ſo very often repeated, that they diſguſt the reader.

† Ver. 128.

See

See thronging millions to the pagod run,
And offer country, parent, wife, or son!
Hear her black trumpet through the land proclaim,
That Not To Be Corrupted is the shame *.

SWIFT tells him, in a letter dated August 8, 1738, that he takes his second dialogue to equal any thing he had ever writ. The same Friend is here again introduced making such remonstrances as before. And several parts of the dialogue are more rapid, and approach nearer to conversation than any lines he had ever before written:

P. The pois'ning dame.—F. You mean.—P. I don't.
F. You do.
P. See now I keep the secret, and not you.
The bribing statesman.—F. Hold—too high you go—
P. The brib'd elector.—F. There you stoop too low.
P. I fain would please, if I but knew with what;
Tell me what knave is lawful game, or not.
Suppose I censure—you know what I mean;
To save a † bishop, may I name a dean?

* Ver. 150.

† Some of the reverend bench, and particularly one of a truly-exalted character, are injuriously treated in line 70.

Ev'n in a *bishop*, I can spy desert;
Secker is *decent*——— ——

The exemplary life, and extensive learning, of this great prelate, are sufficient and ample confutations of the *invidious epithet* here used; which those, who are acquainted with his Lectures and Sermons, in which is found a rare mixture of simplicity and energy, read with indignation.

F. A dean,

F. A dean, Sir?—No—his ſortune is not made;
You hurt a man that's riſing in the trade *.

WEARIED with the ſeverity and poignancy of moſt of the preceding paſſages, we look with delight on the pleaſing enumeration of his illuſtrious and valuable friends:

Oft, in the clear, ſtill mirrour of retreat,
I ſtudy'd *Shrewſbury*, the wiſe and great:
Carleton's calm ſenſe, and *Stanhope*'s noble flame,
Compar'd, and knew their gen'rous end the ſame.
How pleaſing *Atterbury*'s ſofter hour!
How ſhin'd the ſoul, unconquer'd in the Tow'r!
How can I † *Pult'ney*, *Cheſterfield*, forget,
While Roman ſpirit charms, and Attic wit;
Argyle, the ſtate's whole thunder born to wield,
And ſhake alike the ſenate and the field;
Or *Wyndham*, juſt to freedom and the throne,
The maſter of our paſſions, and his own ‡?

* Ver. 35.

† That *Pulteney* had a more manly *underſtanding* than *Cheſterfield*, will not be doubted: but I verily believe he had alſo more true *wit*. The two lines on *Argyle* are ſaid to have been added, on the duke's declaring in the Houſe of Lords, on occaſion of ſome of Pope's ſatires, that if any man dared to uſe his name in an invective, he would run him through the body, and throw himſelf on the mercy of his peers, who, he truſted, would weigh the provocation. *Bolingbroke*'s Letter to *Wyndham*, is one of the moſt curious of his works, and gave a deadly and incurable blow to the folly and madneſs of Jacobitiſm.

‡ Ver. 78.

AMONG

AMONG these, *Atterbury* was his chief intimate. The turbulent and imperious temper of this haughty prelate was long felt and remembered in the college over which he presided. It was with difficulty Queen Anne was persuaded to make him a bishop; which she did at last, on the repeated importunities of Lord Harcourt, who pressed the queen to do it, because truly she had before disappointed him, in not placing Sacheverell on the bench. After her decease, Atterbury vehemently urged his friends to proclaim the Pretender; and on their refusal, upbraided them for their timidity with many oaths; for he was accustomed to swear, on any strong provocation. In a collection of letters lately published by Mr. Duncombe, it is affirmed, on the authority of *Elijah Fenton*, that Atterbury, speaking of POPE, said, there was

Mens curva in Corpore curvo.

This sentiment seems utterly inconsistent with the warm friendship supposed to subsist between these two celebrated men. But

But Dr. Herring, in the 2d vol. of this collection, p. 104, ſays; "If Atterbury was not worſe uſed, than any honeſt man in the world ever was, there were ſtrong contradictions between his public and private character." There is an anecdote, ſo uncommon and remarkable, lately mentioned in Dr. *Maty*'s Memoirs of the Earl of Cheſterfield, and which he gives in the very words of that celebrated nobleman, that I cannot forbear repeating it in this place:—"I went, ſaid Lord Cheſterfield, to Mr. POPE, one morning at Twickenham, and found a large folio bible, with gilt claſps, lying before him upon his table; and, as I knew his way of thinking upon that book, I aſked him, jocoſely, if he was going to write an anſwer to it? It is a preſent, ſaid he, or rather a legacy, from my old friend the Biſhop of Rocheſter. I went to take my leave of him yeſterday in the Tower, where I ſaw this bible upon his table. After the firſt compliments, the Biſhop ſaid to me, My friend POPE, conſidering your infirmities, and my age

and

and exile, it is not likely that we ſhould ever meet again; and therefore I give you this legacy to remember me by it.—Does your lordſhip abide by it yourſelf?—I do.—If you do, my lord, it is but lately. May I beg to know what new light or arguments have prevailed with you now, to entertain an opinion ſo contrary to that which you entertained of that book all the former part of your life?—The Biſhop replied, We have not time to talk of theſe things; but take home the book; I will abide by it, and I recommend you to do ſo too, and ſo God bleſs you!"—Charity and juſtice call on us, not haſtily to credit ſo marvellous a tale, without the ſtrongeſt teſtimony for its truth. In one of thoſe entertaining letters, which the Biſhop wrote about the year 1727, to a Mr. Thiriot *, a French gentleman, we find a ſtriking

* In one of theſe letters he ſpeaks thus of Sir *Iſaac Newton*:—The very lively and piercing eye that Mr. Fontenelle, in his famous eulogium, gives him, did not belong to him, at leaſt not for twenty years paſt, about which time I firſt became acquainted with him. Indeed, in the whole air of his face and make, there was nothing of that penetrating ſagacity which appears in his works. He had ſomething rather languid in his look and manner, which did not raiſe any great expectation in thoſe who did not know him.

ſtriking remark on the Biſhop of Meaux *. "There is a ſerious warmth in all he ſays, and his manner of ſaying it is noble and moving; and yet I queſtion, after all, whether he *ſometimes is in good earneſt.*" *Atterbury* was, on the whole, rather a man of ability than a genius. He writes more with elegance and correctneſs, than with any force of thinking or reaſoning. His letters to POPE are too much crowded with very trite quotations from the claſſics. It is ſaid, he either tranſlated, or intended to tranſlate, the Georgics of Virgil, and to write the life of Cardinal Wolſey, whom he much reſembled. Dr. Warburton had a mean opinion of his critical abilities, and of his diſcourſe on the *Iäpis of Virgil.* He was thought to be the author of the life of Waller, prefixed to the firſt octavo edition of that poet's works.

* Before he compoſed a funeral oration, he uſed to ſhut himſelf up for four or five days, and read Homer. Being aſked the reaſon of this practice, he replied;

———Magnam mihi mentem, animumque
Delius inſpirat vates———

THERE

THERE is a happy imitation of *Perſius*, and of *Boileau*, at verſe 128.

——Come then, I'll comply;
Spirit of *Arnall!* aid me while I lie!
Cobham's a coward, *Polwarth* is a ſlave,
And *Lyttelton* a dark deſigning knave;
St. John has ever been a wealthy fool;
But let me add, Sir *Robert's* mighty dull.

This is the paſſage of *Perſius*, Sat. i. v. 110.

——Per me equidem ſint omnia protinus alba,
Nil moror; Euge, omnes, omnes, bene miræ eritis res;
Hoc juvat?——

And thus *Boileau*, Sat. ix. v. 287.

Puiſque vous le voulez, je vais changer de ſtile,
Je le declare donc, Quinault eſt un Virgile.
Pradon comme un ſoleil en nos ans a paru.
Pelletier ecrit mieux qu'Ablancourt ni Patru.
Cotin, à ſes ſermons trainant toute la terre,
Fend les flots d'Auditeurs pour aller à ſa chaire.

But POPE has plainly the ſuperiority, by the artful and ironical compliments to his friends.

THE beaſtly ſimile, at line 171, may ſafely be pronounced, however difficult it may

may be in many cases to trace resemblances, to be taken from a passage in the Remains of *Butler*, the incomparable author of *Hudibras:*

> Let courtly wits to wits afford supply,
> As hog to hog in huts of *Westphaly*;
> If one, through nation's bounty, or his lord's,
> Has what the frugal dirty soil affords,
> From him the next receives it, thick or thin,
> As pure a mess almost as it came in;
> The blessed benefit, not there confin'd,
> Drops to the third, who nuzzles close behind;
> From tail to mouth they feed, and they carouse,
> The last full fairly gives it to the *House*.

THE passage in *Butler* runs thus:—"Our modern authors write plays, as they feed hogs in *Westphalia*; where but one eats pease or acorns, and all the rest feed upon his, and one another's *excrements*." Thoughts on Various Subjects, p. 497, v. 2.——Though those Remains were not published in the life-time of POPE, yet Mr. *Thyer* informs us, that Mr. *Longueville*, in whose custody they were, communicated them to *Atterbury*, from whom POPE might hear of them. 'Tis impossible any

any two writers could casually hit upon an image so very peculiar and uncommon.

I CONCLUDE this section by observing, that these Dialogues exhibit many marks of our author's petulance, party-spirit, and self-importance, and of assuming to himself the character of a general censor; who, alas! if he had possessed a thousand times more genius and ability than he actually enjoyed, could not alter or amend the manners of a rich and commercial, and, consequently, of a luxurious and dissipated nation. We make ourselves unhappy, by hoping to possess *incompatible* things; we want to have wealth, without corruption; and liberty without virtue.

SECT. XIII.

Of the DUNCIAD.

WHEN the firſt complete and correct edition of the Dunciad was publiſhed in quarto, 1729, it conſiſted of three books; and had for its hero *Tibbald*, a cold, plodding, and taſteleſs writer and critic, who, with great propriety, was choſen, on the death of *Settle*, by the Goddeſs of Dulneſs, to be the chief inſtrument of that great work which was the ſubject of the poem; namely, "the introduction (as our author expreſſes it) of the loweſt diverſions of the rabble of *Smithfield*, to be the entertainment of the court and town; the *action* of the Dunciad being, the removal of the imperial ſeat of Dulneſs from the city to the polite world; as that of the Æneid is the removal of the empire of *Troy to Latium*." This was the primary ſubject of the piece. Our author adds,

"as

"as *Homer*, ſinging only the wrath of Achilles, yet includes in his poem the whole hiſtory of the Trojan war; in like manner our poet hath drawn into this *ſingle action* the whole hiſtory of Dulneſs and her children. To this end, ſhe is repreſented, at the very opening of the poem, taking a view of her forces, which are diſtinguiſhed into theſe three kinds, party-writers, dull poets, and wild critics. A *perſon* muſt be fixed upon to ſupport *this action*, who (to agree with the *deſign*,) muſt be ſuch an one as is capable of being all three. This *phantom* in the poet's mind, muſt have a *name*. He ſeeks for one who hath been concerned in the *journals*, written bad *plays* or *poems*, and publiſhed low *criticiſms*. He finds his name to be *Tibbald* *, and

* Who was a kind of *Margites*. It is a ſingular fact in the hiſtory of literature, that the ſame mighty genius, who by his *Iliad* and *Odyſſey* became the founder of Tragedy, ſhould alſo, by his *Margites*, as Ariſtotle obſerves in the ſecond chapter of his Poetics, become the father of Comedy. This piece was written in various ſorts of metre, and particularly hexameter and iambic. Only three verſes remain of this piece, which was much celebrated by the ancients; one in the ſecond *Alcibiades* of *Plato*;

and he becomes of courſe the hero of the poem."

This deſign is carried on, in the *firſt* book, by a deſcription of the Goddeſs fixing her eye on Tibbald; who, on the evening of a lord-mayor's day, is repreſented as ſitting penſively in his ſtudy, and apprehending the period of her empire, from the old-age of the preſent monarch *Settle*; and alſo by an account of a ſacrifice he makes of his unſucceſsful works; of the Goddeſs's revealing herſelf to him, announcing the death of *Settle* that night, anointing and proclaiming him ſucceſſor. It is carried on in the *ſecond* book, by a deſcription of the various games inſtituted

"Ως αρα πολλα μεν εργα, κακως δ'ηπιςατο παντα.

Another in the ſixth book of *Ariſtotle*'s Ethics;

Τον δ' ετ' αρ' σκαπτηρα θεοι θεσαν, ετ' αροτηρα.

A third is cited by the ſcholiaſt of *Ariſtophanes*, in the *Birds*.

Μεσαων θεραπων, καὶ εκηβολε Απολλωνος.

The poem is mentioned by *Polybius*, *Dion Chryſoſtom*, *Plutarch*, *Lucian*, *Stobæus*, and others.

in

in honour of the new king, in which *booksellers*, *poets*, and *critics* contend. This design is, lastly, completed in the *third* book, by the Goddess's transporting the new king to her temple, laying him in a deep slumber on her lap, and conveying him in a vision to the banks of *Lethe*, where he meets with the ghost of his predecessor *Settle*; who, in a speech that begins at line 35, to almost the end of the book, shews him the past triumphs of the empire of Dulness, then the present, and lastly the future: enumerating particularly by what aids, and by what persons, *Great Britain* shall be forthwith brought to her empire, and prophesying how first the nation shall be over-run with farces, operas, shows; and the throne of Dulness advanced over both the theatres: then, how her sons shall preside in the seats of arts and sciences; till, in conclusion, all shall return to their original chaos. On hearing which,

Enough! enough! the raptur'd MONARCH cries;
And through the ivory gate the vision flies.

 with

with which words, the defign above recited, being perfected, the poem concludes. Thus far all was clear, confiftent, and of a piece; and was delivered in fuch nervous and fpirited verfification, that the delighted reader had only to lament that fo many poetical beauties were thrown away on fuch dirty and defpicable fubjects, as were the fcribblers here profcribed; who appear like monfters preferved in the moft coftly *fpirits*. But in the year 1742, our poet was perfuaded, unhappily enough, to add a *fourth* book to his *finifhed* piece, of fuch a very different caft and colour, as to render it at laft one of the moft motley compofitions, that perhaps is any where to be found, in the works of fo exact a writer as POPE. For one great purpofe of this *fourth* book, (where, by the way, the hero does nothing at all) was to fatirize and profcribe infidels, and free-thinkers, to leave the ludicrous for the ferious, Grub-ftreet for theology, the mock-heroic for metaphyfics; which occafioned a marvel-

lous

lous mixture and jumble of images and ſentiments, Pantomime and Philoſophy, Journals and Moral evidence, Fleet-ditch and the High Priori road, *Curl* and *Clarke*. —To ridicule our petulant libertines, and affected minute philoſophers, was doubtleſs a moſt laudable intention; but ſpeaking of the Dunciad as a work of art, in a critical not a religious light, I muſt venture to affirm, that the ſubject of this fourth book was foreign and heterogeneous, and the addition of it as injudicious, ill-placed, and incongruous, as any of thoſe diſſimilar images we meet with in *Pulci* or *Arioſto*. It is like introducing a crucifix into one of *Teniers*'s burleſque converſation-pieces. Some of his moſt ſplendid and ſtriking lines are indeed here to be found; but I muſt beg leave to inſiſt that they want *propriety* and *decorum*, and muſt wiſh they had adorned ſome *ſeparate* work, againſt irreligion, which would have been worthy the pen of our bitter and immortal ſatiriſt.

But neither was this the only alteration the Dunciad was destined to undergo. For in the year 1743, our author, enraged with *Cibber*, (whom he had usually treated with contempt ever since the affair of *Three Hours after Marriage*) for publishing a ridiculous pamphlet against him, dethroned *Tibbald*, and made the Laureate the hero of his poem. *Cibber*, with a great stock of levity, vanity, and affectation, had sense, and wit, and humour. And the author of the *Careless Husband*, was by no means a proper king of the dunces. "His treatise on the Stage, says Mr. Walpole, is inimitable: where an author writes on his own profession, feels it profoundly, and is sensible his readers do not, he is not only excusable but meritorious, for illuminating the subject by new metaphors, or bolder figures than ordinary. He is the *coxcomb* that sneers, not he that instructs by appropriated diction." The consequence of this alteration was, that many lines, which exactly suited the heavy character of *Tibbald*,

bald, loſt all their grace and propriety when applied * to *Cibber*. Such as,

Sinking from thought to thought, a vaſt profound!

Such alſo is the deſcription of his gothic library; for Cibber troubled not himſelf with *Caxton*, *Wynkyn*, and *De Lyra*. *Tibbald*, who was an antiquarian, had collected theſe curious old writers. And to ſlumber in the Goddeſs's lap was adapted to *his ſtupidity*, not to the *vivacity* of his ſucceſſor,

If we now deſcend, from theſe remarks on the general *deſign* and conſtitution of the Dunciad, to particular paſſages, the following muſt be mentioned, as highly finiſhed, and worked up with peculiar elegance and force. In book i. the Chaos of Abſurd

* 'Tis dangerous to diſoblige a great poet or painter. *Dante* placed his maſter *Brunetto* in his *Inferno*. *Brunetto* was a man of ſenſe and learning, and wrote an abridgment of Ariſtotle's Ethics. It is remarkable that he uſed to ſay, the French language will, one day, become the moſt univerſal and common of all the languages in Europe. And *Michael Angelo* placed the Pope's maſter of the ceremonies, *Biaggio*, in hell, in his Laſt Judgment.

Writings,

Writings, v. 55, to v. 78. In book ii. v. 35, the Phantom of a Poet, to v. 50. The Defcription of the Tapeftry, v. 143, to v. 156. The Adventures of Smedley, and what he faw in the fhades below, v. 331, to v. 350. The Effects of hearing two dull Authors read, v. 387, to the end of that book. In book iii. the Ghoft of *Settle*, v. 35, to v. 66. View of Learning, v. 83, to v. 102. The Defcription of Pantomimes, Farces, and their monftrous Abfurdities, v. 235, to v. 264. In book iv. v. 1, to v. 16. The Modern Traveller, v. 295, to v. 330. The Florift, v. 403, to v. 420. The Butterfly-hunter, v. 421, to v. 436. The Effects of the *Yawn*, from v. 627, to the end. The frequent * parodies introduced on Homer, Virgil,

* Many of the ancients were fond of parodies. It is well known how many *Ariftophanes* has given us on *Euripides* and other tragedians. *Athenæus*, in the 9th book of his Deipnos, p. 406, informs us, that Chamæleon of Pontus faid, that *Hegemon* was the firft author very famous for parodies. He was called, φακη (*Lenticula.*) He was alfo an excellent actor; and the Athenians were fo fond of him, that one day, when news was brought of their defeat in Sicily,

Virgil, Milton, and other great poets, than which nothing has a ſtronger effect in heroi-comic poems, are made with ſingular pleaſantry, happineſs, and judgment.

But juſt criticiſm calls on us alſo to point out ſome of thoſe paſſages that appear exceptionable in the Dunciad. Such, in book i. v. 163, is the hero's firſt ſpeech; in which, contrary to all decorum and probability, he addreſſes the Goddeſs Dulneſs, without diſguiſing her, as a deſpicable being; and even calls himſelf Fool and Blockhead;

Me emptineſs and dulneſs could inſpire,
And were my elaſticity and fire.——
Did on the ſtage my fops appear confin'd?
My life gave ampler leſſons to mankind.——
What then remains? Ourſelf ſtill, ſtill remain,
Cibberian forehead, and Cibberian brain.——

Sicily, they would not quit the theatre, but inſiſted that *Hegemon* ſhould finiſh the piece. He was a great favourite of *Alcibiades*; of whom, and Hegemon, *Athenæus* relates a ſtory worth the reader's peruſal, p. 407. edit. *Caſaubon*. Lugduni, 1612. There are ſome excellent parodies in the *Rehearſal*, in Bramſton's *Art of Politics*, in the *Scribleriad*, and the works of *Fielding*.

For

For a perſon to be introduced, ſpeaking thus of himſelf, is in truth outrageouſly unnatural and out of character.

At v. 300, in this book, alſo, is a ſtroke of profaneneſs that cannot paſs unblamed:

Lift up your gates, ye princes, ſee him come!
Sound ſound, ye viols; be the catcall dumb!

So alſo, book iii. v. 126. (and book iv. v. 562.)

Dove-like, ſhe gathers to her wings again.

And in the arguments he talks of giving a *Piſgah-ſight* of the future *fulneſs* of *her glory*, and of ſending prieſts and *comforters*. In book ii. the filthineſs of the images, v. 93, and v. 160, is extremely offenſive and diſguſting. In book iii. the ridicule on the uſeful and curious publications of *Hearne*, was very undeſerved. In book iv. the Genius of the ſchools is made to declare, v. 148, that,

Words

Words are man's province, words we teach alone;
Confine the thought, to exercise the breath,
And keep them in the pale of words till death.

Surely our author, when he passed this censure, was ill-informed of what was taught and expected in our great schools; namely, besides reading, interpreting, and translating the best poets, orators, and historians, of the best ages, to be able to compose Essays, Declamations, and Verses, in *Greek*, in *Latin*, and in *English*; and in some of these schools, to write critical remarks on Homer, Sophocles, Demosthenes, *Aristotle*'s Poetics, or *Longinus*; an exercise not of the memory, but judgment. And as to *plying* the *memory*, and *loading* the *brain* (see verse 157) it was the opinion of Milton, and is a practice in our great seminaries *, "that if passages from the heroic poems, orations, and tragedies of the ancients were solemnly pronounced, with right accent and grace, as might be taught,

* What is said on this subject by Quintilian, b. i. and 2. is as much superior to Locke's Treatise on Education, in strength of reasoning, as it is in elegance of style.

taught, (*and is*) they would endue the ſcholars even with the ſpirit and vigour of *Demoſthenes* or *Cicero, Euripides* or *Sophocles*." The illuſtrious names of *Wyndham, Talbot, Murray*, and *Pulteney*, which our author himſelf immediately adds, and which catalogue might be much enlarged, with the names of many great ſtateſmen, lawyers, and divines, are a ſtrong confutation of this opprobrious opinion. In book iv. v. 210. is juſt ſuch another breach of truth and decorum as was remarked above, in making *Ariſtarchus (Bentley)* abuſe *himſelf*, and laugh at *his own* labours:

Thy mighty ſcholiaſt, whoſe unweary'd pains
Made Horace dull, and humbled Maro's ſtrains.
Turn what they will to verſe, their toil is vain,
Critics like *Me*, ſhall make it proſe again.
For attic phraſe in Plato let them ſeek,
I poach in Suidas for unlicens'd Greek.—
For thee we dim the eyes, and ſtuff the head,
With all ſuch reading, as was never read;
For thee explain a thing till all men doubt it,
And write about it, Goddeſs! and about it.

Lastly, in this 4th book, the ſudden appearance of Annius, v. 347, of Mummius, 371, and of a gloomy clerk, v. 459, make this part of the poem obſcure, as we know not who theſe perſonages are, nor whence they came. After all, the chief fault of the Dunciad is the * violence and vehemence of its ſatire, and the exceſſive heighth to which it is carried; and which therefore I have heard compared to that

* Which ſour the temper of the reader; inſomuch that I know a perſon, whoſe name would be an ornament to theſe papers, if I was ſuffered to inſert it, who, after reading a book of the Dunciad, always *ſooths* himſelf, as he calls it, by turning to a canto in the Fairy Queen. This is not the caſe in that very delightful and beautiful poem, *Mac Flecnoe*, from which POPE has borrowed ſo many hints, and images, and ideas. But Dryden's poem was the offspring of *contempt*, and Pope's of *indignation*: one is full of *mirth*, and the other of *malignity*. A vein of pleaſantry is uniformly preſerved through the whole of Mac Flecnoe, and the piece begins and ends in the *ſame key*. It is natural and obvious to borrow a metaphor from muſic, when we are ſpeaking of a poem whoſe verſification is particularly and exquiſitely ſweet and harmonious. The numbers of the Dunciad, by being much laboured, and encumbered with epithets, have ſomething in them of ſtiffneſs and harſhneſs. Since the total decay of learning and genius was foretold in the Dunciad, how many very excellent pieces of *Criticiſm*, *Poetry*, *Hiſtory*, *Philoſophy*, and *Divinity*, have appeared in this country, and to what a degree of perfection has almoſt every art, either uſeful or elegant, been carried!

marvel-

marvellous column of boiling water, near mount *Hecla*, thrown upwards, above ninety feet, by the force of a ſubterraneous fire *.

* It is in a valley in Iceland, about ſixty miles from the ſea; it is called the fountain of *Geiſer*. Sir Joſeph Banks, our great philoſophical traveller, had the ſatisfaction of ſeeing this wonderful phænomenon.

SECT.

SECT. XIV. AND LAST.

Of some IMITATIONS *of* HORACE, *the* MISCELLANIES, EPITAPHS, *and* PROSE WORKS.

THE seventh epistle of the first book of Horace, and the sixth satire of the second, are here imitated in a style and manner different from the former imitations, in the burlesque and colloquial style and measure of Swift *; in which our author

* The following is written in the first leaf of a copy of Stevens's Herodotus, now in the library of Winchester college, in Swift's *own hand-writing,* and is a literary curiosity, being a specimen of his Latin.—" *Judicium de Herodoto post longum tempus relecto. Ctesias* mendacissimus *Herodotum* mendaciorum arguit, exceptis paucissimis, (ut mea fert sententia) omni modo excusandum. Cæterum diverticulis abundans hic pater historicorum, filum narrationis ad tædium abrumpit. Unde oritur (ut par est) legentibus confusio, et exinde oblivio. Quin et forsan ipsæ narrationes circumstantiis nimium pro re scatent. Quod ad cætera, hunc scriptorem inter apprimè laudandos censeo, neque Græcis neque barbaris plus æquo faventem aut iniquum; in orationibus fere brevem, simplicem, nec nimis frequentem.

author has not ſucceeded, but falls back, as was natural, from the familiar, into his own more high and pompous manner; as in the following lines, v. 125, Perditur hæc inter, &c.

Thus in a ſea of folly toſt,
My choiceſt hours of life are loſt;
Yet always wiſhing to retreat,
Oh, could I ſee my country ſeat!

And again at line 189; in the fable of the Mice;

Tell how the moon-beam trembling falls,
And tips with ſilver all the walls;
Palladian walls, Venetian doors,
Groteſco roofs, and ſtucco floors.

The difference of ſtyles is more perceivable, from the circumſtance of their being immediately ſubjoined to the lighter and leſs ornamental verſes of Swift.

frequentem. Neque abſunt dogmata e quibus eruditus lector prudentiam tam moralem quam civilem haurire poterit."——Swift, in his diſcourſe on the *Conteſts*, &c. appears to be well acquainted with *Thucydides*, *Polybius*, and *Dionyſ. Halicar.* and to have had a conſiderable knowledge of ancient hiſtory. Of all our poets, perhaps *Akenſide* was the beſt Greek ſcholar ſince *Milton*.

THE

THE firſt ode of the fourth book of Horace, is an elegant compliment to Mr. *Murray*, now *Lord Mansfield*. And it may be worth obſerving, that the meaſure POPE has choſen, is preciſely the ſame that *Ben Johnſon* uſed in a tranſlation of this very ode, in which are ſome lines ſmoother than our old bard's uſual ſtrains; p. 268,

> Then twice a day, in ſacred lays,
> The youths and tender maids ſhall ſing thy praiſe;
> And in the Salian manner meet
> Thrice round thy altar with their ivory feet.

I cannot forbear adding, that there is much harmony and eaſe of verſification in Ben Johnſon's ten *lyric pieces* addreſſed to *Charis*, in page 165 of his works.

THE ſecond ſtanza of the imitation of part of the ninth ode of Horace, book iv, is well expreſſed;

> Tho' daring Milton ſits ſublime,
> In Spencer native Muſes play;
> Nor yet ſhall Waller yield to time;
> Nor penſive Cowley's moral lay.

Pope seems to speak of Spencer with particular complacency. How much this author was his favourite, will appear from what he said to Mr. Spence; from whose anecdotes this passage is transcribed:—"There is something in Spencer that pleases one as strongly in one's old-age, as it did in one's youth; I read the Faery Queen when I was about *twelve*, with a vast deal of delight; and I think it gave me as much, when I read it over about a year or two ago."

Out of the fourth and following stanza, misled by his love of antithesis, he has formed a trifling epigram.

Vixere fortes ante Agamemnona
Multi; sed omnes illacrymalibes
Urgentur ignotique longâ
Nocte, carent quia vate sacro.

Vain was the Chief's, the Sage's pride!
They had no Poet, and they died.
In vain they schem'd, in vain they bled!
They had no Poet, and are dead!

But

But he has made ample amends, by the epiſtle addreſſed to the Earl of Oxford, when he preſented to that nobleman the poems of his old friend Parnelle *; in which epiſtle there is a weight of ſentiment, and majeſty of diction, which our author has no where ſurpaſſed. His † genius ſeems to have been invigorated and exalted by the high opinion he had juſtly conceived of the perſon to whom he was writing; who muſt be confeſſed, now that party-prejudices ‡ are worn away, to have

* He was a writer that improved gradually. Very wide is the difference betwixt his poems on the *Peace*, and on *Unnatural Flights* in Poetry, and betwixt his *Hymn* to Contentment, his *Fairy Tale*, his *Riſe* of Woman, his *Night-piece* on Death, and his *Hermit*. All five of them delicious morſels.

† I am well informed that Lord Bolingbroke was greatly mortified at Pope's beſtowing ſuch praiſes on his old antagoniſt, whom he mortally hated. Yet I have ſeen two original letters of Lord Bolingbroke to Lord Oxford, full of the moſt fulſome flattery, and profane applications of ſcripture.

‡ At the time when the Secret Committee was held to examine the conduct of Sir Robert Walpole, who was the perſon that impeached the Earl of Oxford, Mr. Harley made an admirable ſpeech in the Houſe of Commons, declaring, that he would not treat Walpole, as he had treated his relation; and immediately left the Houſe without giving his vote againſt him. Sir Robert ſeemed much affected with this generous behaviour of Mr. Harley.

had great genius, learning, and honeſty. Strength of mind appears to have been his predominant characteriſtic; of which he gave the moſt ſtriking proofs, when he was *ſtabbed, diſplaced, impriſoned.* Theſe circumſtances are alluded to in thoſe noble and nervous verſes;

> And ſure, if aught below the ſeats divine,
> Can touch immortals, 'tis a ſoul like thine!
> A ſoul ſupreme in each hard inſtance try'd,
> Above all pain, all paſſion, and all pride;
> The rage of pow'r, the blaſt of public breath,
> The luſt of lucre, and the dread of death.

And of which fortitude and firmneſs another ſtriking proof ſtill remains, in a letter which the Earl wrote from the Tower to a friend who adviſed him to meditate an eſcape, and which is worthy of the greateſt hero of antiquity. This extraordinary letter I had the pleaſure of reading, by the favour of his excellent grand-daughter, the preſent Dutcheſs Dowager of Portland, who inherits that love of literature and ſcience, ſo peculiar to her anceſtors and family.

JERVAS owed much more of his reputation to the epiſtle POPE ſent to him, with Dryden's tranſlation of *Freſnoy**, than to his ſkill as a painter. He was defective, ſays Mr. Walpole, in drawing, colouring, and compoſition; and even in that moſt neceſſary, and perhaps moſt eaſy talent of a portrait-painter, likeneſs. In general, his pictures are a light flimſy kind of fan-painting, as large as the life. His vanity was exceſſive. The reaſon why Lady *Bridgewater*'s name is ſo frequently repeated in this epiſtle, is, becauſe he affected to be violently in love with her. Yet his vanity † was greater than his paſſion. One

* This didactic poem of Freſnoy, is but a cold, unintereſting, unpoetical, performance. He was the intimate of *Mignard*, the rival of *Le Brun*. At the end of the life of *Mignard*, are three dialogues on painting, written by *Fenelon*, in a moſt exquiſite taſte, and which are here mentioned becauſe they are little known, and not inſerted in the works of *Fenelon*, and are worthy to be read even after the admirable tenth chapter of the twelfth book of *Quintilian*.

† He tranſlated Don Quixote, without underſtanding Spaniſh, as his friend Pope uſed to ſay. Warburton added a ſupplement to the preface of this tranſlation, concerning the origin and nature of romances of chivalry; which ſupplement Pope extols, in his Letters, vol. ix. p. 352, in the higheſt terms; but the opinions in it are thoroughly confuted by Mr. *Tyrwhitt*, in vol. xi. of *Supplemental* Obſervations on Shakeſpeare, p. 373.

 day,

day, as ſhe was ſitting to him, he ran over the beauties of her face with rapture; but, ſaid he, I cannot help telling your ladyſhip that you have not a handſome ear. " No! ſaid Lady Bridgewater; pray Mr. Jervas, what is a handſome ear? He turned aſide his cap and ſhewed her his own." Anecdotes of Painting, vol. iv. p. 18.

As our author was addreſſing his maſter in this his favourite and delightful art, there is a warmth and glow of expreſſion throughout this epiſtle.

Together o'er the Alps methinks we fly,
Fir'd with ideas of fair *Italy*;
With thee, on *Raphaël*'s * monument I mourn,
Or wait inſpiring dreams at *Maro*'s urn;

With

* In a curious and unpubliſhed letter of *Raffaële* to his uncle, he tells him, that his perſonal eſtate in Rome amounted to 3000 ducats of gold, that is, 862l. 10s. ſterling; that he has 50 crowns of gold per ann. as architect of St. Peter's, that is, 14l. 7s. 6d. and a yearly penſion for life of 300 ducats of gold, that is, 86l. 5s. that he is in *Bramante*'s place; that the church of St. Peter's would coſt more than a million of gold, 287,500l. that the Pope had appropriated for it 60,000 ducats a year, that is, 17,250l. I will add to theſe anecdotes, taken from *Richardſon*, that *Raffaële* with great modeſty conſulted his friend *Arioſto*, who

With thee repose where *Tully* once was laid,
Or seek some ruin's formidable shade!

Though the last line, by the way, is inferior to the rest, because it passes from *particular* images to something *general*. Yet however elegant and finished this epistle must be allowed to be, it does not excel that of *Dryden*, addressed to Sir Godfrey Kneller *; and the following lines, both in point of science and taste, may be compared to any of Pope's;

Thence rose the Roman, and the Lombard line:
One colour'd best, and one did best design.

who was an excellent scholar, on the characters, lives, and countries, of the persons whom he was to introduce in the picture of Theology. All that Raffaële is ever known to have written, is four letters, and a sonnet addressed to *Ariosto*. *Michael Angelo* also wrote verses, and addressed a sonnet to *Vasari*.

* To make an experiment what gross flattery Sir Godfrey was capable of swallowing, Pope one day said to him, "God, we are told, made man in his *own* image; if this figure of *your's* had existed, man would have been made *by it*." Par D. je le crois aussi, Monf. Pope, replied Kneller. This artist little deserved to be consulted by Pope, concerning the arrangement of the subjects represented on the shield of Achilles. See Iliad. B. 18. Pope's notes.

Raphael's

Raphael's, like Homer's, was the nobler part,
But Titian's painting look'd like Virgil's art.
Thy genius gives thee both; where true design,
Postures unforc'd, and lively colours join.
Likeness is ever there; but still the best,
Like proper thoughts in lofty language drest:
Where light, to shades descending, plays, not strives,
Dies by degrees, and by degrees revives.
Of various parts a perfect whole is wrought:
Thy pictures think, and we divine their thought.

ONE cannot forbear reflecting on the great progress the art of painting * has made in this country, since the time that Jervas was thought worthy of this panegyric: a progress, that, we trust, will daily encrease, if due attention be paid to the incomparable discourses that have been delivered at the Royal Academy: which discourses contain more solid instruction on that subject than, I verily think, can be found in any language. The precepts are philosophically founded on truth and nature, and illustrated with the most proper and pertinent examples. The characters are drawn with a *precision* and *distinctness*,

* See Mr. Hayley's fine epistle to Mr. Romney.

that

that we look for in vain in *Felibien*, *De Piles*, and even *Vaſari*, or *Pliny* himſelf. Nothing, for example, can be more juſt and elegant, as well as profound and ſcientific, than the compariſon betwixt *Michael Angelo* and *Raffaële*, page 169 of theſe Diſcourſes. *Michael Angelo* is plainly the hero of Sir *Joſhua Reynolds*, for the ſame reaſons that *Homer*, by every great mind, is preferred to Virgil.

The epiſtle to Miſs Blount, accompanied with the works of *Voiture* *, is full

* Some curious particulars in the life of Voiture are mentioned in vol. ii. p. 409, of the entertaining Miſcellanies of *Vigneul* Marville. An elegant epitaph, to which Pope alludes, was made on him, copied from Martial, and worth peruſal:

Etruſcæ *Veneres*, *Camænæ* Iberæ;
Hermes Gallicus, & Latina *Siren*;
Riſus, *Deliciæ*, & *Dicacitates*,
Luſus, *Ingenium*, *Joci*, *Lepores*,
Et quicquid fuit elegantiarum,
Quo *Vecturius* hoc jacent ſepulcro.

Corneille was invited to read his *Polyeucte*, at the hotel *de Rambouillet*; where the principal wits of the time uſually aſſembled, and where *Voiture* preſided. It was very coldly received; and in a few days, Voiture came to Corneille, and in gentle terms told him, it was the opinion of his friends that the piece would not ſucceed. Such ill judges were then the moſt faſhionable wits of France.

of

of gaiety and gallantry. Our author's attachment to this lady, ended but with his life. Her affectation and ill-temper gave him, however, many hours of uneasiness and disquiet. When she visited him in his very last illness, and her company seemed to give him fresh spirits, the antiquated prude could not be prevailed on to stay and pass the night at Twickenham, because *of her reputation*. She occasioned an unhappy breach betwixt him and his old friend *Allen*. The works of *Voiture*, on which much of this epistle turns, after having been idolized in France, are now justly sunk into neglect and oblivion. The charactiristical difference betwixt *Voiture* and *Balsac* *, is well expressed by *Boileau*, in two letters written under their names, from the Elysian fields, to the *Duc de Vivonne*, in p. 155 of vol. iii. of his works.

* *Descartes*, who, as well as *Leibnitz*, was an elegant scholar, wrote a judicious censure of *Balsac*, in admirable Latin. *Balsac* was, however, much superior to Voiture. But he was affectedly turgid, pompous, and bloated on all subjects, and on all occasions alike. Yet was he the first that gave form and harmony to the French prose: which was still more improved by the Provincial Letters of *Pascal*.

And

And *Boileau*, ſpeaking often of abſurd readers and critics, loved to relate, that one of his relations, to whom he had preſented his works, ſaid to him; "Pray, Couſin, how came you to inſert any other perſon's writings among your own? I find in your works two letters, one from Balſac, and the other from Voiture." In the other epiſtle to the ſame perſon, the calamitous ſtate of an unfortunate lady, baniſhed from town to

Old-faſhion'd halls, dull aunts, and croaking rooks;

and the coarſe compliments of a rural ſquire,

Who with his hound comes hollowing from the ſtable,

are painted with humour.

THE *Town Eclogue* was written in concert with Lady Wortley Montague, who publiſhed four more of this ſort. Gay wrote a *Quaker*'s eclogue, and *Swift* a Footman's eclogue; and ſaid to Pope, I think the *paſtoral* ridicule is not exhauſted: what think you of a Newgate paſtoral, among the

the whores and thieves there? When Lady M. W. Montague would ſometimes ſhew a copy of her verſes to Pope, and he would make ſome little alterations, "No," ſaid ſhe, "Pope; no touching; for then, whatever is good for any thing will paſs for yours, and the reſt for mine."

NEXT follows a cloſe tranſlation of a fable from *Boileau*; which fable *Boileau* removed from the end of his Epiſtle to the King, by the advice of the great Prince of Condè, as unſuited to the ſubject, and finiſhed with it an epiſtle to L'Abbé des Roches, tom. i. p. 285. It will be no unuſeful or perhaps unpleaſing amuſement to compare theſe two pieces *. And I will not think of making any apology for ſo frequently quoting a writer ſo pure, ſenſible, and claſſical, as *Boileau*.

Once (ſays an author, where I need not ſay)
Two trav'lers found an oyſter in their way †;
Both

* In the fifth, ſixth, ſeventh, ninth and twelfth verſes, Pope is inferior to the original.

† I cannot forbear mentioning a work, not ſo well known as it deſerves to be, the Latin Fables of J. Deſbillons, a Jeſuit,

Both fierce, both hungry; the diſpute grew ſtrong,
While, ſcale in hand, dame Juſtice paſt along.
Before her each with clamour pleads the laws,
Explain'd the matter, and would win the cauſe.
Dame Juſtice, weighing long the doubtful right,
Takes, opens, ſwallows it, before their ſight.
The cauſe of grief remov'd ſo rarely well,
There take (ſays Juſtice) take ye each a ſhell.
We thrive at Weſtminſter on fools like you!
'Twas a fat oyſter—live in peace.—Adieu.

Un jour, dit un Auteur, n'importe en quel chapitre,
Deux voyageurs à jeun rencontrerent une huître,
Tous deux la conteſtoient, lorſque dans leur chemin,
La Juſtice paſſa, la balance à la main,
Devant elle à grand bruit ils expliquent la choſe.
Tous deux avec depens veulent gagner leur cauſe.
La Juſtice peſant ce droit litigieux,
Demande l'huître, l'ouvre, & l'avale à leur yeux,

Jeſuit, printed firſt at Paris, and afterwards at Manheim, 8vo. 1768, in a moſt chaſte and unaffected ſtyle. To ſpeak in his own words;

Me Fabularum ſuavis indoles capit,
Capit venuſta munditie latinitas
Simplex, & arti prænitens facilis color
Laborioſæ———

The fables in your *Eſop*, ſaid Pope to Vanbrugh, have the very ſpirit of *La Fontaine*. It may be ſo, replied Vanbrugh; but I proteſt to you I never have read *La Fontaine*'s Fables. *Patru*, who was conſulted as a capital critic, by all the wits of France, diſſuaded La Fontaine from attempting to write Fables: fortunately he diſregarded his advice.

Et

Et par ce bel arreſt terminant la bataille:
Tenez voilà, dit elle, à chacun une écaille.
Des ſottiſes d'autrui, nous vivons au Palais;
Meſſieurs, l'huître étoit bonne. Adieu. Vivez en paix.

We will paſs over the next ten little pieces, ſtopping only to commend the verſes on the Grotto, and the lines addreſſed to *Southerne*, when he was eighty years old. In the former, is a paſſage of a ſtriking and awakening ſolemnity.

Approach! great Nature, ſtudiouſly behold
And eye the mine, without a wiſh for gold!
Approach, but aweful! Lo, th' Ægerian grot,
Where nobly penſive *St. John* ſate and thought;
Where Britiſh ſighs from dying *Wyndham** ſtole,
And the bright flame was ſhot thro' *Marchmont*'s ſoul.

In

* Who was one of the moſt able and eloquent of that reſpectable body of patriots, that leagued together againſt Sir Robert Walpole. Indeed almoſt all the men of wit and genius in the kingdom oppoſed this miniſter, who in vain paid the enormous ſum of above fifty thouſand pounds, to paltry and dull ſcribblers in his defence. Soon after Mr. Glover had publiſhed his *Leonidas*, a poem that was eagerly read and univerſally admired, he paſſed ſome days with Mr. Pope at Twickenham, where they were one evening honoured with the company of the Prince of Wales, attended by Mr. Lyttelton; the latter privately deſired Mr. Pope and Mr. Glover (who himſelf kindly related to me this fact) that he begged they would join with him in diſſuading

In the latter, the venerable father of *Isabella* and *Imoinda*, is said to have raised by his eminence,

> The price of prologues and of plays.

For Southerne was the first author that had two benefit-nights, the third and sixth, at the exhibition of his comedy, entitled, Sir Anthony Love, 1691. By the custom, which had something illiberal in it, and was first dropt by *Addison*, of distributing tickets, Southerne gained 700l. for one play. In the year 1722, he received of a bookseller 120l. for copy-money; when,

dissuading the prince from riding a vicious horse he was fond of. And among other things urged on the subject, Pope said with earnestness to the prince; "I hope, Sir, the people of England will not be made miserable by a *second* horse:" alluding to the accident that befel king William. "I think (added Pope, turning and whispering to Mr. Glover) this speech was pretty well for me!"

In a letter dated May, 1737, Swift asks Pope; "Who is that Mr. Glover who writ the poem called Leonidas, which is reprinting here, and hath great vogue?" Pope's answer does not appear: it would have been curious to have known his opinion concerning a poem that is written in a taste and manner so different from his own, in a style formed in the Grecian school, and with the simplicity of an ancient.

the year before, Dr. Young could get no more than fifty pounds for his *Revenge*. But to drive a bargain, was not the talent of this generous and disinterested man.

THE fifteen *Epitaphs*, which conclude our author's poetical works, do not seem to merit a particular discussion. The three best * are that on Mrs. *Corbett*, *Fenton*, and the Duke of *Buckingham*. They are all in general over-run with point and antithesis, and are a kind of panegyrical epigrams. They are, consequently, very different from the *simple sepulchral* inscriptions of the ancients, of which that of *Meleager* on his wife, in the Greek Anthology, is a model and master-piece. And in which taste a living author, that must be nameless, has written the following hendecasyllables:

* As that on *Kneller* is the worst, in imitation of two wretched lines on Raphaël, which had a much better turn given to them by Mr. W. Harrison, of New College, a favourite of Swift;

Here Raphael lies, by whose untimely end,
Nature both lost a Riyal, and a Friend.

O dulcis

O dulcis puer, O venuſte Marce;
O multi puer et meri leporis,
Feſtivi puer ingenî, valeto!
Ergo cum, virideis vigens per annos,
Aevi ver ageres novum tenelli,
Vidiſti Stygias peremptus undas?
Tuum, moëſtus avus, tuum propinqui,
Os plenum lepida loquacitate,
Et riſus facileis tuos requirunt.
Te luſus, puer, in ſuos ſuètos
Aequales vocitant tui frequenter.
At ſurdus recubas, trahiſque ſomnos
Cunctis denique, Marce, dormiundos.

As it was the profeſſed intention of theſe papers to conſider POPE *as a poet*, the obſervations on his * *proſe-works*, will not be long.

THE rich vein of humour that runs through the Memoirs of *Scriblerus*, is heightened by the variety of learning they contain; and it may be worth obſerving, that the chief of thoſe who have excelled in works of wit and humour, have been

* The ſtyle of which is certainly not ſo melodious and voluble as that of Dryden's enchanting proſe. Voltaire, it muſt be owned, writes proſe with remarkable elegance, preciſion, and force.

men of extensive *learning*. We may instance in *Lucian*, *Cervantes*, *Quevedo*, *Rabelais*, *Arbuthnot*, *Fielding*, and *Butler*; for no work in our language contains more *learning* than *Hudibras*. This life of the solemn and absurd pedant, Dr. Scriblerus, is the only imitation we have of the *serious* manner of *Cervantes* *; for it is not easy to say, why Fielding should call his *Joseph Andrews*, excellent as it is, an imitation of *this* manner. Arbuthnot, whose humour was exquisite, had a very large share in these Memoirs; and I should guess that the fifth, sixth, seventh, eighth, tenth, and twelfth chapters are by his hand; as they contain allusions to parts of learning

* Don Quixote is the most original and unrivalled work of modern times. The great art of Cervantes consists in having painted his mad hero with such a number of amiable qualities, as to make it impossible for us totally to despise him. This light and shade in drawing characters, shews the master. It is thus Addison has represented his Sir Roger, and Shakespeare his Falstaff. How great must be the native force of Cervantes's humour, when it can be relished by readers, even unacquainted with Spanish manners, with the institution of chivalry, and with the many passages of old romances, and Italian poems, to which it perpetually alludes.

and

and ſcience, with which POPE was little acquainted.

THERE are few of the many faults and abſurdities, of which modern writers are guilty, but what are well expoſed in the *Bathos*; particularly in chapters tenth, eleventh and twelfth; and in the Project for advancement of the Stage, in c. 16. It is rather ſingular, that ſome of the moſt uſeful criticiſm in our language, ſhould be delivered in two *ludicrous* pieces; the *Rehearſal* and the *Bathos*. For there is ſcarcely a fault or abſurdity of which a dramatic poet can be guilty, but what is ridiculed in the *Rehearſal*.

THE familiar goſſiping ſtyle of *Burnet* in his hiſtory, is ridiculed in the Memoirs of a Pariſh Clerk. The Diſcourſe on the office and creation of the Poet *Laureat*, might be much enriched by the curious particulars, which our author's own tranſlator, the ingenious Abbé *Du Reſnel*, has given us in the 15th vol. of the Memoirs of Li-

 terature,

terature, in his learned researches on poets *Laureat*. The eight papers in the *Guardian* are elegantly written, particularly number 61, on cruelty to animals, and number 91, on a club of little men.

The *Preface* to his translation of the Iliad, is a declamatory piece of criticism, in the way of Longinus; it is written with force and spirit, but deals too much in *generals*. The most exceptionable passage in it, is where he compares the different great Epic poets to different sorts of *fire*. The *Postscript* to the Odyssey is better written, and more instructive. So also is the *Preface* to his Shakespeare; though it appears, by what later authors and editors have done, that he was not sufficiently acquainted with the history of our poetry, nor with the works of Shakespeare's predecessors and contemporaries. The *Letters* to various friends, occupy three volumes in that * col-

* His translation of Homer is therefore not here included; the discussion of whose beauties and faults (for faults

collection of his works, which we professedly made use of in drawing up these remarks. They appear to have been written with a design to have them one day published. They contain, it must be allowed, many interesting particulars; but they are tinctured and blemished with a great share of vanity, and self-importance, and with too many commendations of his own integrity, independency, and virtue. Pope, Swift, and Bolingbroke, appear by the letters, to have formed a kind of haughty *triumvirate*, in order to issue forth *proscriptions* against all who would not adopt their sentiments and opinions. And by their *own account* of *themselves*, they would have the reader believe that they had engrossed and monopolized all the genius, and all the honesty of the age, in which, according to their opinion, they had the *misfortune* to live.

faults it has) well deserve a separate volume; a work, which if well executed, would be of the greatest utility in forming a just taste, by shewing readers, especially of the younger sort, how very inferior and unlike it is to the original, and how much overloaded with improper, unnecessary, and Ovidian ornaments.

THUS have I endeavoured to give a critical account, with freedom, but it is hoped with impartiality, of each of POPE's works; by which review it will appear, that the *largeſt* portion of them is of the *didactic*, *moral*, and *ſatyric* kind; and conſequently, not of the moſt *poetic* ſpecies *of poetry*; whence it is manifeſt, that *good ſenſe* and *judgment* were his characteriſtical excellencies, rather than *fancy* and *invention*; not that the author of the *Rape of the Lock*, and *Eloiſa*, can be thought to want *imagination*, but becauſe his *imagination* was not his predominant talent, becauſe he indulged it not, and becauſe he gave not ſo many proofs of *this* talent as of the *other*. This turn of mind led him to admire French models; he ſtudied *Boileau* attentively; formed himſelf upon *him*, as *Milton* formed himſelf upon the Grecian and Italian ſons of *Fancy*. He ſtuck to deſcribing *modern manners*; but thoſe *manners*, becauſe they are *familiar*, *uniform*, *artificial*, and *poliſhed*, are, in their very nature, unfit for any lofty effort of the Muſe. He

gra-

gradually became one of the moſt correct, even, and exact poets that ever wrote; poliſhing his pieces with a care and aſſiduity, that no buſineſs or avocation ever interrupted: ſo that if he does not frequently raviſh and tranſport his reader, yet he does not diſguſt him with unexpected inequalities, and abſurd improprieties. Whatever poetical enthuſiaſm he actually poſſeſſed, he withheld and ſtifled. The peruſal of him affects not our minds with ſuch ſtrong emotions as we feel from *Homer* and *Milton*; ſo that no man of a true poetical ſpirit, *is maſter of himſelf while he reads* them. Hence, he is a writer fit for univerſal peruſal; adapted to all ages and ſtations; for the old and for the young; the man of buſineſs and the ſcholar. He who would think the *Faery Queen*, *Palamon* and *Arcite*, the *Tempeſt* or *Comus*, childiſh and romantic, might reliſh POPE. Surely it is no narrow and niggardly encomium to ſay he is the great Poet of Reaſon, the *Firſt* of *Ethical* authors in verſe. And this ſpecies of writing is, after all, the ſureſt

road

road to an extensive reputation. It lies more level to the general capacities of men, than the higher flights of more genuine poetry. We all remember when even a *Churchill* was more in vogue than a *Gray*. He that treats of fashionable follies, and the topics of the day, that describes present persons and recent events, finds many readers, whose understandings and whose passions he gratifies. The name of *Chesterfield* on one hand, and of *Walpole* on the other, failed not to make a poem bought up and talked of. And it cannot be doubted, that the Odes of Horace which celebrated, and the satires which ridiculed, well-known and real characters at Rome, were more eagerly read, and more frequently cited, than the Æneid and the Georgic of Virgil.

Where then, according to the question proposed at the *beginning of this Essay*, shall we with justice be authorized to place our admired POPE? Not, assuredly, in the same rank with *Spencer*, *Shakespeare*, and *Milton*;

ton; however juſtly we may applaud the *Eloiſa* and *Rape* of the *Lock*; but, conſidering the correctneſs, elegance, and utility of his works, the weight of ſentiment, and the knowledge of man they contain, we may venture to aſſign him a place, *next* to *Milton*, and *juſt* above *Dryden*. Yet, to bring our minds ſteadily to make this deciſion, we muſt forget, for a moment, the divine *Muſic Ode* of *Dryden*; and may perhaps then be compelled to confeſs, that though *Dryden* be the greater genius, yet *Pope* is the better artiſt.

THE preference here given to POPE, above other modern Engliſh poets, it muſt be remembered, is founded on the excellencies of his works *in general*, and *taken all together*; for there are *parts* and *paſſages* in other modern authors, in *Young* and in *Thomſon*, for inſtance, equal to any of POPE; and he has written nothing in a ſtrain ſo truly ſublime, as the *Bard* of *Gray*.

APPENDIX,

APPENDIX, N° I.

THE ALMA of PRIOR, page 126. This is not the only composition of Prior, in which he has displayed a knowledge of the world, and of human nature. For I have lately been permitted to read a curious manuscript, now in the hands of her Grace the Duchess Dowager of Portland, containing Essays and Dialogues of the Dead, on the following subjects, by Prior.

1. HEADS for a Treatise on Learning. 2. Essay on Opinion. 3. A Dialogue betwixt Charles the Fifth and Clenard the Grammarian. 4. Betwixt Locke and Montaign. 5. The Vicar of Bray and Sir Thomas More. 6. Oliver Cromwell and his Porter. If these pieces were published, Prior would appear to be as good a prose-writer as poet. It seems to be growing a little fashionable to decry his great merits as a poet. They who do this, seem not sufficiently to have attended to his admirable Ode to Mr. Charles Montague, afterwards Earl of Halifax; his Ode to the Queen, 1706; his Epistle and Ode to Boileau; most of his Tales, the Alma here mentioned, the Henry and Emma (in which surely are many strokes of true tenderness and pathos) and his Solomon: A poem, which however faulty in its plan, has very many noble and finished passages:

and

and which has been ſo elegantly and claſſically tranſlated by Dobſon, as to reflect honour on the college of Wincheſter, where he was educated, and where he tranſlated the firſt book as a ſchool-exerciſe. I once heard him lament, that he had not, at that time, read Lucretius, which would have given a richneſs, and variety, and force to his verſes; the only fault of which, ſeems to be a monotony, and want of different pauſes, occaſioned by tranſlating a poem in rhyme, which he avoided in his Milton. It is one mark of a poem being intrinſically good, that it is capable of being well tranſlated.

The political conduct of Prior was blamed on account of the part he took in the famous Partition-treaty; but in ſome valuable *Memoirs* of his life, written by the Hon. Mr. Montague, his friend, which are alſo in the poſſeſſion of the Ducheſs Dowager of Portland, this conduct is clearly accounted for, and amply defended. In thoſe Memoirs are many curious and intereſting particulars of the hiſtory of that time.

APPEN-

APPENDIX, Nº II.

The following is a Summary of the Arguments of each *Scene* and *Act*, in L'ADAMO of G. B. ANDREINI, mentioned above, page 183.

ATTO PRIMO.

SCENA 1. Iddio di creta forma Adamo, quale incontanente forzasi di lodarto ma divinamente addormentatosi, mentre in estasi scorge altissimi misteri della santissima Trinita, & Incarnatione del verbo eterno: dalla costa di lui ne viene formata Eva: la quale egli, dopò suegliato, caramente abbraccia, & accetta per compagna onde benedetti da Dio, e fecondati, acciò riempissero il mondo d'huomini, riceuono il precetto di non mangiare del albero, che suela il bene, & il male, e cominciano à contemplare la bellezza delle creature.

SCENA 2. Lucifero uscito dall' Abisso contempla il Paradiso terrestre, biasmando tutte l'opre di Dio.

SCENA 3. Lucifero essorta Sathan e Belzebu à forzarsi di far peccare Adamo, acciò macchiato di peccato, sia in odio à Dio, e non s'incarni il Verbo Eterno.

SCENA 4. Lucifero manda Melecano, e Lurcone à tentar Eva, quelli di Superbia, & questi d'Invidia, acciò

ciò si dolga di Dio, perche non l'habbi creata prima di Adamo.

Scena 5. Si mandano Ruspicano, & Arfarat, à tentarla d'Ira, & di Avaritia.

Scena 6. Maltèa và à tentarla d'Accidia; Dulciato, di Lussuria; & Guliar, di Gola.

ATTO SECONDO.

Scena 1. Quindeci angeli à gara lodono tutte l'opre divine.

Scena 2. Adamo pone il nome à tutti gli animali, & insieme con Eva loda con molti encomii il sommo Dio.

Scena 3. Serpe s'apparecchia per tentar Eva, e dice per qual cagione habbi preso quella forma, & non altra.

Scena 4. Volàno narra a Sathan l'infernal consiglio del modo di assaltar Eva.

Scena 5. Vana Gloria e Serpe congiunti d'accordo entrano nel Paradiso terrestre, e si nascondono sù l'albero della scienza del bene, e del male, per tentar Eva à gustare i frutti di quello.

Scena 6. Eva gloriandosi dei tanti favori, e gratie riceuute da Dio, rimira il Serpe sopra l'albero, e con molte ragioni da quello persuasa, prende il pomo, lo gusta, e và cercando Adamo, per farlo fare l'istesso.

ATTO

ATTO TERZO.

SCENA 1. Adamo dopo l'haver descritto leggiadramente la fonte che irrigava il Paradiso terrestre fù da Eva persuaso a gustare il pomo, e lo mangiò per non contristarla; onde ambidue conobbero d'esser nudi, soggetti a morte & a mille altri mali & si nascosero.

SCENA 2. Volano rallegrandosi d'el peccato d'Adamo, col suono di roca tromba chiama tutti gli spiriti Infernali.

SCENA 3. Sathan certificato d'ella caduta d'Adamo, essorta gli altri spiriti a far festa.

SCENA 4. Serpe con Vana Gloria tornando trionfanti d'Adamo sono da Sathan, e da gli altri spiriti perciò adorati: e da Canoro vengono cantate le lodi loro.

SCENA 5. Gli Folletti per allegrezza della caduta d'Adamo danzano insieme: ma sentendo trombe celesti e scorgendo la divina luce tutti fuggono all' abisso.

SCENA 6. Il Padre Eterno chiamando Adamo & Eva e da loro confessato l'errore, ad ambidue publica le pene nelle quali sono incorsi, maledice il serpente & si nasconde da loro.

SCENA 7. L'Angelo porta due vesti di pelle ad Adamo & Eva, e da quelli partendo à volo gli lascia dolenti, a lagnarsi de gli errori loro.

SCENA

Scena 8. L'Archangelo Michaele con ſpada di foco ſcaccia Adamo & Eva dal Paradiſo, & eſſortando gli altri Angioli, che ſolevano ſtare con loro, ad andar ſeco in Cielo, fa che reſti un Cherubino con la ſpada di foco a guardare la porta del Paradiſo.

Scena 9. Gli Angeli pria che partirſi, licentiatiſi d'Adamo, l'eſſortano a piangere il ſuo errore, promettendoli allegrezza, e canto.

ATTO QUARTO.

Scena 1. Volàno a ſuono di tromba chiamando tutti gli ſpiriti de gli elementi, che vengano ad incontrare Lucifero, eglino vengono tutti.

Scena 2. Lucifero chiamati tutti gli ſpiriti a conſeglio, dimanda a ciaſcuno il ſuo parere, ſi delle attioni d'Adamo, come delle Divine; ma non ſapendo quelli bene interpretarle, egli loro le dichiara.

Scena 3. Lucifero emulo di Dio, nella creatione del mondo, da una maſſa di terra confuſa fa uſcire quatro moſtri a danno dell' huomo, Mondo, Carne, Morte, e Demonio, poi con tutti gli altri torna all' Inferno.

Scena 4. Adamo ſolingo narra come gli animali, e tutte l'altre coſe hanno cangiato forma, e coſtumi, per il ſuo peccato, & amaramente lo piange.

Scena 5. Le fere ſeguendoſi, & amazzandoſi tra

loro, mettono gran terrore ad Adamo & Eva che perciò si nascondono.

Scena 6. Appariscono ad Adamo quattro mostri cioè, Fame, Sete, Fatica, e Desperatione, e la Fame gli dice, che mai questi da lui partiranno.

Scena 7. La Morte minaccia di troncare la vita ad Eva, & Adamo, e subito il Ciel turbato con tuoni, saette, grandini, pioggie, e venti, gli spauenta.

ATTO QUINTO.

Scena 1. La Carne tenta Adamo, e trouandolo ritroso, gli mostra, come tutte le cose sentono amore.

Scena 2. Lucifero s'aggiunge, alla Carne, e tenta di persuadere Adamo a congiungersi con essa; fingendosi Adamo celeste.

Scena 3. Adamo con l'agiuto dell' Angelo suo custode supera la Carne & Lucifero.

Scena 4. Il Mondo narra le sue grandezze, e ciò che faranno gli huomini per l'oro, e s'apparecchia per tentar Eva.

Scena 5. Il Mondo propone ad Eva tutte le sue pompe, e gli fa apparire un vago, e ricco palazzo d'oro.

Scena 6. Dal palazzo del Mondo uscito un choro di Donzelle, con molti ornamenti vogliono ornarne Eva,

Eva, ma alla voce & precetto d'Adamo reſtano confuſe, & il tutto ſpariſce: onde il Mondo minacciando ad Adamo, chiama contra di lui tutti gl' Infernali Moſtri.

Scena 7. Lucifero, Morte, Mondo, e chori di Diavoli, s'apparecchiano per far violenza ad Adamo, e combattere con Dio.

Scena 8. L'Archangelo Micaele, con chori d'Angeli, combatte con Lucifero, & i chori di Demonii, & ſuperati gli ſcacciano ſino all' Abiſſo.

Scena 9. Adamo & Eva riveriſcono l'Archangelo Micaele, e da lui ſono conſolati & aſſicurati, che per la penitenza loro, an dranno a goder in cielo: on de per allegrezza gli angeli cantano lodi a Dio, della vittoria, & felicità dell' huomo, per l'immenſa pieta & Amor divino.

The lovers of Paradiſe Loſt will, we truſt, be entertained with having an opportunity of ſeeing how greatly and judiciouſly our ſublime and divine poet has heightened and improved any the leaſt hints or images, he has been ſuppoſed to have taken from this ancient drama, copies of which are extremely ſcarce and uncommon: and therefore a ſpecimen of the verſification is ſubjoined. Not that it can be imagined, that the copious, comprehenſive, and creative mind of Milton, ſo rich in the ſtores of *nature*, could condeſcend to be a meer *borrower*, as Voltaire would inſinuate: nor can we aſſent to the opinion of that critic who ſays, "that the poetical fire of Milton glows like a furnace, kept up to an uncommon ardour by the force of *Art*."

ATTO QUARTO, SCENA QUINTA.

ADAMO. Doue men fuggo ahi laſſa, oue m'aſcondo?
Corri ne le mie braccia,
E chi ha inſieme peccato
Sia da le fere inſieme anco ſbranato.

EVA. Ahi ch' ogni ſcampo è fatto
Varco di morte, a chi di vita è indegno,
Pur di quell' antro in ſeno
Sommergiamoci Adamo.

ADAMO. Laſſi partiro al fin, ma gia non partoro
Da l'Huomo le ruine, il duol mortale:
Strano caſo infelice, il riſo piange,
L'allegrezza ſta meſta,
Hoggi la vita more.

EVA. Quanto m'affligo Adamo,
Ahi quanto piango ò Cielo,
Quanto ſoſpiro ò Dio, quanto m'accoro,
Nè ſon viva, nè moro.

ADAMO. Ma quai ruggiti horrendi
L'aer fa rimbombar fremer le valli?

MORTE. Tù pur fuſti, ò vil Donna,
Che prima mi chiamaſti
Con voce di peccato
Sin dal Tartareo oſcuro.
Tù tù putrida carne, e poca terra,
Queſto terribil moſtro

D'oſſa

D'oſſa humane conteſto
A rimirar le ſtelle hoggi chiamaſti.
Hor, che vuoi? di? favella,
Stanca ſè de la vita?
Ecco la falciatrice, ecco la falce
Che la luce à laſciar hoggi t'invita.
Gia con occhio lincèo
Scorgo mirando la futura etate
Ch'al mio nome, a queſt' armi à l'empietate
Trofei s'ergon funeſti.
Ma, che? non finiran qui le ruine
Chà tè minaccia il Cielo; altre ſuenture
T'appreſt'anco l'Inferno,
Colme d'horror ſi grande;
Ch'io che la Morte ſono
Bramo morir, per non mirarle in volto:
Gia tu ſè reo di morte,
Già tua ſtanza è l'Inferno,
Fatto rubello al tuo Fattor ſuperno.

ADAMO. Ahi lagrime, ahi dolore
Ahi crudo peccatore.

EVA. Ahi dolente, infelice
Eva gran peccatrice.

ADAMO. Ahi, che s'annera il Cielo, ahi che ne toglie
Com' indegni di luce ogni ſua luce.
Ma qual toſto nel Ciel s'auuina, e more,
Fiamma, ch' abbaglia, e ſerpeggiando fugge
Fatta ſerpe di foco?

EVA. Ahi, che fin non hauran quì del Ciel l'ire
Ne conuien pria morire.

ADAMO. Deh qual rimbombo là sù in alto ascolto?
Forse con simil voce
Ne discaccia dal Mondo, il Cielo irato,
E ne condanna de l' abisso al fondo?
Quante saette, ò quante
Atterran selue, e boschi, ò quanti, ò quanti
Venti fremon per l'aria;
Quanto scende dal Cielo
Humor converso in grosse palle, in gielo.

EVA. Lassi noi, che da l'alto
Diluviano tant'acque,
Che trabboccano i riui,
E'n superbiti i fiumi
Van le belue fugando,
E di boschi, e di selue
Gli humidi pesci habitator si fanno.

ADAMO. Fuggiamo, ohimè fuggiamo
Dè monti à quelle cime
Où il Ciel sembra c'hoggi
Dal lungo fulminar stanco s'appoggi.

The names of the persons represented, are as follows:

INTERLOCUTORI.

PADRE ETERNO.
CHORO di SERAFINI, CHERUBINI, & ANGELI.

ARC-

ARCANGELO MICAELE.

ADAMO.

EVA.

CHERUBINO custode d'ADAMO.

LUCIFERO.

SATHAN.

BELZEBU.

GLI SETTE PECCATI MORTALI.

MONDO.

CARNE.

FAME.

FATICA.

DISPERAZIONE.

MORTE.

VANAGLORIA.

SERPE.

VOLANO, messaggiero infernale.

CHORO di FOLETTI.

CHORO di SPIRITI IGNEI, AEREI, ACQUATICI, & INFERNALI.

FINIS.